The Leyland Man

THE HISTORY, REDISCOVERY
AND RESURRECTION OF THE EARLY
LEYLAND OMNIBUS

MIKE A. SUTCLIFFE

The Crowood Press

First published in 2003 by
The Crowood Press Ltd
Ramsbury, Marlborough
Wiltshire SN8 2HR

www.crowood.com

British Library Cataloguing-in-Publication Data
A catalogue record for this book is available from the British Library.

ISBN 1 86126 572 7

Photographic Acknowledgements
All photographs are credited to 'The Mike Sutcliffe Collection' unless
otherwise stated.

Dedication
This book is dedicated to Leyland Motors.

Typeface used: Bembo.

Typeset and designed by
D & N Publishing
Lowesden Business Park, Hungerford, Berkshire.

Colour origination by Black Cat Graphics Ltd., Bristol

Printed and bound by Times Offset (M) Sdn. Bhd., Malaysia

Contents

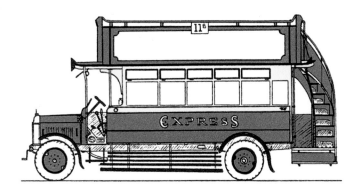

Foreword

Mike Worthington-Williams

I write this foreword with both pride and gratitude. As many of you know, I have been closely involved with the early vehicle movement since leaving school in 1954, and my features have appeared every year since then (and every month since I became a full-time freelance in 1974). It has to be said, however, that I am largely perceived as being a car and motorcycle man – but my interest in commercials goes back much further than 1954. As a child there was no money for lavish entertainment, and so every day I amused myself by lorry, bus and tram spotting. I learned to drive on a Standard Fordson (iron-tyred and Cork-built) on a Sussex farm in 1953, and graduated to an ex-RAF Leyland that was relegated to off-road menial farm duties. At that time I was already aware of the longevity of Leyland vehicles, as our school bus ('the Old Tin Ticker') was an elderly Leyland Lion PLSC1 half-cab dating from around 1926.

By 1956 I was writing for *Veteran & Vintage Magazine*, and I remember the announcement in the November issue of that year concerning the possible formation of an 'Old Lorry Club'. The eventual outcome of that was, of course, the Historic Commercial Vehicle Club (now the HCVS), which then merged with the Vintage Passenger Vehicle Society. However, it was not until I joined the late Prince Marshall as assistant editor of *Old Motor* magazine that I became more involved in commercial vehicles, and aware of the activities of a young chap called Mike Sutcliffe.

Since those days I have followed Mike's career closely, and with increasing respect (not to say incredulity) as each succeeding restoration project has been announced, undertaken and successfully completed. As a car man who has himself rescued many wrecks from oblivion, and fully restored two of them, I am fully cognisant of what a full-scale restoration entails, both in terms of outlay and commitment. My own achievements in this respect, however, pale into total insignificance when compared to what is involved in bus restoration (or indeed that of any heavy commercial). If I have learned anything, however, it is that successful restoration requires a combination of several things, the most important being enthusiasm, knowledge, skill, dedication, finance and organization.

Not the least of these is organization, and a visit to Valley Forge impresses on every newcomer the fact that Mike Sutcliffe is well organized. It is this factor, I believe, that not only enables Mike to carry out his restorations to the very highest standards and within incredibly short time-scales, but also inspires enthusiasm and confidence in his helpers, such that they have no doubt that a project, once commenced, will proceed to a successful conclusion. It is the lack of this conviction that is responsible for the failure of so many enthusiastically conceived, but flawed restoration projects.

Although I myself am totally disorganized, I do share with Mike a number of common interests. They include history (in particular the individual history of each vehicle owned), the

rescue and restoration of derelict vehicles, matters of minute detail (to the point of obsession), and a respect for fine engineering. His feelings about Leyland products echo my own concerning the early products of the Austin Motor Company Ltd, so I suppose that it is natural that we should be kindred spirits. In this book Mike has happily combined his love of history (of Leyland Motors Ltd, the individual operators of the vehicles featured and the vehicles themselves), the rescuing of derelict examples, and the painstaking and loving restoration that has followed (with all the elements of luck, coincidence, serendipity and chance that invariably attend the brave), and has so organized the contents of the book that each section flows evenly and logically to form a brilliant chronicle of all his endeavours. Mike's individual contribution to the preservation of Britain's transport heritage is, in my view, absolutely unique and without equal – he is clearly the most prolific restorer of some of the earliest motor buses – not only here in Great Britain, but anywhere in the world.

Should anyone, having read this book, still be in any doubt as to why we do these things, I think I can do no better than quote from *Punch* which, in its inimitable way, once summed it all up for me: 'And there is still, for the man with the right gifts and the proper appreciation, the tremendous moment when the old engine, cold these forty years, fires and comes noisily to life. This is much more than the collectors' discovery of a period piece: it is resurrection.'

Introduction

Michael Plunkett's Thames Valley Tilling Stevens B9A with the author at the wheel, not a Leyland but a magnificent vehicle that is a pleasure to drive. It is also a very relevant vehicle due to his early interest in Thames Valley.

This is the story, so far, of my interest in vehicles generally, but more importantly early Leyland buses, explaining how it all started from when I was a young boy. I have always been interested in vehicles of all sorts, and also railways, and this interest has become more intense as I have grown older. Despite my financial circumstances being very modest, particularly in my earlier years, I have always been able to indulge myself in my interest, and as my financial situation has improved, entirely through my own efforts, I have been able to progress to restore a magnificent fleet of early Leyland buses. My wife Pat is immensely supportive, and since we have been together we have gone from strength to strength.

Over the last 25 years or so, with collecting so many bits for the restoration of my Leylands, badges, Leyland brochures and manuals, etc, and also with my involvement with The Leyland Society, many people who do not necessarily know my name have often referred to me as the 'Leyland Man' and the title seems to fit, hence the title of this book.

It was very flattering to be asked to write this book – not many people get the opportunity to write an autobiography, though mine is clearly aimed at the vehicle interests in my life. There are so many interesting tales to tell with regard to each of my Leyland restorations, and it gives me great pleasure to recall some of these anecdotes, and to

give others an insight into how the vehicles were found and ultimately restored. Fortunately I have always taken photographs of my finds and of the restoration work in progress, and these help to illustrate the various stories. The only one I missed was the White Rose body, which was set on fire the day before I reached it.

It also gives me the opportunity to detail the development of Leyland petrol-driven vehicles over the first quarter of the twentieth century. This was an immensely important timespan to cover, and it has given me great satisfaction to relate the history of what turned out to be the greatest British commercial vehicle manufacturer of all time: Leyland Motors Ltd.

Each of the eight chapters on the early Leyland bus restorations is split into three main parts. The first part covers the development of the Leyland petrol models, up to my restored bus; the second part traces the history of the vehicle's operator when it was in service; and the third part tells the story of the vehicle's discovery and rescue, its restoration, and its activities since the work was completed. I am frequently asked 'How do you achieve so many restorations to such a high standard in such a short time?' The answer is, by sheer hard work and determination, and meticulous planning. From the chapters in this book you will see that I have always had a soft spot for the vehicles from Todmorden, Yorks. The motto on the Todmorden coat of arms is 'By industry we prosper' – and how true this is. Pat and I *never* stop working, and by seizing all opportunities when they arise (some people call it luck) you can make it happen.

I hope you enjoy reading the book as much as I have enjoyed writing it. Its preparation has been very diverse and complicated, and I would like to thank those who have assisted with photographs for inclusion, particularly the Archive of the British Commercial Vehicle Museum. My greatest thanks of all, however, go to Pat.

This is the state in which most of my vehicles have been found, or even worse! The Tilling body of the Leyland X2, part of the nearside having been cut up for firewood.

Outing at one of the Valley Forge Open Days.

CHAPTER ONE

The Start of the Passion

So, how did it all start? I was christened Michael Anthony Sutcliffe, having been born in High Wycombe, Bucks on 19 December 1942. My mother, Freda Ashworth (now more affectionately known as Fredi) and father, Harold Sutcliffe, had moved to High Wycombe when they married earlier in the previous year, to make a new life for themselves, having previously lived in the small cotton-mill town of Todmorden, in the West Riding of Yorkshire, in the heart of the Pennines, near the Lancashire border. Both families had lived in Todmorden for many generations – in fact, the name Sutcliffe (meaning South Cliff) comes from the Calder Valley between Todmorden, Hebden Bridge and Halifax, where the Sutcliffe clan had profusely populated the area over several centuries.

Todmorden, and a Fascination with Numbers

The town of Todmorden, and its surrounding districts, was to play a major part in the development of my interest in both road and rail transport, particularly as a great deal of the long school holidays was spent staying with my grandparents in Todmorden. In the early 1950s, if a young lad was asked the question 'What do you want to do when you grow up?', 90 per cent of the answers would be 'I want to be an engine driver'. I was no exception, and in fact spent much of my holidays train spotting in Todmorden – watching the locomotives negotiating the triangular layout of track in Todmorden caused by the meeting of the three valleys; watching the WD class 'Austerity' 2-8-0

locomotives acting as pilot and pushing the heavily laden goods trains up the hill towards Burnley; and, most exciting of all, watching the only 'namer' of the day to come through Todmorden on the Manchester to Leeds express at midday. For years it was headed by a 'Jubilee'-class 4-6-0 locomotive, either 45698 'Mars' or, less frequently, 45717 'Dauntless'.

Numbers have always fascinated me, and this may have had something to do with the fact that I later became a Chartered Accountant! However, after starting to collect engine numbers, I soon realized that buses had numbers too – and not only the fleet numbers, but registration numbers, chassis numbers and body numbers too: this was an opportunity not to be missed! At that time the Todmorden Joint Omnibus

The locomotive that usually headed the Manchester to Leeds Express through Todmorden was this 'Jubilee' Class 4–6–0, 45698 'Mars'.
(National Railway Museum, Treacy Collection)

Committee had a very modern fleet of Leyland Titan double deckers, all with lowbridge, fifty-three-seater, Leyland-built bodies. Their fleet numbering system was rather haphazard, using a 'gap-filling' procedure, though this made the whole subject much more interesting to me. Not only that, but following railway practice (Todmorden Joint Omnibus Committee was half owned by the Corporation and half by the LMS Railway, later British Railways), when a bus was replaced but not disposed of, the older vehicle's number was given an X prefix – these were called 'supernumeries'. The Todmorden buses were painted in a very attractive Brunswick green livery, with no adverts – although latterly they became a bit shabby – and they carried a magnificent double garter on their sides.

High Wycombe and the Thames Valley Traction Co. Ltd

A young lad's interest in vehicles usually starts with those that he sees every day, and I ran true to type – my junior school was across the other side of High Wycombe, and even at the tender age of nine, with younger sister Jill, age seven, in tow, it was sometimes necessary to catch the service bus home. This was operated by the Thames Valley Traction Company (High Wycombe was on the easterly boundary of Thames Valley's operating area), and it would frequently be a Leyland

ABOVE: *Todmorden Joint Omnibus Committee retained two of their 1940 Leyland Titan TD5s with Leyland lowbridge bodies for about ten years after they had been replaced. They were renumbered X23/4 and were regarded as 'supernumeries'. At the age of seventeen, I well remember sitting on the upper deck of one of these knowing that it was to be scrapped in a month or two and thinking to myself 'however could I manage to save one of them' – but it was all in vain. (G. Lumb)*

Thames Valley 267, a Leyland Tiger TS7 with Brush coachwork, rests at High Wycombe station ready to take the young Sutcliffes home from junior school. (W. J. Haynes)

ABOVE: *The grammar school was at Marlow, which necessitated a trip on a Thames Valley Bristol LWL6B working the route 28. (S. N. J. White)*

RIGHT: *F. H. Crook sold two AJS buses to Thames Valley in 1937, with the Booker to High Wycombe via Sands route. Here is an artist's impression of the bonnetted AJS Pilot and forward control AJS Commodore as they might have looked, standing in the forecourt of Wycombe Station. (Pencil drawing and watercolour by Mike Sutcliffe in his younger days)*

BELOW: *Another coloured drawing, done at the same time, of a Maudslay ML3B with all-weather, twenty-six-seat coachwork passing over Marlow Bridge. It had been taken over by Thames Valley in 1929 from the Great Western Railway, and they had put it into their Marlow & District fleet, No. 11.*

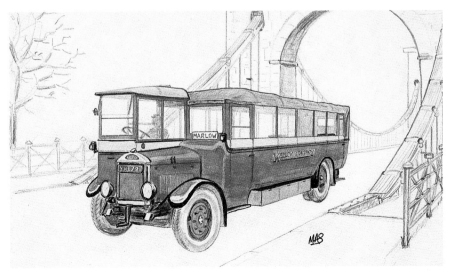

Tiger TS7 or TS8, with Brush or Eastern Coachworks body. On entering the bus at the rear, there was a single seat over the wheel arch on the near side, and *that* was the place to sit. It was the subject of many arguments. These buses had what looked like a small letterbox in the back panel below the window, and I always wondered what these were – in fact they had been used as a small destination box when new.

I well remember that, during an English lesson at the junior school, a Thames Valley Tiger TS8 with Harrington coach body stopped in the road outside at the belisha beacon crossing (as they were called in those days). Having not seen one of this batch before, BMO 989, this was a real treat; at last I could restrain myself no longer, and said in a loud voice to *all* my classmates: 'Just look at that!' I was instantly reprimanded by 'Old Ma Cabbage', the rather strict headmistress of the junior school, who never seemed to appreciate the young Sutcliffe's mischievousness and who at that time seemed to be my lifelong enemy.

These old Leylands of Thames Valley were disappearing fast from the fleet, being replaced at a very rapid rate by

Thames Valley Buses at the Fairground

Buses with showmen were still around in the mid-1950s, providing a glimpse of buses from an earlier age. A visit to the local fairground was a real treat as nearly every vehicle operated by showmen had been converted from a bus. These would include not only buses converted to living vans, but also frequently one would see double-deckers with their upper deck windows taken out, the roofs lowered and in use as a van. Favourites among the showmen were those buses fitted with Gardner engines, and also Tilling-Stevens petrol electrics, which were ideal for generating electricity to power the rides. At the time there was no thought of bus preservation – what a lost opportunity!

1. Typical of the many remaining ex-LGOC 'B'-type bodies, and latterly on a TV Thornycroft 'J', seen in a garden in Reading.
2. Hanging out the washing on a Tilling Stevens B9A, MO 9325.
3. An especially 'low bridge' version of an early TD1 Titan, still in Thames Valley colours and with upper deck windows removed.
4. Another customized TD1 in excellent order, photographed at Booker.
5. This Lion LT2, RX 6245, fitted with a ladder, appears to have had its headlamps adjusted to spot low-flying aircraft!
6. A Brush-bodied Leyland Tiger TS4 lurks behind the bushes.
7. A later Brush-bodied Tiger, this time TS7, pictured near Booker.
8. ARX 982, a Tiger TS8 with ECW (BEF design) body shows its rear 'letter-box' destination, with pushchair.

Eastern Coachworks and Windovers bodied Bristols, until they had all gone in 1954, although many of them had a second lease of life with showmen. In those days, a trip to the fairground was a sight to behold, since nearly every vehicle operated had been converted from a bus. One would be treated to sights from a previous generation of motor buses – many of these I had never seen in service, particularly the Leyland Titan TD1s and Tilling Stevens Express buses, let alone petrol electrics. These ancient vehicles had a special interest to me, although at that stage there was no thought of preservation.

F. H. Crook, Booker

By 1952 we had moved to the outskirts of High Wycombe, on Cressex Road, near Booker aerodrome; this meant even longer journeys home on the bus that was invariably Thames Valley No. 507, EJB 229, a Bristol K6B with ECW lowbridge body, and which became my favourite 'modern' bus of the time. The local coach operator at Booker was F. H. Crook, a firm that had built up a stage carriage service in the area, which it had sold to Thames Valley in 1937, along with the whole of its fleet of ten vehicles. With the proceeds, a fleet of brand new coaches was purchased, although some of these did not last very long as they were requisitioned by the War Department in 1940. Their livery, which had been green, was changed in 1937 to cream and red, and they proudly carried the Union Jack on their sides to celebrate the Coronation of 1937.

Their fleet introduced me to a selection of vehicles, including AECs and Albions, an unusual WestNor (West Norwood)-bodied Tilling Stevens K6LA7 registered DDP 572, a Maudslay Marathon 3, and of course three of the statutory Bedford OB/Duple Vista. The most interesting vehicle, however, was not in the modern fleet of runners

RIGHT: *The rotting remains of REO Speed Wagon YK 9541 with twenty-seater body by Wray stands next to the F. H. Crook Garage in Limmer Lane, Booker. (Still wearing its green livery, although by now mainly brown rust – what an evocative sight this was, and eminently restorable!)*

BELOW: *S 512, seen here in London General colours, was identical to S 888, the latter as a static caravan; it was absolutely complete, but disappeared in 1953. (J. Higham)*

– it was very much a non-runner, with its nose buried in a hedge next to the garage at Limmer Lane: it was the remains of an REO Speed Wagon registered YK 9541, with a small saloon body built by Wray. Being green in colour it had probably been in this derelict condition since before 1937, and was eminently restorable; for me, however, at the age of eleven, restoration was restricted to repainting Dinky toy buses into my own fleet livery – but it did start my mind thinking! This was not the only wreck in the area, because just around the corner was an ex-London General S-type single decker, S 888. Absolutely complete, it was painted grey and in use as a caravan: another bus from a bygone age.

F. H. Crook (t/a Advance), Booker, High Wycombe

My local independent bus operator was F.H. Crook of Limmer Lane, Booker, High Wycombe, who had started in business operating under the fleet title 'Advance' on stage carriage services from High Wycombe to Sands, Booker, Marlow and Bledlow Ridge. By June 1937 the fleet had grown to a size of ten buses and coaches, at which time they sold the stage carriage services to Thames Valley, together with the ten vehicles, painted in a green livery. These included four REOs, an AJS Pilot, an AJS Commodore, one Bedford WLB and three Albions (a Valkyrie and two Victors).

With the proceeds of sale, five brand new coaches were purchased and painted in a cream and red livery with a large Union Jack on each side (to show their patriotism as it was Coronation Year). Several of these coaches did not last very long as they were requisitioned by the War Department in 1940, never to return to the F.H. Crook fleet. After World War Two they replenished their fleet, mainly with quality-built full-size coaches, back to a fleet of ten including three Bedford OB/Duple Vistas.

ABOVE: *YT 4520, a REO Sprinter of 1927 with all-weather body by Wray, became Thames Valley No. 358.*

RIGHT: *Also sold to Thames Valley was No. 357, the 1932 Duple-bodied Bedford WLB.*

LEFT: *Two of the new fleet were these AEC Regals, DXT 591/3, with Duple bodies. Both were requisitioned by the War Department in 1940.*

BELOW LEFT: *This Albion Victor EPP 484 with Duple coachwork escaped the War Department and survived until 1957. It is seen here with a war-time headlamp mask. (R. H. G. Simpson)*

RIGHT: *The first post-war purchase was this AEC Regal I, with Duple A body, in December 1946.*

Adventures into Deepest Lancashire

A terrible blow struck in 1954 when my father died at the age of forty-four, when I was only eleven. Thus I never had the opportunity to get to know him properly and to share interests with him, and from then on, virtually everything I did with my hobby was self-initiated. At the time, my sister Jill and I were whisked away by my grandparents for a holiday in Lytham St Annes, and this was my first introduction to the Leyland 'gearless' bus: Titans and Lions with the Lysholm-Smith hydraulic torque converters. What a magnificent sound the Titans made, with their Leyland 8.6-litre oil engines – there has never been an engine noise that quite matched their melodic sound.

In 1955 I was treated to my first camera, a 'VP Twin' that cost the princely sum of 7s 6d (37½p): now some serious recording of these vehicles could take place. However, there was little money to spare, and a financial evaluation had to be made before taking each photograph. I well remember one of my adventures by bus into mid Lancashire, from my Todmorden holiday base: I was at Wigan, having visited the Corporation Bus Garage, and with only two frames left on my film. I was also in full school uniform, and a policeman stopped me because he thought I was playing truant, and asked which school I went to. Being totally amazed at the reply 'I come from High Wycombe, sir', he instantly took me to Wigan Pier, and insisted that I took a photograph of this historic monument. What should I do? Not wishing to waste one of my precious frames, or to invoke the wrath of the law, I pretended to take a photograph, making the appropriate clicking noise with my mouth, and then pretended to wind on the film. He was obviously convinced and let me go on my way.

These forays into deepest Lancashire became quite a regular thing, and I looked forward to the long school holidays; I would load up my bag with notebooks, pencils, camera and film,

ABOVE: *Lytham St Anne's BTF 28 was an all-Leyland Titan TD4c with full-fronted body and the radiator proclaiming 'gearless bus'. (R. H. G. Simpson)*

RIGHT: *On holiday in Bournemouth in 1955; with my first camera over my shoulder ready for some serious photography, I posed in front of one of the most attractive coaches of the time, a Royal Blue Bristol L6B, with Beadle 'Camel Back' body.*

and, of course, enough currant tea cakes to last me for the day, and set off from Todmorden, catching the bus from town to town. I travelled across Lancashire as far as I could get, going there and back in a day, visiting all the municipal bus garages, studying buses in their proud municipal liveries, many of them fully lined out and without an advert in sight. Can you imagine a boy of between eleven and fourteen being *allowed* to do that these days, let alone having the inclination and the initiative to make his own entertainment?

Forays from Todmorden into Deepest Lancashire

Some of the delights to be found in the late 1950s.

Wigan Corporation's Leyland Tiger TS4, its body built by Santus to Leyland design, was in use as a driver trainer vehicle with dual controls.

Lurking in the back of the Bury Depot, now unused, was EN 2903, a 1925 Leyland A13 converted to a tower wagon.

Rawtenstall had three of these all-Leyland Tiger TS8 buses converted to mobile polling stations. Behind it was the Lion LT3 snowplough/towing bus, which fortunately lasted into preservation.

Municipal Pride, a Blackburn all-Leyland TD5, waits next to Darwen Corporation's Leyland PD1; both are profusely lined out, and were in commission before advertising was generally applied to municipal buses. What a magnificent sight they made!

Lytham St Annes operated this breakdown wagon converted from bus No. 2, TC 4898, a Guy B dating from 1923.

Blackburn Corporation's towing vehicle was this Leyland Titan TD2, with its giant front balloon pneumatics – those were the days!

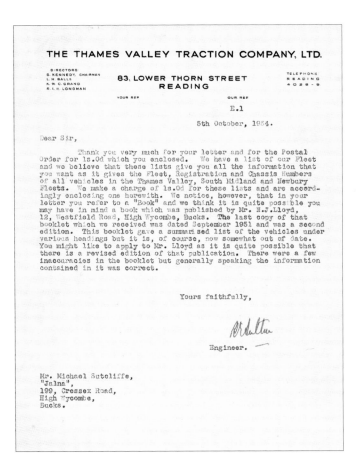

THE THAMES VALLEY TRACTION COMPANY, LTD.

DIRECTORS:
S. KENNEDY, CHAIRMAN
L. H. BALLS
A. W. C. GRAND
R. L. H. LONGMAN

83, LOWER THORN STREET
READING

TELEPHONE
READING
4028-9

YOUR REF   OUR REF
                           E.1

5th October, 1954.

Dear Sir,

Thank you very much for your letter and for the Postal
Order for 1s.0d which you enclosed. We have a list of our Fleet
and we believe that these lists give you all the information that
you want as it gives the Fleet, Registration and Chassis Numbers
of all vehicles in the Thames Valley, South Midland and Newbury
Fleets. We make a charge of 1s.0d for these lists and are accordingly enclosing one herewith. We notice, however, that in your
letter you refer to a "Book" and we think it is quite possible you
may have in mind a book which was published by Mr. N.J.Lloyd,
12, Westfield Road, High Wycombe, Bucks. The last copy of that
booklet which we received was dated September 1951 and was a second
edition. This booklet gave a summarised list of the vehicles under
various headings but it is, of course, now somewhat out of date.
You might like to apply to Mr. Lloyd as it is quite possible that
there is a revised edition of that publication. There were a few
inaccuracies in the booklet but generally speaking the information
contained in it was correct.

Yours faithfully,

B R Sutton

Engineer.

Mr. Michael Sutcliffe,
"Jalna",
199, Cressex Road,
High Wycombe,
Bucks.

LEFT: *One of the first letters that I wrote to bus companies at the age of eleven brought this reply from Basil Sutton, the chief engineer of Thames Valley, in October 1954.*

It was always exciting to see the Thames Valley tree lopper No. 29 in service, converted from a Leyland Titan TD1; it is seen here at the Colonnade, Reading. (A. M. Wright)

BELOW: *Captured on film at the Colonnade, Reading, on one of the earlier trips, was this group of Titans and Tigers of Thames Valley, awaiting disposal (No. 267 is again in the background). (Michael Plunkett)*

Further Local Forays

Another activity that would be considered undesirable these days, was for my school friend Peter Wilks, from Flackwell Heath, and myself to set off on our bicycles for the day and cycle from High Wycombe to Maidenhead, Stokenchurch, Twyford, Reading and other far-flung places – again, all at the ages of twelve to fourteen, initially on a small-wheeled 'Gresham Flyer', soon to be replaced by a second-hand full-sized bicycle (on which my odometer clocked up 25,645 miles (41,263km) over the time I had it – once round the world!).

Comet and Pioneer

Already seriously 'bitten by the bug', my first attempt at amateur bus building was around the age of twelve to thirteen, when I built 'Pioneer'. Peter Wilks and I visited one another's houses regularly to compare notes on Thames Valley. With the help of his grandfather, he had converted an old box into a single-decker bus with the use of some pram wheels and plenty of sacks; the resulting vehicle was named 'Comet', and we had great fun pushing one another about in it along the paths in his large garden. Shortly afterwards Peter added an open-top upper deck on the contraption, and Comet Mark II, from a distance, could almost be confused with a London General B type! However, neither of us dared ride on the upper deck as it

(the drivers seat was replaced by a broken lavatory !!)

RIGHT: *Michael Plunkett gave illustrated directions to Goodey's Yard at Twyford, where we may find an ex-Thames Valley Tilling Stevens B9A, with unusual driver's seat, sitting next to a 1920s Lancia.*

BELOW: *Having cycled to Twyford with Peter Wilks, we inspected the remains of Leyland Titan TD1, RX 6244, which was in use as a store shed.*

was so unstable – it would almost fall over if you so much as looked at it!

Comet inspired me to build my own bus. Wheels were in short supply, as every boy wanted to build his own trolley, but having found some that were suitable, I first built the chassis. My grandfather found a box that was just right, side pillars were affixed, and even a curved plywood roof! I painted it green with a white stripe and a grey roof (the latter being copied from Manchester early post-war livery). It was fitted with a steering wheel and electric lighting, powered by a small battery, with switches and jam-jar tops for reflectors. This was the 'bees knees': it could sit two small boys, one behind the other, and needed a lot of pushing with its bus body on. We had

Comet, in Peter Wilks' back garden at Flackwell Heath.

Comet Mark II – rebuilt as a double decker, but extremely unstable when cornering!

Pioneer, with its electric lighting set, tax-disc holder and rear-view mirror, shortly before its unfortunate end.

an immense amount of fun with Pioneer, either with its body on, or in chassis-only form; but unfortunately it came to a sticky end. A friend and I were playing with it on the wonderfully smooth tarmac surfaces in front of the Cressex Road shops, when five youths hijacked us and made off with Pioneer, two inside it, two pushing and one pulling. They ran off with it at an alarming rate, but when turning the first corner and going far too fast, it turned over, and the pillars and roof were smashed to firewood. Poor old Pioneer! The only good thing that came out of it was that the ringleader of the louts was one of the two passengers, both of whom were badly shaken and grazed.

Early Literature

In the 1952–53 period there were very few publications aimed at bus enthusiasts. Ian Allan Ltd was the only serious publisher with the quarterly *Buses Illustrated* magazine, and the ABC books covering some of the major fleets; among these was *The ABC of Ribble Buses and Coaches*. This was a fleet of immense interest to me, being Lancashire based and currently operating so many Leyland buses and coaches. I well recall riding on a Ribble all-Leyland Royal Tiger bus to visit relations on a farm near Barnoldswick. There were no bus stops in the countryside – you merely asked the driver to stop where you wanted to get off. Having reached the farm, and it being the first time my sister and I had ever visited such an establishment, we were excited to watch the cows being milked. However, standing directly behind the cow to study the process is not the thing to do, and the inevitable happened: both Jill and I were plastered from head to toe in hot, steaming cow manure – and it was no consolation to discover later that the cow's name was

'Blow Bags'! After a complete hose-down in the farmyard we were ready to travel back on another Royal Tiger – and I will never forget the sounds that vehicle made, with its low-revving and powerful O600 engine. What lengths an enthusiast will go to in order to hear the sounds of a Leyland engine!

Buses Illustrated opened my eyes to the bus industry, and every issue was a treat to behold, with 'provincial developments' giving up-to-date details of fleet movements. It also contained advertisements by people such as W. J. Haynes, R. H. G. Simpson, *Aviation & Transport* photographs, S. N. J. White, Ascough & Taylor, and a host of other people who sold postcard-sized bus photographs, and much of my very limited pocket money went in sending off for these. I also discovered a fellow enthusiast, Prince Marshall, who ran a small shop in Vauxhall Bridge Road, London, selling bus magazines and photographs, and I persuaded my mother to take me there on one of her occasional shopping trips to London. It was a disappointment not to find any Thames Valley pictures, but Prince put me in touch with Michael Plunkett (*the* expert on the early fleet of Thames Valley, and of course, the Leyland Titan TD1). Both Prince and Michael were to become very good friends who gave me support and encouragement in the future.

The attractive cover of the 1934 Thames Valley timetable showing a Leyland Titan at Windsor Castle.

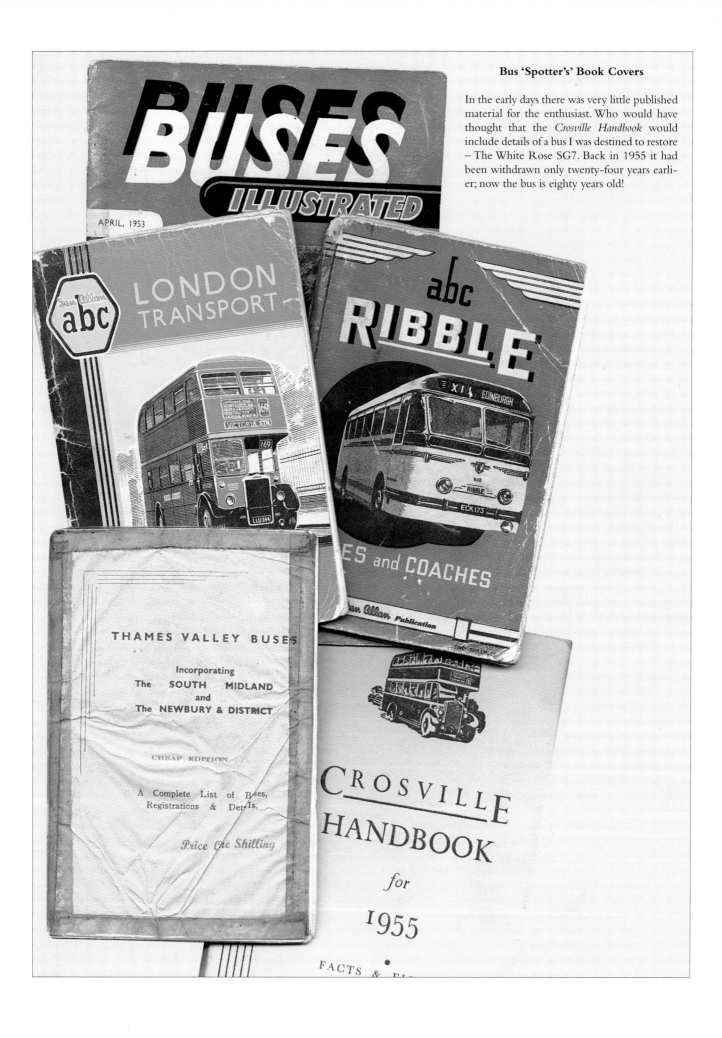

Bus 'Spotter's' Book Covers

In the early days there was very little published material for the enthusiast. Who would have thought that the *Crosville Handbook* would include details of a bus I was destined to restore – The White Rose SG7. Back in 1955 it had been withdrawn only twenty-four years earlier; now the bus is eighty years old!

Letterheads

From the age of eleven, in 1954, I wrote numerous letters to bus operators asking for fleet lists and to bus manufacturers requesting chassis and body numbers, most of whom replied with helpful details. This assisted the learning process for the young Sutcliffe and it was very exciting to rush to the front door when the postman arrived to see what goodies he had brought. How many of these names still survive? (Note the Meccano letter starts 'Dear Sutcliffe'.)

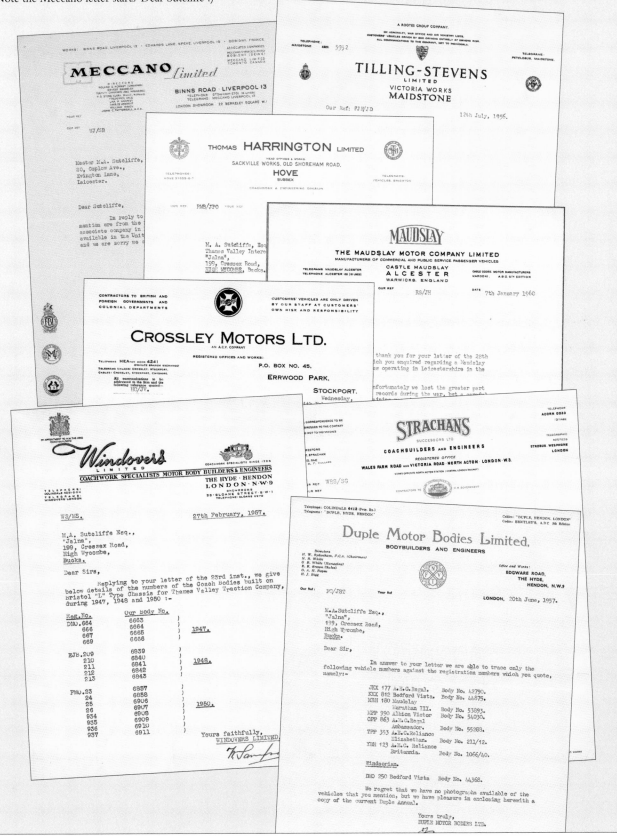

We Move to Leicester

In August 1957, at the age of fourteen, we moved house to Leicester, the land of the AEC Renown Six-Wheelers. These enormous beasts were grossly underpowered: in the words of one of the Leicester City Transport employees, 'They couldn't pull the skin off a rice pudding!' It wasn't difficult to chase them on my bicycle, armed with my new Brownie Cresta camera on my back, and corner them at the next bus stop to record them for posterity. I met new friends – John Paine, Derek Bailey, Peter Smith, Paul Banbury and Maurice Darnes – and every weekend was spent investigating the

ABOVE: *Returning from Allen's of Mountsorrel, Leicestershire, with destination boards from a solid-tyred Dennis and a Dennis Dart coach. Paul Banbury leads the articulated bicycle train, followed by myself, while John Paine gives advice on stability and cornering techniques. It was approximately 10 miles from home – would anyone dare to do this today? (These boards are now mounted on my garage wall at 'Valley Forge'.)*

The South Notts Bus Co. of Gotham was an interesting company to visit, especially as they ran this ex-Todmorden all-Leyland Titan TD5, CWR 286.

independent operators of Leicestershire, and others further away. Four of these fellow enthusiasts were to become joint owners with me of the first vehicle we acquired for preservation (more of that later). Over the next three years we travelled further and further afield (Derek had a car), and by 1960 I had traded in my Brownie Cresta for an Ilford Sportsman 35mm camera, and had taken nearly 200 35mm films (7,000 photographs). However, my interest in modern buses came to an abrupt end around 1968 – with further nationalization and the formation of the National Bus Company, local government re-organization with wholesale

slaughter of municipal operators, and of course, the last of the half-cab double deckers.

In Search of a Gilford

One of the first photographs I took was of a Gilford 168OT with Strachans bodywork that had operated for a local independent, Astill & Jordan of Ratby, Leicestershire. It had clearly been withdrawn from service before the war, and laid up on a farm in Ratby where it had been used as a chicken shed – what a rarity this was – absolutely complete apart from its seats and with its Gruss air suspension very visible. I had never seen a Gilford

before; the firm had gone out of business in the mid-1930s and always held a special intrigue for enthusiasts, so this bus should surely be saved for posterity: but how?

There were no Gilfords remaining in service, but on searching through the 1958 edition of the *Passenger Transport 'Little Red Book'*, it was discovered that a firm called Mulley's Motorways of Ixworth, near Bury St Edmunds, had three Gilfords, reputedly with Wycombe bodies (built in High Wycombe). So early in 1959, off we went to have a look at them, and at the Ixworth depot Jack Mulley gave us permission to look around. There were many wrecks of old buses

Astill & Jordan's chickens, at Ratby, Leicestershire, did not know how lucky they were to reside in a Gilford 168OT with Gruss suspension and Strachans bodywork.

ABOVE: *Mulley's Motorways had these two Duple-bodied Bedford WLBs round the back of the garage. Both went into preservation, but only one finally survived.*

LEFT: *A sketch I did on returning from Mulley's showing the little Chev coach, and escaping feral cats!*

scattered around his premises, but the best ones were inside, in the dry. There were no fewer than four Gilfords, including an AS6 lorry that had once belonged to the Danish Bacon Company. There was a rebodied 168OT (complete with Gruss air suspension), having originated in Scotland, and two AS6 buses, all in as-withdrawn-from-service condition, and all very restorable. Should we ask if we could buy one?

In a lean-to between two garages, and behind two of the Gilfords, was another unusual little coach: a fourteen-seater Chevrolet LQ, with Bush & Twiddy body. We had never seen one of these before, either! It was clearly a breeding ground for Jack Mulley's feral cats, and as I opened the front door of the Chev, cats ran everywhere!

The Start of Bus Preservation

Up to 1956 there were few, if any, motor buses preserved by private collectors, despite the fact that a number of horse buses had survived, most of these having been saved by horse owners, along with all sorts of other carriages and conveyances. A few far-sighted operators had put motor buses and trolleybuses by for preservation, notably London General, followed by London Transport. Their collection of twelve or so historic buses remained virtually unused in store at their Reigate Depot for many years, and these formed the nucleus of the collection that now resides at Covent Garden and The Depot, Acton. A few other operators had held on to older vehicles, including the Portsmouth Thornycroft J, Hastings Tramway's open-top Guy Trolleybus, Southdown's open-top Leyland Titan TD1, and the famous LGOC 'Ole Bill', B43, owned by the Old Comrades Association and kept in commemoration of the part played by such vehicles on the battlefields of Europe in World War One. Barton Transport of Chilwell, Notts, had in 1952 built a replica char-a-bancs body on an early 1920s, solid-tyred Daimler chassis, to look like their first bus, a 1908 Durham-Churchill. This chara was never regarded highly by enthusiasts due to its lack of authenticity; however, the chassis itself is now eighty years old!

By the mid-1950s some far-sighted people had already started collecting early cars and commercials, notably the Sword Collection and Jack Sparshatt, who had a number of early lorries. Interest had also started with the restoration and rallying of traction engines, but in those days anyone who bought and used an old vehicle was regarded as a bit of a 'crank' – it was just not the done thing to have an old car.

In October 1956 the first privately owned preserved bus was purchased by a group of seven people, who included Prince Marshall and Ken Blacker. It was, of course, the ex-London Transport, formerly LGOC AEC Regal, T31, which had been retained for use as a driver-training vehicle; on purchase it was driven to a yard at Swiss Cottage. Restoration commenced by removing some of the side panels, but in doing so, large chunks of the framework came away too: the only remedy was to rebuild the frame. It is frequently at this stage that bus restoration becomes too much of a problem for the owner, especially working out in the open, and a project has faltered. Thus T31 passed through the hands of several owners until Norman Anscomb acquired it; he carried out an excellent major restoration of the bus, finishing it around 1977.

Gradually other vehicles were rescued – a Gilford 168SD with Gruss air suspension, followed by an ex-Leicester six-wheeled AEC Renown, Ken Blacker's Leyland PLSC Lion, and Prince Marshall's ex-Valiant Gilford 168OT. The London-based group formed the Vintage Passenger Vehicle Society (VPVS) in 1957, and by the time the first VPVS vehicle display was held at the Red Lion at Hatfield, Herts in September 1960, seventeen buses were owned by various members.

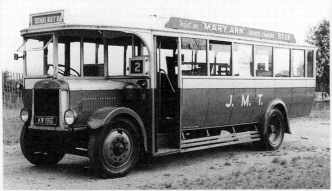

Ken Blacker brought this Leyland Lion PLSC3 back from Jersey in April 1958, and re-registered it with its original registration number, KW 1961. (A. A. F. Bell)

The Leicester Renown six-wheeler with Northern Counties body, seen here in September 1958 at the HCVC rally at Southall. (Paul Banbury)

Prince Marshall was the signatory to this letter to my friend Paul Banbury at the beginning of 1960. The seven founder members are shown at the bottom of the page.

continued overleaf

Running parallel with this, the Historic Commercial Vehicle Club had been inaugurated in 1958 with some important names on its letterhead: Henry Spurrier of Leyland Motors was the president, Lord Montagu of Beaulieu the chairman, and vice presidents included J. E. Foden and Geoffrey Rootes. The first HCVC rally was held at the end of May 1958 at the Leyland factory, and of the twenty entries, only two were privately owned buses, the Jersey Lion and the normal control Gilford 168SD. Further rallies took place at Southall, Beaulieu and Basildon, and in April 1962 the VPVS, the Vintage Taxi Club and HCVC merged, thereby creating a stronger unit. The following month the first annual London to Brighton Run took place, and from then on the preservation movement has gone ahead in leaps and bounds.

The VPVS closed its books when it merged in 1962 with a 'fleet' of thirty-two preserved buses and coaches, and this total grew in geometric proportions to approximately 1,100 vehicles, recorded by Keith Jenkinson in his book *Preserved Buses* in December 1974. The current total would appear to be over 5,000, although it is questionable as to whether all of these are really preserved, and there is a lot of duplication of types. Clearly anyone should be allowed to buy, and get enjoyment from, whatever vehicle they like, but a large number of these cannot be regarded as forming part of any national collection of buses that should be saved for future posterity – more on that later.

The first major bus restoration carried out by anyone was probably Michael Banfield's LGOC S type, which was finished in 1967, followed by Barry Weatherhead's LGOC K type, although there had already been some very significant goods vehicle restorations, for example the Tate & Lyle McCurd. However, the restoration of a lorry is nowhere near as complicated as a bus when it comes to the bodywork – from a restoration point of view there is about three times more work in a bus body than in its chassis – with a lorry there frequently isn't much to the bodywork, apart, of course, from its coachbuilt cab.

With ever-increasing money in peoples' pockets for leisure activities, the acquisition of buses and coaches for preservation may well continue to expand – however, buying a bus is the easy part! Finding accommodation for it under cover is the first major stumbling block, and the next, and by far the biggest, is having the money, skill, effort and staying power to see the job through. And if all of these things can be achieved, the final major hurdle is that of providing long-term security for the restored masterpiece: that is not easy to achieve, and may well be out of our hands!

Prince Marshall's Gilford 168OT ex-Valliant is seen here taking part in an early London to Brighton Run, its Weymann, fabric-covered saloon body now fitted with steel panels. (Steve Stevens-Stratten)

LEFT: *Norman Anscomb's newly restored London General T31. This bus now belongs to the London Bus Preservation Trust and resides at Cobham. (Steve Stevens-Stratten)*

My good friend Michael Plunkett walks around his Brush-bodied Thames Valley Tilling-Stevens B9A at the start of the 1997 London to Brighton Run.

CHAPTER TWO

Holiday in Jersey – The Turning Point

In the late 1950s many bus enthusiasts turned to Jersey for a holiday in the sun, a paradise island where many Leyland buses built in the late 1920s/ early thirties were still actively in service and in original condition – in fact, a 'working museum'. Some of these enthusiasts, notably Ken Blacker and Michael Plunkett, had already been there and purchased Leyland Lions (one 'Long' Lion PLSC3 and one LT1), bringing them back to the mainland for preservation. These were some of the first PSVs to be preserved, other than London Transport's own collection of vehicles taken straight from service. I spent two weeks in Jersey in August 1959 with friends Paul Banbury and Maurice Darnes, and we spent the entire fortnight riding on the buses and recording them. The most memorable journey of all was on a 1931, lowbridge, all-Leyland Titan TD1, J 1199, which tore along the whole length of St Brelades Bay at 40mph (65km/h), with its petrol engine purring and virtually every joint in its ancient bodywork oscillating – what a magnificent machine this is! (It is preserved and now owned by Peter Stanier.)

The Snow Hill bus station was an interesting place. It was in a deep railway cutting with high rocks on either side, being on the site of the previous railway line. There was no room to turn buses around, and a railway-style turntable was provided at one end for that purpose: buses drove onto the turntable and stopped in a predetermined position for the balance to be absolutely right, after which the conductor/driver could manually turn the bus round. Some of the more skilful and daring drivers would screech to a halt on the turntable, turning the steering wheel violently at the last minute, and the sideways momentum

ABOVE: *In 1958 Michael Plunkett sent me this Christmas card of Leyland Lions snowbound in St Helier – enough to entice any enthusiast to visit the island of Jersey.*

From left to right, Maurice Darnes, myself and Paul Banbury pose in front of a 1932 Titan TD2 in St Helier. The bus is now preserved by Michael Banfield. (Paul Banbury)

Treasure Island! Jersey, 1959

JMT Lion LT2 tears along St Brelades Bay.

JMT Titan TD2 at St Helier with an RTL.

Ex-Red Line Gilford 168OT with JMP body in a quarry.

A Leyland Cub once with Jersey Airlines.

Ex-Tantivy Motors Cheetah LZ2/Alexander in a quarry.

Jersey Tours ran this Bedford WTBI with Duple rear-entrance body.

JMT had three of these ex-Southdown Leyland KPZ1 Cubs.

Typical of Joe's Bus Service fleet of Morris-Commercials.

(All pictures courtesy of Paul Banbury)

of the bus would start the turntable in motion!

At the other end of the bus station and across the main road was the Jersey Motor Transport bus garage, again converted from railway buildings, and part of the parking area for the elderly, disused Leyland buses was along the top of a railway embankment. A number of real treasures were to be found here, including No. 3, a PLSC1 Lion. There were also LT1 and LT2 Lions, a Cheetah, the ex-King George V Lioness, a remarkably handsome Burlingham-bodied Lioness Six that had once operated for Brookes Brothers (White Rose) of Rhyl, and two further hybridge Leyland-bodied Titan TD1s, No. 36 and No. 39.

Major Blakeway had been the manager of JMT since the early 1930s, and he was very much a Leyland man. He kindly took us in his car to show us the various sights, and I clearly remember him expressing his disappointment that Leyland had finished body building in 1954. They had recommended that his next two Titans were bodied by Metropolitan Cammell Carriage & Wagon Works, but he didn't like them, and commented that the best place for them was 'Where a monkey stuffs its nuts', or something like that (I never quite got the point of it); so future bodies on Titans were built by Reading.

One evening over dinner the three of us resolved that we could not possibly go back home without taking a bus with us, and furthermore, it would have to be one of the TD1s – No. 39. We visited the Major the next morning and told him of our intentions, and he let us test drive No. 39; the sum of £40 was agreed for its purchase, and a deposit was handed over there and then. We had bought a bus – and now the problems really started!

While in Jersey we also visited the garage of A. A. Pitcher, who traded as 'Tantivy', another long-established Jersey bus and coach operator. Inside the garage and totally hemmed in was another vehicle that had just been taken out of service: a rear-entrance, Burlingham-bodied, forward-control

Leyland Cub (or possibly even a Lion Cub), in absolutely immaculate condition and with extremely comfortable seats. I couldn't help but sit there for a good half hour thinking that this magnificent coach would soon go to the scrap heap, but really must be saved for posterity – but how? I couldn't even record it on film as the surrounding vehicles were too close, and I always wondered what happened to it. J 10740 had spent the

Tantivy Motor's little Burlingham-bodied SKP3 Cub, sporting what appears to be a later radiator, and with Leyland 'By Appointment' coat of arms. (Photobus)

whole of its life in Jersey, and I'll bet it didn't have many miles on the clock. What a terrible waste of such a handsome little coach!

Titan Struggle

On the flight back to Birmingham airport (on a Douglas DC3 Dakota) we discussed what we would do next. Clearly we had to arrange transport for No. 39, and we would also have to get Customs' clearance to bring it into the country. I volunteered to go down to the local H. M. Customs & Excise Office to find out just what had to be done, and what procedures had to be followed. The next day I found myself in the Customs Office in Leicester, explaining to these two nice men that

we had bought a double-decker bus in Jersey, and wanted to bring it home: what should we do, 'What forms do you need filling in?' They whispered to one another, and I'm sure two of the words were 'nut case', and asked me to repeat my question, which of course I did, with even more vigour. To my amazement and sheer annoyance they both fell about laughing, exclaiming 'You've bought a bus in Jersey, ha ha!' I tried to re-establish some sort of credibility, but it was absolutely useless – they laughed even louder!

What could an inexperienced boy of sixteen do in these circumstances? I walked out, and recall the tears flooding into my eyes as I made my way down the steps. Paul enquired into the costs of shipping No. 39, and was given quotes of around £100 – two-and-a-half times its purchase price! It was becoming absolutely hopeless now – how could we save No. 39? I don't recall what happened next, but the whole project was abandoned, and Major Blakeway kindly returned our deposit. No. 39 ended up derelict on a farm, but its engine did survive, and was brought back to the mainland to assist in the preservation of another early Leyland.

Back to Mulley's Motorways

Having recovered from the Titan trauma, and seeing the bus preservation movement expanding every month, we had no intentions of being left behind: if we could not rescue a double decker, perhaps we should rescue two single deckers. Paul Banbury was delegated to write to Jack Mulley to see if he would sell one of his Gilford AS6s – UT 7836 the Willowbrook twenty-seater, new in 1930 to Whetton, Coalville, Leicestershire – together with the Chevrolet LQ, namely VF 8157, with Bush & Twiddy fourteen-seat coach body, built in 1930. A letter came back by return from Mulley's Motorways to say that the Gilford AS6 was not for sale, but the Chevrolet could be bought for £40 – this seemed to be about the going rate for an old bus in those days, possibly just above scrap value. We replied that we would very much like to buy the Chevrolet, and then proceeded to look for somewhere to keep it – though not very successfully, and out in the open in a breakdown recovery firm's yard in Leicester.

Three months elapsed, and then on 19 December 1959, my seventeenth birthday, I received a telegram

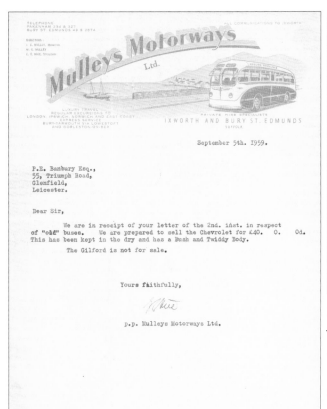

LEFT: *The reply came back from Mulley's Motorways that the Chevrolet LQ was for sale, but not the Gilford AS6.*

ABOVE: *The Chev, ready for collection on my seventeenth birthday, 19 December 1959, carrying slogans 'Not to be opened 'til Xmas', 'Ban the Bomb', and suchlike.*

BELOW: *A friendly tow from Mulley's ex-London Transport STL helped to get the Chev started.*

from Jack Mulley and off we went to Ixworth, a journey of 108 miles (174km). When we arrived we found that the Chev had been removed from the garage and the tyres pumped up; it stood in the corner of Mulley's yard looking very dirty, with chalk signs saying 'Frying Tonight', 'Ban the Bomb', and 'Not to be opened until Christmas'. Jack Mulley informed us that she was 'a runner', but the battery was flat and we had to get a tow start from Mulley's STL (EGO 426, itself now preserved and taking pride of place at the Cobham Bus Museum).

The journey home was very eventful and exceedingly frustrating due to a combination of a flat battery and continual petrol blockages, but we finally reached the yard in Leicester at 11pm. The story of this journey home was told in an article, 'Frying Tonight', that I wrote for *Buses Illustrated* magazine, being published in issue No. 85, dated April 1962.

There were originally seven shareholdings in the Chev, each contributing 2s 6d (12½p) per week. This meant that we could just afford to rent a small garage to house the vehicle, costing 15s 0d (75p a week) with 2s 6d left over to spend on restoration costs. The garage was behind Leicester Station in a very seedy part of Leicester, and opposite a brothel, which caused us great amusement to see the comings and goings, and the ferrying of clients back and forth in a clapped-out mid-thirties Wolseley car! The bus preservationists' biggest nightmare is finding somewhere to store and restore your treasure, and this was solved, at least for the moment.

The next step was to pull everything apart, with the intention of restoring each piece individually and putting it back in due course – a major potential problem, and the downfall of many well intentioned restoration projects, where the owner has not had the resources or the determination to get on with the restoration and complete it quickly. Within ten months the inevitable happened, and the majority of the shareholders wanted to pull out and dispose of the Chev. So I took the lead, still aged seventeen, and with the help of my mother, bought the others out, with John Paine and Derek Bailey owning part shares. Over the next five years John and I spent every Saturday working on the restoration, and when this was completed, took it for its first outing on the May 1965 London to Brighton Run.

With the change in ownership in late 1959, the bus restorer's nightmare again became a reality: with our reduced number of shareholders, we could not afford to keep up the rent payments, and soon after found ourselves under a sheet of tarpaulin in a demolition contractor's yard. It was two steps forwards and three steps backwards every week, another major blow coming when we were given notice to move out because the space was needed for a bulldozer. The situation was absolutely desperate, and many a bus preservationist, in such circumstances, has given up.

The Tin Blackbird

Having left school and taken articles to study as an accountant, I was guaranteed to earn only a pittance for the next five years; but despite these financial restraints I was absolutely determined that we should not lose the Chev. After much searching, a kind elderly gentleman living in Scraptoft, a village near Leicester, offered us a tumble-down barn, most of which had been destroyed in recent gales. The deal was that if John and I rebuilt it, we could lease it for a 'pepper-corn' rent. This was an offer that could not be refused! The same gale had fortunately destroyed a corrugated-iron Nissen hut in another Leicestershire village and the owner needed the site clearing: John and I leapt at the opportunity. It took us six months of Saturdays and holidays to complete the restoration of the building, and at last we moved the

TOP: *Before: the skeleton of the 'Blackbird'.*

ABOVE: *'The Tin Blackbird': after – sheer luxury. (With my mother's Ford Anglia that I 'tarted up to the eyebrows', as an eighteen-year-old son would do.)*

'The Chev'

The restoration of this little coach is not covered in detail here, as the emphasis in this book is on the early Leylands in my collection. However, the five and a half years taken to restore the Chev were very important in the learning process of restoring a bus. The vehicle was owned by me for a period of over forty-two years (a very long time!), until in January 2002 I sold it to the Ipswich Transport Museum. It is therefore in good hands, and nice to see it back in its own operating area, East Anglia.

Set out on these two pages are some of the more important pictures relating to the restoration of that attractive little coach. The 1930 Chevrolet LQ coach, VF 8157, with fourteen-seater body by Bush & Twiddy, Norwich, made its first appearance after restoration on the London to Brighton Run in May 1965.

I made this sketch of the Chev at the age of seventeen in February 1960, before removing the Mulley's paintwork, as a reminder of what it originally looked like.

John Paine working on the Chev in the demolition contractor's yard in 1961.

I am at work rubbing down the rear dome on a borrowed ladder with no rungs.

1965 – Derek Bailey (left), John Paine and I (the year before I grew my beard!) pose with the Chev ready for setting off for Brighton.

BELOW: *The two Bush & Twiddy-bodied Chevrolet LQs meet at Brighton, VF 6618 being owned by Michael Banfield.*

BELOW RIGHT: *For a short period I owned another Chevrolet LQ, this time a small truck registered KP 8118, which I sold many years ago to buy a World War One Karrier lorry.*

BOTTOM: *The Chev looks resplendent after the restoration work was completed, in the livery of T.O. Osborne of Ixworth, the colours that it carried just before its acquisition by Jack Mulley.*

Chev into the 'Tin Blackbird': what luxury – a building of our own, though not secure. We made an inspection pit out of an old water tank, which unfortunately almost immediately filled up with water. It had a dirt floor, and even an electricity supply, albeit an exceedingly dangerous one for using electric drills – in damp weather one experienced a sort of tingling, vibrating feeling coming from the metal-cased drill whenever it was used. This would not be tolerated these days!

The next five years were a tale of sheer determination and a lot of hard work. At such a tender age a young man has very few skills, particularly when trying to copy some of the craftsmanship that went into the original product. Many jobs that we undertook we did again at a later stage because we were not satisfied with the first result – and sometimes did them even a third time. Both John and I had a flair for artistic tasks, and the job we enjoyed the most was to hand paint the garter on each side of the Chev with the initials of the owner, in whose livery we had painted the coach: T. Osborne of Ixworth, the owner in 1937, just prior to Jack Mulley acquiring the bus in 1941. By comparing notes we each produced a garter that turned out to be almost identical the one with the other!

From May 1965 the trip to London and then the Brighton Run became annual pilgrimages, and the little Chev coach became very well known among vintage bus enthusiasts. We attended many other rallies with it, and it was always a pleasure to drive, and gave us a great deal of enjoyment.

The Years Between

The next fifteen years or so were particularly quiet in terms of vehicle restoration. In 1964 I had bought a 1928 Swift 3P, 10hp tourer (registered UR 1931), and this was my first every-day car. Not satisfied with its condition – it had been restored by its previous owner – I eventually pulled it completely to pieces, and then re-restored it over a number of years. The

Swift is still mine and is quite a nice, driveable little car; but since its restoration now dates to thirty years ago, it is in need of some tidying up and a re-paint.

In 1966 I married Molly and there were a number of house moves, coupled with changes in job: first to Enfield, then Brentwood, followed by a move to Lower Stanton St Quintin in Wiltshire in 1974 – this a momentous occasion, as will be recounted later. In the meantime, still having little money to spare and bringing up a young family, most of my efforts were aimed at photography, copying many manufacturers' and operators' official collections, and ending up with a collection of over 60,000 photographs of vehicles, mainly buses and coaches from the earlier years. The time was also taken building up the nucleus of what is now a massive collection of

commercial vehicle-related books, histories, magazines and vehicle badges. It has since grown into what must be one of the largest private collections of this kind of material. Part of the collection includes forty commercial vehicle radiators dating from 1910 to 1960, which can be found on display all over the house and my garages.

A Second Turning Point

1974 was an important year. First, I had accepted a job promotion to Swindon; then, two weeks before the house move, two friends, Roy Marshall and Vic Blackmore, turned up at my front door in Brentwood, saying they had little time to spare, but '… did I know that there were two old Todmorden buses in a hedge only five miles away?' This had to be a joke! What were Todmorden buses doing in Essex? And

My 1928 Swift 3P, 10hp tourer, UR 1931, photographed at a Swift gathering at Warwick Castle one very cold day at the end of April 1981.

in a hedge? But I could not ignore it, especially when the word 'Todmorden' was uttered: a visit became essential. So we drove up and down the country lanes around Navestock, with Vic constantly saying things like, 'It must be around here somewhere', and on numerous occasions 'This must be the place!' – and then suddenly it was 'This is it!' and we screeched to a halt. We approached the farmhouse and explained that '… we would like to see the old bodies in the corner of the field'; the farmer obviously thought we were completely mad and gave us

although I was able to rescue the upper part of the front and rear bulkheads that still proclaimed the maker's name: 'Leyland Motors Ltd'. We hacked our way through the undergrowth to find the lower saloon of the other body still fairly intact, although in a dreadful state after being forty-six years out in the open – in fact it was a total wreck! On the rusted side panels one could only just make out the wording on the garter surrounding the Corporation Coat of Arms: it read 'Todmorden Corporation'. My goodness! So it was true, and not just a

Over the next two weeks, frantic preparations were made not only to move our household contents and so on in one removal van, and to put the Swift car and another little 1929 Chevrolet LQ truck (that I had acquired in the meantime) into a second removal van, but a third van was ordered to transport the Todmorden body. To manhandle it to the van, all my neighbours were seconded, together with Michael Plunkett, Bob Hearn and many of my vehicle friends, about eighteen of us in all: using a frame of planks, and with G-clamps fastened

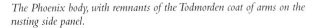
The Phoenix body, with remnants of the Todmorden coat of arms on the rusting side panel.

The magnificent interior of the Phoenix body showing the front bulkhead. When wet it gleamed in the sunshine, and it was clear that this Phoenix had to rise from the ashes!

permission to inspect 'the bodies'; but then would have nothing more to do with us.

They stood fifty yards apart; complete with upper decks and staircase, they had been used for sleeping accommodation for temporary farmworkers back in 1928. They lay at the edge of a field, and a dense hawthorn hedge had grown up around them and through them, until they were hardly visible. One was a Leyland body of *c.* 1923 that had completely collapsed and was just a pile of rotting wood,

wind-up! Soaked by a recent shower, the oak and inlaid mahogany front bulkhead glistened in the sunlight – as it would look when it was varnished! The sun shone through the six remaining (out of twelve) ventilator windows that were glazed in sparkling yellow hammered glass: *this* magnificent bus just had to be saved! Not only that, but this body was one of about five made by the Phoenix Cabinet & Joinery Co. of Milwood, Todmorden and, more importantly, by a man called E. Sutcliffe and his brothers.

underneath it, we bodily picked up the body, walked it across the field, over a little bridge and into the Pickfords removal van, with less than half an inch to spare at each side! Again, the farmer thought we were completely mad, would not take any money for the body, and was glad to see the back of us. Once in Wiltshire, the wreck was placed on oil drums in my back garden and covered with a black polytarp to keep the weather out. The story of what happened next is told later in Chapter 8.

The Hobby that Got Out of Hand?

This was the start of something a lot bigger than I realized at the time. By 1977 we had moved to Studham, near Dunstable in Bedfordshire, following yet another job move. That year was spent buying a plot of land and building my own house and garage, something I had always wanted to do; but it took every spare minute of weekends, holidays, evenings and early mornings before going to work. However, there was room for my vehicles, although the bigger ones had to be content with a larger car port – or should I say, bus port – big enough for three vehicles, but open on two sides. It is here that the *serious* restoration was to begin.

In the late 1970s/early 1980s I became very good friends with Barry Weatherhead of LGOC K-type, Tilling Stevens, Sentinel and so on fame; he and I went out virtually every weekend with his little Bedford pick-up, collecting vehicle parts or even complete buses and lorries. In those days there were still a few early vehicles to be acquired, but the numbers were declining rapidly and soon would virtually dry up altogether. However, we did our bit! In a relatively short time Barry himself acquired many vehicles and parts, we jointly acquired vehicles, and as well as some other makes, I recovered the remains of no fewer than fifty-two Leylands – from major units, for instance chassis frames and wheels with no engine, to complete vehicles. It is these that have formed the nucleus of my collection and provided spare parts where things have been missing in order to complete a restoration.

House Demolition

In some cases it has been necessary to demolish a house in order to rescue the bus that sits inside it! Barry and I have accomplished this on four occasions. You might ask 'What is a bus doing inside a house?', but in the years between the two World Wars many people would buy a bus out of

service, park it up and convert it into a static caravan. Most of these buses would not necessarily be very old when purchased, and had probably become obsolete in the fleet of its operator when new vehicles of a much more up-to-date design had been delivered. In the 1950s and sixties, which is as far as my memory goes back, there were literally hundreds of fields full of these old buses, particularly near seaside resorts or natural beauty spots – for instance, Matlock in Derbyshire, where you could see AEC Qs, trolleybuses, and all sorts of goodies when passing through on the train.

Of course, some also still remain in the Wye Valley. One such 'goldfield' was Purley Park, near Reading, an area close to the River Thames where it was felt desirable to live in a bus with its floor resting on the chassis frame, so that in case of flooding your house was well off the ground – I suppose a bit like those houses you see on stilts in China and such countries! Many of

these 'caravans' would have been enlarged, the first step being to put a pitched roof over, and then cladding around the sides in order to try to disguise its 'bus-iness'. Possibly the family would increase and another room was required and added, then another, and then a brick-built fireplace installed. At the end of the day it would be almost impossible to recognize the bus from the outside – except of course to the trained eye! This led to countless hours spent by Barry and myself driving and walking around these shanty towns looking for evidence. There was even Lucky Forman's ex-Maidstone & District Tilling Stevens TS6 double decker, in which he used to keep his racing pigeons. I well remember viewing its interior and sliding around in wet pigeon droppings, trying desperately not to fall over while inspecting its remains (since rescued by Chris Newman). What wonderful days those were, but we just didn't have the time, energy or money to rescue them all! Now, they have gone!

'Bus in a house' at Newark. This chalet bungalow was situated on the outskirts of Southwell Racecourse, near Newark – would you know that there was a bus inside? A tell-tale sign is the flight of steps up to the front door, as the floor of the house rested on the chassis frame. This was in fact my Barnsley & District 1913 Leyland as originally found, and before demolition work started – see Chapter 5.

CHAPTER THREE

Serious Restoration

Having acquired the remains of my first Leyland in 1974, and accumulated many more major parts for Leyland RAF types, what I would call 'serious restoration' started in 1981. This has continued ever since, being halted only temporarily due to divorce; moving house again; then marriage to Pat, who supports my vehicle restoration activities enormously; buying a seventeenth-century, Grade II listed thatched cottage; both Pat and me being made redundant on the same day, and nearly losing the cottage; preparing drawings and getting planning permission and listed building consent (not easy!); thoroughly renovating and extending the cottage (really just like a chassis-up restoration, but much easier); erecting three enormous, quality built garages to accommodate nine buses; and last but not least, starting up a new chartered accountant business from scratch. Each one of these could be described as a 'life crisis', but with Pat's help and support we have gone from strength to strength, and restoration work has continued throughout most of this time.

The Mike Sutcliffe Collection of Leyland Buses

During the period 1981 up to the time of writing, we have restored seven elderly Leylands dating from 1908 to 1924, all of which have been major restoration jobs; and we are currently working on a former Barnsley & District Electric Traction, Leyland S3.30.T 'Combination Car' of 1913.

These Leylands now form not only the biggest, but also the most significant collection of really early motor buses in the whole world – double the quantity of the next largest collection of solid-tyred buses (namely

the London Transport Museum at Covent Garden). Apart from the fact that they are all Leylands (Leyland became the biggest commercial vehicle producer in the UK, and was once the fifth biggest motor manufacturer in the world), mine cover a very varied cross-section of early bus and coach operation in this country, both in terms of the style of bodywork and also the operating fleets.

There are four double deckers, one of which is the oldest restored British-built motor bus (and also the oldest surviving Leyland vehicle). This Leyland X2 was built in 1908 and operated for the London Central Motor Omnibus Co., which became a major component part of London General, later London Transport. In fact its body is older than the chassis, having been built in 1906 and operated by Thomas Tilling, before being sold second-hand to London Central. This vehicle is probably of the most significant importance in the collection, though this is very difficult to say.

The 'newest' double decker in the collection is another London bus, once operated by not only the first, but the most famous of the London 'pirate operators' of the 1920s and thirties. Formed in 1922 by the infamous Arthur Partridge, the Chocolate Express Omnibus Co. was later compulsorily taken over by London Transport in 1934. This bus was originally built on solid-tyred wheels, but was converted to pneumatics in 1930. It carries a body built by Christopher Dodson of Willesden, built to a design used extensively for the 'pirates'. The pirate buses were faster than the 'General' buses, and creamed off the passengers from the more lucrative routes until they were legislated off the road. Chocolate Express was one of the last to survive.

The other two double deckers come from provincial operators, although the design of one of them, the 1913 Wellingborough Motor Omnibus Co. Leyland S3.30.T bus, was almost 100 per cent influenced by London operations. It is one of the second generation of British motor buses built to a low weight specification, following the 1909 Metropolitan Police weight limits, and was contemporary with the London General 'B type'. It carries a body built by Birch Bros, the longest lived, privately owned London bus operator (and coachbuilders), to a relatively simple specification in order to achieve the low weight. This is the oldest surviving British provincial double-decker bus.

The other provincial double decker, the 1921 Todmorden Leyland G, is typical of the very small number of double deckers operating outside London at the time, belonging to a municipality. Todmorden Corporation had a very important early history of motor-bus operation. It was also built on a chassis of a model primarily developed for War Office/Royal Flying Corps work in World War One, I later developed for civilian use. It carries a body locally built by the Sutcliffe Brothers who traded as Phoenix of Todmorden, cabinet makers.

The next four are single deckers, all on solid tyres – and there are hardly any other British-built single deckers remaining on solid-tyred wheels. The earliest in the collection, built in 1913, is the oldest surviving, full-sized, British-built, single-decker bus. It is of particular interest as it was one of the first built for a tramway operator belonging to the British Electric Traction Group, and was therefore the forerunner of one of the biggest bus-operating groups in this country. BET was nationalized in 1968 and became

1908 London Central Leyland X2.

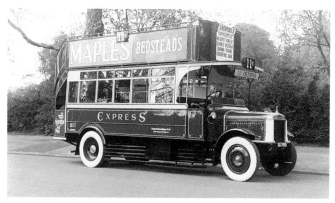

1924 Chocolate Express Leyland LB5.

ABOVE: *1913 Wellingborough Leyland S3.30.T.*
RIGHT: *1921 Todmorden Leyland G.*

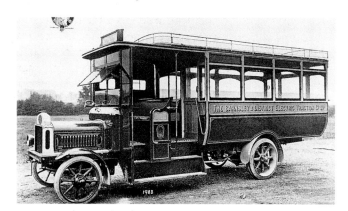

1913 Barnsley & District Leyland 'Combination Car'.

1914 L&NWR Leyland char-a-bancs.

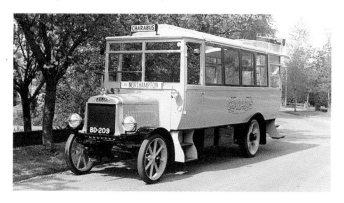

1921 Leyland G7 – 'The Charabus'.

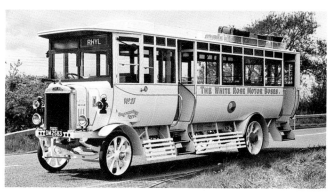

1923 White Rose Leyland SG7.

part of the National Bus Company. This Barnsley & District Electric Tramways Leyland S3.30.T bus has a 'combination car' style of body, with 'toast-rack' bench seats in front and an enclosed saloon behind – very typical of early tramway practice.

Next comes the London & North Western Railway 1914 Leyland S4.36.T3 char-a-bancs (French for 'carriage with benches'). It has a 'Torpedo' type of body, and is the only surviving, genuine full-sized char-a-bancs. (There are two or three remaining unrestored post-war charas.) It is also one of only two remaining former railway-owned buses, the railways having played a very major role in the development of the bus-operating industry in this country.

The 1921 'Charabus' is now completely unique, and was one of a number with this type of body built by Christopher Dodson of Willesden, one of the most important of the English coachbuilders; this company started by building horse buses, and went out of business in the early 1930s. This particular example of a 'convertible' bus (with removable side windows) was the first 'Charabus' built by Dodson, who exhibited it on their stand at the 1921 Commercial Motor Show at Olympia, afterwards using it as a demonstrator. It then passed to United Counties Omnibus and Road Transport Co., who went on to become one of the major companies within the Tilling Group, nationalized in 1948, and going into the National Bus Company in 1968.

The White Rose, Leyland SG7 of 1923 is an example of one of the first British, high-capacity, single-decker buses ever built, with dual doorways, first-class and second-class passenger compartments, and seating accommodation for forty passengers – in fact, it was a real monster (or should I say dinosaur?) of its day. The White Rose fleet, operated by Brookes Brothers of Rhyl, was typical of the small, prosperous, independent operators of the day which sold out to the larger companies around the time of the Road Traffic Act of 1930. White

Rose was a very famous company, being absorbed by Crosville Motor Services, a company then owned by the LMS Railway, and which went into the nationalized Tilling Group in 1948, later to become part of the National Bus Company.

These eight buses therefore represent most of the major building blocks of the British bus industry in its formative years. A ninth Leyland in the collection, and next in line for restoration, is rather more modern: a 1934 Leyland Tiger TS6, with 8.6-litre Leyland oil engine (diesel). Apart from being the oldest surviving Northern Counties-built body, this bus originally operated for the Todmorden Joint Omnibus Committee, a fleet jointly owned and operated by Todmorden Corporation and the London Midland & Scottish Railway. Only four municipalities had this sort of joint ownership with railway companies, the others being Halifax, Huddersfield and Sheffield. This bus therefore has important railway links, and even carries the LMS crest as part of its joint coat of arms. It is also a very important representative of bus operations in Yorkshire (and Lancashire).

So, with seven Leylands restored, one currently undergoing restoration, and one more to go, this is the total of what I am realistically going to be able to achieve through my own efforts and with the help of a small group of friends.

Standard of Restoration

When looking at the vehicles on a rally field, or paraded along Madeira Drive on the Brighton Run, one sees a complete range of restoration work, from a poorly repainted or bodged-up job to the over-restored eight wheeler, over-sign-written and with a polished wood flat-bed body. Frequently vehicles, usually lorries, are almost 'customized', with extra bumpers, lights and so on, reflecting their current owners' preferences rather than what the vehicle may have actually looked like either in service or when new. These vehicles never ran like that in service and in

my opinion should be *authentically* restored. Sometimes they carry a modern 'SV' or 'DS' 'age-related' number plate with little attempt made to obtain the original registration (although this is not always possible for an imported vehicle).

The restoration of buses and coaches is usually a little more restrained, with their owners usually wanting to present the vehicle in its original livery, or at least one that it carried during its operating lifetime. I do not like to see a bus in a livery that it never wore – would you repaint a GWR 'Castle' class locomotive in your own personalized livery of purple and black? I think not! There are frequently poorly restored buses, but not often do you find one that is over-restored. Some of the nicest examples, although they are few and far between, are those that have been maintained in good 'out of service' condition. Frequently, however, the term 'out of service' is used as an excuse to present a shabbily restored vehicle that has had little work carried out on it since it left the service, possibly with a building contractor many years after normal PSV operation. Genuine 'out of service' vehicles do not last in that sort of state for very long, since even the most carefully preserved vehicles deteriorate over time. In my view the most successful restorations are those that have been brought to the best possible condition with what is already there, with everything restored in a sympathetic, authentic and accurate way. No attempt should ever be made to 'gild the lily', and make any part of the vehicle better than it was when it was new.

I would classify all of my Leyland restorations as 'major restorations'. Because of their enormous age, far fewer of these older vehicles have survived, unlike buses from the 1950s and later, when it may have been easy to buy an 'out of service' Leyland Atlantean, PD2, or an RT/RM. In the early days of the motor bus, when technology was leaping ahead, buses became obsolete in a very short space of time. For example, my London

Central X type lasted for four years, being withdrawn from service in 1912. Likewise the White Rose SG7 of 1923 only just lasted into Crosville ownership in 1930, by which time the Leyland PLSC Lion had been introduced, followed by the 'T'-series Leyland Lion and Tiger; the White Rose must have been exceedingly cumbersome and sluggish compared with these modern new buses.

should also be said that there are very few vehicle restorers who have been prepared to go to these extreme lengths in order to see the vehicle brought back to its former glory.

With the first five of my Leyland restorations, where I have come across the bus body, it has meant finding a suitable chassis, of exactly the right model, in order to make the restoration possible at all: if this is not done,

not gone to this trouble, there would be virtually no genuine full-size buses in preservation dating from before 1925 (except for the handful in the London Transport Collection). *All* of these people have carried out what I would describe as 'major restorations' of *specific* vehicles without having produced replicas or re-creations – both of these words are often used incorrectly, and I will try and put the record straight, as I see it.

Replicas and Re-Creations

The *Oxford English Dictionary* defines the word 'replica' as 'an exact copy or reproduction, especially on a smaller scale', and 're-creation' as 'something reproduced/created anew'. Both of these when applied to vehicles conjure up in most preservationists' mind something like an Asquith van, the Beaulieu and Devon 'London General B types', the Beamish replica Daimler double decker, or even a Ford Model T/Morris one-tonner or International bus, with a clearly new and certainly not authentic char-a-bancs or small bus body (there is a growing number of these latter vehicles). These are not genuine historic vehicles, and for most *real* enthusiasts they are not at all nice (to put it politely), and certainly not worth a second glance. Some do, however, have a very important role to play, particularly in museums such as Beamish and Beaulieu where they give a novelty ride to the general public without wearing out the real thing. The Beamish replica of a *c.* 1913 Daimler is probably the best example of these and, like many replicas, it is built on a modern diesel chassis. I feel that the non-authentic re-bodies of earlier chassis should always be regarded very much as 'second rate', as they are likely to deceive people of future generations as to what the original vehicle was precisely like, even though the restorer may have done the job with the best of intentions. If a job is worth doing, it should be done *properly*.

So, where do my vehicles fit in? Especially when much of the woodwork of the body, for example, has

This is the state in which most of my vehicles have been found, or even worse! The Todmorden Leyland G, devoid of engine, gearbox and many other bits and pieces.

After withdrawal, most buses had their bodies removed and were fitted with lorry bodies, which would probably double the life-span of the chassis. The bus bodies, that were still quite sound, were then sold off for sheds or living accommodation, and this is how some of them managed to last into more modern times. But having endured fifty or sixty years of English weather, most of the bodies that I have rescued have been in a pretty poor state, and have needed a major restoration to bring them back to life. It

the vehicle could not be restored and would never run again. With the next two Leyland restorations – the L&NWR 'Torpedo' Char-a-bancs and the White Rose, Leyland SG7 – it is the chassis that I have found, and I have needed to find the correct body. Some 'purists' might say that these are not then genuine restorations of original vehicles, but I would argue very strongly against that. If people like me, or Prince Marshall, Michael Banfield, Barry Weatherhead, Richard Peskett and Bill Thornycroft at Amberley had

had to be replaced, but where all the ironwork, fittings and so on have been retained, and with, of course, an original chassis. I would classify them as being 'major restorations', since they all start with the remains of a *specific* vehicle, even if a lot of bits are missing and have had to be replaced. Each of these vehicles has its own 'pedigree' in that it actually ran for the operator in question, and the bus can be identified as a particular vehicle, even down to the retention of its original registration number and livery. They cannot possibly be called replicas or re-creations because they have not been re-created from new. Admittedly if you have major components missing – for instance an engine, a gearbox or axles or wheels – then *correct* originals (not made from new) have to be found. Besides, when a vehicle is in service these are frequently replaced anyway. So where do you draw the line? If you were restoring a railway locomotive that had stood in the Barry scrapyard for many years devoid of most of its fittings and its tender, it would be rescued and all the missing parts would be found from other surviving examples, or made from new to the original pattern. The end result would be a restoration job, albeit a very major one. If, however, an additional Class A1 Pacific locomotive is built from scratch, as is currently happening –

'Tornado' – that cannot be called a restoration in any sense of the word: it is a re-creation. A 'Thomas the Tank Engine' lookalike would be a replica, even though it is not an exact copy of an original locomotive.

Why do I discuss this in so much detail? Because on rally fields I hear so many different questions and opinions, many quite heated, that I want to put forward my own points of view, together with my reasons for holding them.

Authenticity

Why does anybody, especially a chartered accountant who ought to know better, spend so much time and money on an asset that will never be worth what he puts into it? This is a good question! 'Is he mad?', I imagine many people have wondered. But the answer is no: I am a true enthusiast, and I don't mind admitting that this is a hobby that has got out of hand. I don't smoke, or drink (much!), or have expensive holidays – Pat's and my hobbies are gardening and early vehicles respectively, and we are both intensely interested in them. I get a tremendous 'buzz' carrying out the research, not only into the particular vehicle's history and so on, but how it is made. When there are many bits missing or to be replaced, there is a lot of 'detective work', investigating what

the vehicle was like when it was built. The restoration work has to be absolutely authentic, to the minutest detail, totally irrespective of cost and the time involved in getting it right. It has to be correct in every last detail, and in the following chapters you will see the lengths to which I will sometimes go in order to achieve this. As an example, I will not use any cross-head screws; also all the nuts and bolts must have Whitworth or BSF threads, and none of that nasty metric rubbish. I will even file off the initials of Mr Guest, Mr Keen and Mr Nettlefold from bolt heads, and any initials other than 'LML'; and I have had brass nuts specially made at times, just to get the job absolutely authentic. OK, so I may be a bit eccentric, but surely, that's part of being British! I find it an immense challenge, and take the view that 'if it's been done before, it can be done again'. There is a large element of discovery, and tremendous satisfaction when you know you have got something just right. It also gives me enormous pleasure to prepare scaled drawings of parts that we need to make, or even of the whole vehicle, and also planning the weekly restoration activities so that we accomplish them in the most efficient way possible.

Saturday is 'restoration day' at Valley Forge (the Sutcliffe household), and every weekend I have help from Steve Elliott, a model engineer: Steve

Finding the bits – these pictures are typical of one of the many expeditions of Barry Weatherhead and myself – struggling through the brambles amongst a massive pile of 1910–1920s engines and gearboxes at a 'secret location' not far from my home. We even extricated two Rolls-Royce Silver Ghost engines and gearbox from this heap, one of which was completely buried under the ground.

ABOVE: *Four acetylene interior lamps for the Leyland X2, all painstakingly made by hand, including the gas burners and having had a graphite mould made in which to blow four glass globes, all to the exact original shape even with 'Ross Patent' moulded into their sides.*

ABOVE RIGHT: *The rear door latch mechanisms for the White Rose SG7, scaled off from an original photograph and made precisely as they were originally.*

RIGHT: *Compound curves and tapered, hand-carved in ash: the front door of the White Rose SG7, and there's much more behind the panels that you don't see, including the winding mechanism.*

FAR RIGHT: *The tapered steel mudguard irons on the Leyland X2, together with twenty-six spring-loaded grease caps of a special type for early Leylands. I originally had six and three halves of these, and the rest all had to be made by hand.*

is absolutely brilliant and can make anything out of anything. He has deservedly won many gold and silver prizes at the major model-makers' exhibitions – for example at Olympia – with working scale-model, steam-powered traction engines, and so on. His latest quarter-scale working model of a Fowler ploughing engine is being put forward for the Duke of Edinburgh's Award. Another friend who has worked with me virtually

every Saturday since he was seventeen in 1981 is Mike Street, an expert at joinery: he has frequently ended up cutting curved timbers out of the solid on a trial-and-error basis until they were just right. My youngest son, Ricky, who is training to be a carpenter/joiner, also helps, and I have had assistance from others from time to time. All this work needs a huge amount of planning, and throughout a restoration I prepare comprehensive

weekly lists of who (including myself) is to do what, and with what priority. I also have help from Chris, who does much of the painting and wood varnishing, and Pip, the excellent sign-writer. I generally do any job that needs doing, and I always insist on doing the coach painting of the final coats, and the varnishing, myself.

Most of the work done is carried out at Valley Forge, with only a few of the jobs being put outside – for example, making seat spring bases and some of the upholstery, although these are all done to my own drawings and with strict control over their quality and accuracy. With some of the restorations we have had to make new radiators from scratch, or replace major parts of the radiator, and this is one of the biggest jobs in the restoration of a vehicle. Here again, we will do all the pattern-making in house, but obviously have to go to a local foundry to have the castings made and then machined. Over the years I have built up a large library of contacts for sourcing materials and services.

Preservationists' Nightmare

There are two key factors that help me to achieve so many quality restorations in such a short time. The first is that I have overcome the accommodation problem, which is most bus preservationists' nightmare: where to keep your enormous treasure safely under cover, and with a power supply, and near enough to your home to be able to work on it. I have lived through all of these nightmares, first, in the course of restoring the little Chev coach, and subsequently during the initial restoration of the Todmorden 1921, Leyland

G, when it was kept under a scaffolding frame covered with plastic sheets; and later, for the next four restorations in an open car port. In fact the car port (or should I say, bus-port) was quite acceptable in that it was outside my front door, and this enabled me to work on the vehicles in my spare time at home. Now at Valley Forge we are even more favoured, with half an acre of land and three superb large purpose-built garages, each of which has thermal qualities (including double glazing) at least as good as, if not better than, a new domestic house; this is a tremendous advantage, and it means

ABOVE: *Desperate stuff! Trying to restore the Chev under a tarpaulin, after a windy night.*

RIGHT: *Under a scaffolding frame and plastic sheeting, and in the snow – how can anybody possibly restore something properly in these conditions? But my first four Leylands were restored in just such conditions.*

The solution: buy a tumble-down cottage with some land, and build your own thermally clad garage.

The L&NWR Chara poses in front of the 'White Rose' garage: big enough to keep two long single deckers in absolute luxury – and next to my house.

Preparing to move house – never again! A line-up of nine Leyland engines wait their turn for the lorry with crane. (There were six full lorryloads of spares!)

that I can work on the vehicles in comfort, and whenever I choose in my spare time.

The second factor is that I personally own the vehicles, so I can control and direct how they are to be restored, and at what pace we should proceed. This is of huge advantage to the efficiency of the operation, particularly with the enormous amount of planning and research that I carry out myself so as to keep the restoration work moving at a quick pace. I am always looking for the critical path through any job or problem, and this helps to prioritize the workload, and the sourcing of materials and services. Compare this with a museum project, where not only does the vehicle have to be restored, but the museum buildings have to be kept in order, and visitor shops run, and time is taken up looking after the general public. With many group restorations there may be differences of opinion: some members

will regard the exercise as being purely a bit of relaxation, getting away from the wife and kids, whereas others may spend a lot of the time just chatting, drinking cups of tea and not working very efficiently. These are extremes, I know, but a major restoration is a very big job, and if it is to be done in a sensible timescale it needs to be pushed on *all the time* and to a deadline. Set a deadline, and you will achieve it! Some of my restorations have taken up to 10,000 man hours, much of which has to be paid for, although my own time is free. Most of this work is carried out every Saturday, irrespective of weather conditions, but I also put in a lot more additional time, frequently getting up at 5.00 or 6.00am, and doing a few hours before work during the week, as well as in the evenings, and on Sundays and holidays.

From a financial point of view, each restoration has cost a significant sum and, as I have no capital, it all has come

from my own earnings. This is why I have to be realistic about what more I can achieve, given a reasonably sensible expected retirement age (from work, of course!). I have also been very successful in winning a number of prizes for the restoration work, and these have all been ploughed back into restoration, as is the money earned on the occasional film and television work, and of course sales of surplus vehicles. One little bonus has been that, since I started to work from home in 1993, I do not have to travel to and from work. Before that my journeys to and from north London used to take 1¼ hours each way – that is, 2½ hours out of every working day of your life, or 12½ hours per week, which is the equivalent of 1½ working days, equating to seventy-five working days per year (or 3½ months!). Over a three-year vehicle restoration, this equates to nearly one year of full-time work! I know that only an accountant

THE ANATOMY OF THE MOTOR BUS

(DRAWING BY MIKE SUTCLIFFE)

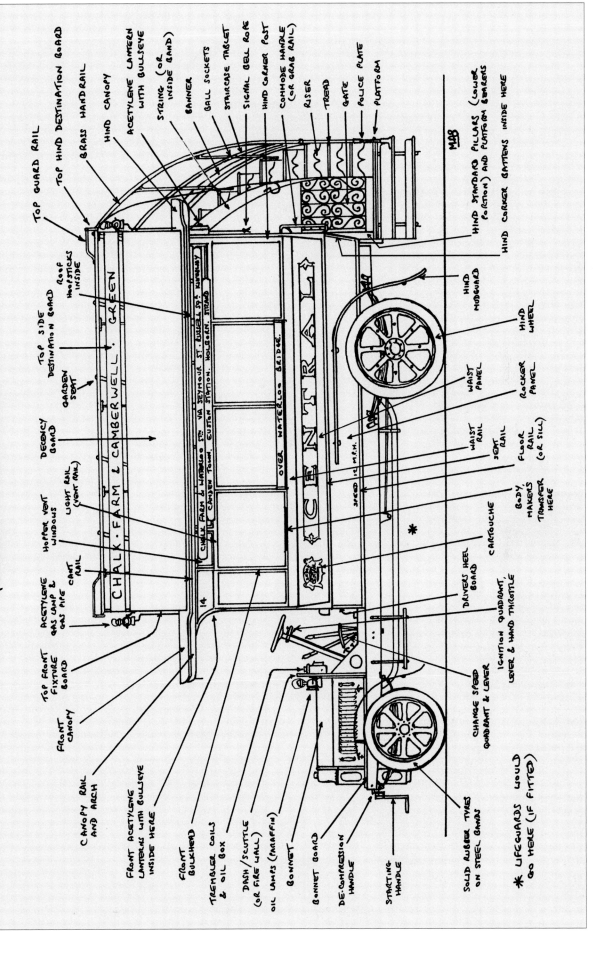

Part of my new stores for small spares – in one of two lorry containers utilizing the tea-chests from the house move. Larger parts, for instance axles and wheels, are housed under cover separately in 'The Grotto'.

vehicle, but that is not so. Many people could win £100,000 or more on the lottery, but they would not have the skills or the determination to carry out an *authentic* restoration on the scale of, say the London Central, Leyland X2 or the L&NWR 'Torpedo' char-a-bancs, and get it right.

The above comments therefore give an insight into my motivation, and the operation of the restoration work overall; the next few chapters are devoted to each vehicle in chronological order of their manufacture by Leyland. Set out below are the dates when the restoration of each vehicle was started and completed, some of which overlap:

1981–84
Todmorden, Leyland G
1984–87
Chocolate Express, Leyland LB5
1986–89
The Charabus, Leyland G7
1988–91
Wellingborough, Leyland S3.30.T
1991–96
London Central, Leyland X2
1996–2000
L&NWR Torpedo Char-a-bancs
1999–2002
The White Rose, Leyland SG7
2002 to date
Barnsley & Dist. Combination Car
2005–08
Todmorden Leyland Tiger, TS6

The next nine chapters tell the story of each of the nine Leylands in my collection. Each chapter is divided into three main parts: first, some details are given about the development of each Leyland model, which in itself gives a brief history of vehicles produced by Leyland Motors over the period. The second section of the chapter covers the operating history of the vehicle and its operator; and this is followed by the story of its rescue and restoration. There are numerous incidents and stories recalled in this book, all absolutely true, however far fetched they might seem to be, especially co-incidences; but as I said earlier, I believe that you make your own luck!

would work out these things, but it does go to show that I now get the work of a 'free full-time worker' with every restoration! What a total waste of time it is sitting in your car in traffic jams, especially when you could be restoring old buses!

Apart from my own time, I have invested a lot of money in the vehicles, more than many could afford, but I have a good job, and work very hard *all* the time. I have no capital, but do not have any other vices. Pat is intensely interested in the garden, to the extent that we open the gardens once a year for charity under the National Garden Scheme; but that is not an expensive hobby. Some might say that, with those sums of money being spent, anybody could restore a

CHAPTER FOUR

The London Central, Leyland X2, of 1908

Leyland's Early Days, and Steam Power

The history of Leyland Motors Ltd is always said to go back to 1896. This is the date that the company recognized as being its formation, and it has been perpetuated by subsequent histories and books. However, this is not really correct, and I believe that picking this date does the company a disservice! In fact, 1896 is the year in which the Spurrier family invested in the business, which was already in existence at that time, and had been for several years. Similarly, 1896 has little relevance with regard to the legal entity of the company. From the Spurrier involvement in 1896 it was a partnership, and the business was not taken over by a limited company, The Lancashire Steam Motor Co. Ltd, until its incorporation on 29 August 1903. It merged with T. Coulthard of Preston in 1907, and changed its name to Leyland Motors Ltd on 5 April 1907 by special resolution. A new company, Leyland Motors (1914) Ltd, was formed in that year, and in 1919 a further company, Leyland Motors Ltd, was incorporated on 27 September, and so on.

Forgetting the Spurriers' involvement, the *real* history of the business goes back to 1880, when James Sumner commenced building his 5-ton steam lorry; this was completed in 1884, and sold to Stanning's Bleach Works of Leyland. It operated for a period of 'one or two years', but was not found to be a commercial success, and was laid up and used as a stationary engine driving a saw mill. Later the boiler was used to power the Sumner Works at Water Street, Leyland.

The 1908 Leyland X2, newly restored in time for the 1996 Leyland 100 Celebrations. It was fitting that the oldest surviving Leyland vehicle should be used to commemorate 100 years of Leyland, 1896–1996.

In 1892 James Sumner built an experimental steam tri-car with a two-cylinder compound engine, seating two people. It was based on a Starley Sociable 'two-penny farthing' tricycle, bought second-hand from Squire Bretherton of Runshaw Hall. The following year, 1893, saw the

James Sumner.

Sumner's steam lawnmower and roller, made by J. Sumner Ltd.

development of the first steam-powered lawnmower, of which many were built; and in 1895 Theodore Carr, the biscuit manufacturer of Carlisle, purchased a steam-powered tri-car, followed by an improved version in the summer of 1896.

By this time the company was short of money, and T. Coulthard & Co., a Preston engineering firm, invested in the business, taking a 60 per cent share in a new company, J. Sumner Ltd. It was later in 1896 that the Spurrier family bought out Coulthard's interest and

changed the name of the business to The Lancashire Steam Motor Co., producing a steam-powered, 30cwt covered van with two-cylinder, 10–14hp compound engine in late 1896. Most of the early steam-powered vehicles were oil-fired (using paraffin), whereas the original Stanning's lorry was coal-fired; but in 1900 Henry Spurrier designed their first coke-fired wagon. From this time onwards, The Lancashire Steam Motor Co./Leyland Motors were very successful, with their new steam wagon production

designated 'Class B'. This was followed in 1905 by the Class H and, later, Class F steam wagon, though the latter did not really take off in any great volume until 1911/12. There were other steam wagons that were built in small numbers, too, but there is not space enough to go into their details here. The class designation for the steam wagons started at A and went through the alphabet to reach K (including some of the Coulthard models), although it is difficult to follow the order of introduction of the models.

RIGHT: *Henry Spurrier, the First.*

FAR RIGHT: *Lancashire Steam Motor Co.'s first steam vehicle in 1896, a 30cwt van with two-cylinder, 10–14hp compound engine.*

ABOVE: *Dundee & District Tramways Co. had the first LSMCo. steam bus, with eighteen-seat body by J. Stirling, Edinburgh, 31/5/1899. It is seen here after its sale to Henry McNeill, Larne, N. Ireland. (Bill Montgomery collection)*

RIGHT: *Typical of the Leyland steam wagons is this early Class F wagon built in 1911 and exhibited at the Royal Agricultural Show, Norwich, in June of that year.*

The First Petrol-Driven Vehicles

The Class Z 'Lurry'

The manufacture of petrol-driven vehicles started in 1904 with the experimental Class Z, the classification thereafter going backwards through the alphabet as models were introduced, and reaching Q just prior to World War One. Drawings for the Class Z 30cwt were begun in July 1903, but it was nearly eighteen months before the vehicle was built. There was probably only one, and this carried a Leyland 12hp two-cylinder engine (not Crossley, as has otherwise been stated) and a three forward-speed gearbox. The engine had a bore and stroke of 4½ × 6in (3.1 litres). It had a platform lorry body, and was not liked by the men who produced it, who had steam in their blood; and with low-tension ignition, it was difficult to start. Being a two-cylinder engine, as many were at the time, it would not have been very smooth running, and due to the animal-like grunting noises that it emitted, it was nicknamed 'The Pig'.

After running on trade plates for two years, it was finally registered B 2072 in about October 1906, and spent its working life as a Leyland Works 'lurry' (as they tended to call them).

The Class Y 24/28hp Bus

Next, in early 1905, came the Class Y, with a 3-ton chassis that was fitted with a Crossley 24/28hp four-cylinder

ABOVE: *The first petrol 'lurry' (as they called them in Lancashire), a Class Z nicknamed 'The Pig'. (BCVM Archive)*

BELOW: *The first Leyland-Crossley Class Y, 24/28hp bus with Scammell & Nephew body, Letter 'A', P 1944, delivered in March 1905 to The New London & Suburban Omnibus Co. Ltd. (Note that William Benjamin Richardson was the managing director.)*

Birch Bros built bodies for other customers, but they also ran two Leyland-Crossley Y2, 24/28hp buses, the first being LC 3680. (The Y2 had the fluted radiator.)

engine. It was generally known as the Leyland-Crossley, and was very successful in terms of sales (approximately thirty-three produced over sixteen months). However, commercial vehicle technology was at an early stage, and there were design problems, particularly with the shaft-driven back axle, and many did not last in service more than eighteen months to two years. The bore and stroke of the Crossley engine were $4\frac{1}{4} \times 5\frac{1}{8}$in (4.8 litres). The first two (possibly three) originally had front axles and springs similar to the Class Z, and carried a 'Milnes Daimler'-type radiator, similar to the first Crossleys. However, an improved design came out in June 1905, classified Y2, and the remainder of the Y types were the same. A new radiator with fluted header tank was used (designed by J.S. Critchley of Daimler fame), and apart from later changes to the header tank, this radiator was used in various forms until 1927. Even the PLSC Lion radiator had the same basic dimensions, and its core would have been interchangeable! Leyland didn't change anything unless they had to – a policy pursued right to the end! As can be seen from the photographs, the Y2 is instantly recognizable, in particular by its fluted radiator and curved dumb irons. The majority of Y2s went into service with double-decker bus bodies in London with a number of operators, though Belfast Corporation Tramway bought no fewer than four chassis fitted with tower-wagon bodies.

The Class X Type

Detailed drawings commenced in November 1905 for the Class X $3\frac{1}{2}$-ton chassis, and the first example appeared in April 1906, with double-deck body by Birch Bros. This was the first reliable petrol-engined vehicle built by Leyland, and probably the most famous of the pre-World War One period, despite the fact that the S and ST range was built in larger quantities. The Class X deserves a whole article all to itself, but I will try to summarize the many variations. It was a completely new design, with Leyland-designed and built 35hp engine (sometimes known as 35/40hp) with 4¾in bore × 5½in stroke (6.4 litres). This was a development from the Crossley engine, and was basically the same but much bigger. The cylinders were cast in pairs, with a 'T'-head arrangement and two camshafts, the inlet valves being on the offside, and exhaust valves on the nearside, usually with dual ignition. The fan ran directly off the front of the propshaft, thereby enabling a low radiator position. The first models ran with low tension magneto ignition, with high tension magneto ignition being more general from 1908. A new double-reduction bevel-drive back axle was a feature of this class, and this arrangement was to continue in production until 1930.

The first two Leyland X types had unusual radiators with a flat panel at the top, with the oval makers' plate, but the next eight or so had an enormous top tank to the radiator. This was re-designed again in January 1907, with the introduction of the Class U.50hp engine, and it remained on all X types until, in 1912, the X2.40hp was introduced (sometimes referred to as 40/50hp). This X2.40hp

was an 'L'-head engine, derived from the S range but larger. It required more space, and the length of the bonnet was extended and raised, as was the top tank of the radiator, with a space above and below the oval Leyland badge on the header tank. It also had more bonnet louvres.

Up to January 1907 all the Leyland chassis had frames made out of channel section steel 'inside out', but from February 1907 pressed-steel frames came in (initially with the Todmorden Corporation No. 4, Class U.50hp). The next development was the second development of double-reduction bevel rear axle for the X type in 1908, the 'X2', and from then onwards the class became X2.35hp. A further complication was that the straight frame chassis (38in/96.5cm wide overall) was

described as the 'X2 Straight', and the joggled frame chassis was described as the 'X2 Bus'. This was 38in (96.5cm) wide at the front, and 43in (109.2cm) wide from the driver backwards. These two dimensions were used consistently in all larger Leyland chassis right up to the mid/late 1920s, being referred to as 'wide' or 'narrow' frames. The London Central Motor Omnibus Co. had a complete mixture of these models, and my 1908 Leyland is one of the 'X2 Straight' chassis. Another major change with the X2 was the introduction of the spherical ball thrust for which Leyland became famous. It was first shown by Leyland at Olympia in 1908 on a London Central bus. This device was placed at the front of the torque tube, just behind the gearbox; it retained the back axle in the correct

RIGHT: *The first Class X vehicle was AP 2015, which saw only two months' service due to licensing difficulties. It was later sold to Todmorden Corporation. (Note the elaborate curtains at the windows.)*

BELOW: *The Great Central Railway operated B 2186, a Class W, 5-ton chassis (W12/401). It is seen here in this delightful picture flanked by a Ryknield, FA 132, on the left, and a Westinghouse, N 4839, on the right.*

position relative to the gearbox to avoid putting undue strain on the propshaft and universal couplings. The Class X then remained with few alterations up to 1912; its story will be continued later in this book.

The Classes W and V

In the meantime, a few other models are worthy of mention. The Class W, 5-ton chassis, although first drawn up in May 1906, did not materialize until 1909. This was basically a heavier version of the X2, with a special single-beam, forged back axle designed to carry heavier loads and sprung directly underneath the chassis frame. Again, these had the double-reduction bevel-driven axle gearbox that sat above the forged beam, and with exposed half shafts, and it lasted as such until the outbreak of World War One.

The Class V, with 3-ton back axle, was initially a scaled-down version of the Class W, with separate forged axle beam to carry the load. There were probably none of these built until 1911, by which time the Class S 'L'-head engine was in production, the three-tonners then becoming Class SV (or in more detail, S2.30.V).

The Class U

The Class U referred to the 50hp engine, which could be fitted into the Class X chassis. Basically it used the same crankcase as the X.35hp but much bigger cylinder blocks, to give a capacity of about 10 litres. Only a handful were built, and one was fitted to the first fire engine produced by Leyland in 1909 (for Dublin). Further details of Leylands' petrol vehicle development will follow in the next chapter, but it is worth recording here that, up to the outbreak of war in August 1914, 440 X types had been built, and by that time the designation had reached Class X4. In 1912 the X2's 35hp twin-cam T-head engine was replaced by a 40hp version of the Class S 'L' head, and the model was re-designated X2.40hp. An updated version was the X3.40hp which came out in 1913, followed by the X4 in late 1913. This latter development not only had a much higher radiator, above the chassis frame, but it also had a new, one-piece, 'electric steel' cast-back axle. This referred to a new method of casting stronger back axles, that had previously been made in three sections bolted together.

The London Central Motor Omnibus Co.

The history of the London Central Motor Omnibus Co. Ltd goes back to horse-bus operating days, when it ran under the title of the London & Suburban Omnibus Co. Ltd. William Benjamin Richardson was a horse-bus driver on the service to Surbiton, and he became managing director of the company, which changed its name in 1895 to The New London & Suburban Omnibus Co. Ltd. (Ben Richardson, by some remarkable coincidence, was the manager of three of the companies of which I have restored vehicles, and his name appears as manager on all of them: the London Central Leyland X2; the Wellingborough Leyland S3.30.T; and the Charabus, Leyland G7 – I'm sure there's another story there!)

William Benjamin Richardson's name appears as manager on three of my vehicles (including the Wellingborough bus depicted here).

Along with many other horse-bus operators, The New London & Suburban Omnibus Company decided to experiment with the mechanically powered motor bus in March 1905, and placed in service the very first Leyland petrol-driven bus (NL&SOC letter 'A'). It was a Leyland-Crossley Class Y with 24hp Crossley engine, and carried a thirty-four-seater, double-deck bus body built by Scammell and Nephew (who went on to produce Scammell lorries). The following month New London & Suburban added a 24hp Dennis (letter 'B') to their fleet, this being the first worm-driven

The first Class U with 50hp engine was delivered to Todmorden Corporation in February 1907. It was the last Leyland chassis to have a channel-section frame, and it carried a UECC body, numbered 3 in the fleet, B 2079. (BCVM Archive)

The only known photograph of a New London & Suburban Omnibus Co. Ltd horsebus, a 'garden seat' bus probably dating from the 1890s.

ABOVE: *The driver cranks the handle of a letter 'H', NL&SOC Leyland-Crossley Y2, operating on the Kingsway service.*

BELOW: *The first four buses of London Central, all early X types. P 2994 (on the left) was later converted to a single decker, and all four had the radiator with deep top tank.*

Dennis bus (more on this in the next chapter). These two vehicles were quite a progressive new start for such an enterprise, which went on to buy approximately five more Leyland-Crossley Y2 buses in 1905, followed by two more in 1906. It is noteworthy that these were all *British*-made chassis, compared with most other London operators who were experimenting with buses mainly of German and French manufacture. NL&SOC then purchased one of the first two Leyland Class X buses with X.35/40hp engines

in May 1906, followed by a second X type later in that year.

However, motor-bus operation was in its infancy, and most operators of them lost substantial sums of money in the early period. The company went into liquidation early in 1907, but the operation was saved by a fresh injection of capital directly from Leyland, with the London Central Motor Omnibus Co. Ltd being formed late in 1906. This new company took over the newest X type (P 2994) from NL&SOC, and went on to buy new

Leyland X types – three in November/December 1906, followed by six more in 1907. A further batch of six, including my No. 14, LN 7270, was added in 1908, by which time the X2 was in production; the fleet then remained constant with these sixteen Leylands until 1910.

These X types carried thirty-four-seat, open-top bodies obtained from various sources. Some had been fitted to withdrawn buses from the New London & Suburban fleet, others were built new by the United Electric Car

Co., Preston (UEC), and some, it is thought, by Birch Bros. Among those with second-hand bodies was No. 14; it carried a body purchased from Thomas Tilling, and this had been formerly used on a 1906 Milnes Daimler. In 1908, Thomas Tilling was successful in obtaining a contract for the Royal Mails. They immediately built up a fleet of Milnes Daimler mail vans, some of which were built on former bus chassis, the bus bodies then becoming surplus to requirements; this is how LN 7270 received its body, which is two years older than the chassis.

Merger of the London Companies

In 1908 the three major London motor-bus operators merged. First the London Motor Omnibus Co. Ltd ('Vanguard'), which itself had acquired four smaller companies, was absorbed by London General Omnibus Co., despite having 370 motor buses compared with the General's 243. Shortly afterwards, the London Road Car Co. Ltd ('Union Jack'), with its 226 buses, was also absorbed by London General. The merged operation found itself with a large fleet of double-decker buses that could be described as of the 'first generation' of design of the motor bus, many of which were in need of replacement. This led to a search for a more reliable motor bus and, after combining the best features of all those currently operated, the first of sixty-one experimental LGOC X types (made by the LGOC) appeared on 12 August 1909. These were followed by the first B type, on 7 October 1910.

'Second Generation' Buses

This 'second generation' bus was a much lighter vehicle than previously operated, and conformed to the new Metropolitan Police requirements to have a bus at under 3½ tons unladen. Leyland Motors retaliated, and in June 1910 the London Central MOC took delivery of No. 17, LN 9930, the first of a new generation of lightweight Leyland buses. They had the Class T worm-driven back axle and Class S 30hp ('L' head) engine,

London Central No. 5, LN 2272, a Leyland X with 'joggled frame', and UECC body; it is shown before delivery in March 1907. It had a four-speed, Panhard-type gearbox. Note the elaborate paintwork and lining-out on the chassis frame and even on the road springs. This was copied religiously on my X2. (EEC)

One of the first batch of Leyland ST buses – a 'second generation' bus designed as a lightweight (similar to my Wellingborough bus).

and were an instant success. After taking delivery of eighteen Leyland STs in 1910/11, on 3 January 1912 London Central was re-capitalized as the New Central Omnibus Co. Ltd. The new company ordered a total of 100 more of these Leylands, and also

expanded into the provinces with a fleet of fourteen buses in the Bedford area (the history of these services is written up in a booklet entitled *London's Forgotten Bus Operations – Public Motor Transport in Bedfordshire, 1899–1919*, by John Cummings – it is an

A selection of tickets of NL&SOC and LCMOC.

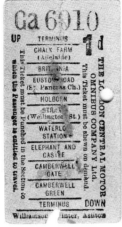

excellent history of these operations).

Before the last of these 100 buses entered service, an arrangement was introduced whereby the New Central Omnibus Co. was leased to London General from 1 January 1913, later being sold outright to the Underground Electric Railway Group in October 1913. By that time the Underground Group controlled the LGOC, and from then on, the Leylands were gradually replaced by AEC B types; the last of the Leylands survived until 1921. By that time, of course, the last of London Central's Leyland X types were long gone (full details of the vehicles operated by these companies are included in the Leyland Vehicle Production Listings, currently being compiled by myself; they are available from me at Valley Forge).

Rescue and Restoration

Following withdrawal in 1912, No. 14, the Leyland X2, vanished for the next sixty-seven years, and nothing is known of its history over this period. However, in 1979 an enthusiast spotted a rather interesting-looking shed in a field in Warwickshire. After discovering inside it what might have been the remains of an old bus, word soon got around and my friend, Barry Weatherhead, and I went to have a look.

The body was clearly the lower saloon of a 'first generation' thirty-four-seater double decker, being of a much heavier build than the 'second generation' London General 'B-type' bodies. Another clue to its earlier age was that the body is extremely narrow, being some 4in (10cm) narrower than a 'B type' at the waist rail. Remains of the original paintwork could be found on both bulkheads, giving clues to its identity, and it was clear that originally it had had a very ornate interior, with gas lamps and a lot of polished woodwork. There were also the remains of rails for curtains, whereas some bodies had roller blinds.

What a sorry sight it was! The body had been removed from the chassis to be used as a store shed having been

The mortal remains of the 1906 Tilling body sits on Barry's trailer after its recovery from the field in Warwickshire in 1979 – a very sorry sight and with half of the nearside missing as it had been cut up for firewood.

stripped of its upper deck, platform and stairs – as happened with virtually all of these elderly double-deck bodies at that time: they were sold off cheaply for use as sheds. Over sixty-seven years the elements had taken their toll: most of the glass had fallen out and broken, and the rain had started to come through the calico sheet between the roof and floorboards, and consequently the lower deck floor had rotted and fallen out. To make matters worse, the owner had decided to cut up the bus for firewood, and his fire had already consumed three-quarters of the nearside woodwork. He had, however, very carefully saved all the iron bracing bars and brackets, which was very kind of him!

The X2 chassis had been relieved of all its mechanical parts in order to make it lighter to carry what could only be described as a massive workmens' caravan sort of body; latterly, hay bales had been stored in it for horses at the local riding school. It was merely a frame, springs, axles and wheel. There was no engine and no gearbox, and the radiator, steering column and box, gear-change quadrant and pedal controls had all been removed, as had the propshaft and torque tube – even the gears had been removed from the back

axle and thrown away in order to make the chassis lighter: how inconsiderate can people get? They were, however, kind enough to leave the half shafts in place.

In two separate journeys these rotting remains were carefully loaded up and brought home. The living van body was jacked up using two bottle jacks, and with the help of some very unstable columns of bricks we were able to lift the body high enough to drag the chassis out, having in the meantime a few nearly fatal disasters with the piles of bricks. Initially it was Barry who owned the remains of the X2, but shortly afterwards he and I swopped ownership of various vehicles and parts, and I proudly acquired what most people would consider to be a pile of rubbish, not even fit for the scrap heap – who said I was mad! These remains were put into storage while restoration continued on the Chocolate Express Leyland LB5 double decker, followed by the Charabus, and then the 1913 Wellingborough Leyland S3.30.T (oddly enough the model that replaced the X types in the London Central fleet).

Finding the Engine
In 1987 I had a remarkable find: an X-type 35/40hp engine in 'show

condition' and on display in a private museum in Lytham, Lancashire. I had been trying to track this engine down ever since I saw a photograph of it in a 1947 issue of the *Leyland Journal* when it was displayed with other engines by Leyland, showing the development of the Leyland power unit. To my knowledge there is only one similar engine like this in existence, in the 1910 (not 1908!) Carter Paterson Leyland X2 Straight lorry that now belongs to the Science Museum, and is currently on display in the British Commercial Vehicle Museum.

After lengthy discussions with the owner of the museum, he fortunately agreed that it would be nice to see it running again in a restored vehicle, and kindly agreed to exchange the X.35hp engine for a slightly later Leyland 'RAF'-type 36/42hp engine. This now made the restoration of the X2 a definite possibility

Finding the Other Parts
Next came a search in earnest for the other bits. I recalled a previous trip made a few years before to a well known scrapyard in Bingley, West Yorkshire, where there were some remains of very early Leylands, albeit in an extremely rusty and damaged state – but where else would you find

ABOVE: *Vic Elliott (Steve's father) gets to grips with the X-type 35hp engine. Note the two large drive wheels for the two camshafts – twin-cam engines are nothing new!*

LEFT: *The Leyland X2 'Straight' chassis was underneath an enormous workmen's living van, that had to be jacked up before the chassis could be pulled out in November 1979.*

a model X3 four-speed gearbox? This was slightly later than the X2, but almost exactly the same design, and it would fit without any adjustment. Not only that, but on lifting it from the position where it must have lain for about sixty years, underneath was yet another X3 gearbox! Considering that its top cover had gone and that it was full of water, it was still in remarkably good condition. These gearboxes were purchased, together with a rebuilt 'RAF'-type S5 36hp engine, a slightly later 40hp engine, and a steering column and box; they were all in a dreadful state, but the engines were useful for spares for my other restorations.

An unbelievable stroke of luck – in fact, two strokes of luck – happened just before finding the X2 engine. I had a telephone call from a friend in Lancashire who told me that the old Leyland drawing office was being demolished, and a number of early Leyland bonnets had been found underneath the floorboards, sitting in the dirt, still with their original coats of paint and all properly lined out. There were two model Q (15cwt to 1ton model of 1911–14) and two X-type bonnets dating from the same period. How ever did they get there? It must be fate! And within the same week, another colleague told me about an old brewery at Charnock Richard in Lancashire that had latterly been used by a haulage company, and which at one time also ran a char-a-bancs. They had used one of the upper rooms of the brewery to store spare parts, and as the brewery was to be demolished, these parts had to be removed. They included eight Leyland 'RAF'-type bonnets; two other bonnets, one that fitted straight on to the Chocolate Express bus; nine petrol tanks; five fire walls (scuttles); four engine and gearbox under-trays; and a whole host of Leyland mudguards of varying shapes and sizes, all with their ironwork – what an amazing find! All of these were very rusty indeed and many could not be used, but all the brass fittings, handles, hinges and so on, could be removed and used again. There was even a char-a-bancs windscreen

Some of the bonnets and other bits and pieces that were found under the floorboards of the Leyland drawing office when it was demolished, stand in front of the RAF-type chassis rescued from Florence Nightingale's house. Three of these bonnets have already been used in my restorations.

(complete with Leyland Motors builder's transfer) and a char-a-bancs front door with handles, latch and fittings. Realizing the importance of this find, some of the Friends of the British Commercial Vehicle Museum kindly rescued them all, and the next day a 16-ton Leyland box van, with 'Leyland Bus' on its sides, arrived at my house with all this scrap in. When it was unloaded it initially took up a major part of my driveway, until I was able to squirrel it all away under cover.

The annual Beaulieu autojumble is an excellent place for finding bits and pieces, although I was lucky enough already to have the Claudel Hobson carburettor and Bosch high-tension magneto with the X2 engine. The X type, however, ran with dual ignition, the magneto being used for running, and with four trembler coils operating through a crude sort of distributor for starting. I was lucky enough to find a four-coil trembler box at Beaulieu in perfect original condition, looking magnificent in its polished mahogany box. The only thing against it was the ridiculous price the owner was asking for it; *but*, on the other hand, this was

The magnificently original trembler coil box.

the *only* one I was probably ever going to find, so I felt I should buy it – but what a silly price. Pat suggested that I walk up and down the autojumble field, wrestle with my conscience, and then go and buy it. Thanks to Pat, this is what I did, and it took the whole of the prize money that I had just won from The Transport Trust Award Scheme; but at least the money was put to good use. I also found at Beaulieu a 1908 Smith's square brass speedometer, with cardan shaft, leather belt drive, together with many other fittings such as acetylene lamp burners, oil lamps, rear-view mirrors, special connectors for connecting the HT leads to the sparking plugs, a period oil can for mounting on the front seat by the driver, the horn, and many more smaller items.

Having previously rescued the mortal remains of many Leylands, mainly from the 'RAF-type' generation of models, I have built up a vast collection of spare parts. The 'RAF type' was a development of the X type, and unless there was a need to change the design of a component, Leyland did not change it. This meant that a whole host of these parts fitted either with no modification, or with only slight adjustments, including the clutch and

clutch brake, that were missing from the X.35hp engine. Even the gear lever quadrant (in the old days called 'the change speed lever'), the cardan shaft brake behind the gearbox, the propshaft and pedal shafts, all fitted with no major problems.

Making up Spare Parts

The Radiator

The radiator was a different story – I had to make that from scratch, and this was an enormously time-consuming job. Luckily the 1910 Carter

Paterson, Leyland X2 Straight, in the British Commercial Vehicle Museum, helped give me the dimensions, although that has had a replacement and more angular header tank fitted at some stage. We carefully made new wooden patterns and core boxes out of Jellutong, and had the top and bottom tanks and two side standards cast in LM6 aluminium at a local foundry. Round crinkled gills then had to be made, and threaded one by one (15,400 of the little blighters!) on to eighty-six tubes, afterwards being soldered onto ½in copper tubes. The completed tubes, after making appropriate bends to go round the starting handle, were soldered into the two ¼in brass tube plates. On any major restoration of an early vehicle the radiator is one of the most complicated problems to overcome, especially when you have to start from scratch!

The Steering Wheel

We laminated patterns in plywood to have the four-spoke brass steering wheel cast, and this pattern later came in useful again for the Barnsley & District Leyland. The castings are in brass, to which we fastened ten curved wooden segments, with each of the 100 or so finger grips carved by hand – another major job. It is interesting to note that the 18in (45cm), five-spoke brass steering wheel, part no. 699A, Leyland private code JUPYE, was priced at £1 17s 6d (£1 87½p in modern money) – if only! We then fabricated the ignition levers, quadrant and so on, that fit below the steering wheel. These consist of a hand-operated throttle (as well as the foot throttle) and ignition lever for advancing and retarding the magneto.

The body frame was cut in half lengthways in order to save as many of the original parts as possible.

The body framework takes shape, and Mike Street clamps up the canopy rail that we had just laminated out of thin strips of ash.

The Gears in the Back Axle

The next major problem (or as the Americans would say, 'opportunity'!) was the back axle: how do you make a bus go when there are no gears in the back axle? There was no propshaft or torque tube, and to make matters worse, the 'RAF-type' axle (that was model X4) was not only bigger, but the gears were of a different pitch. Nor

We had to make the large bevel wheel, bevel pinion and its bearing housing and several other parts for the back axle. We had no plans or drawings to work from, merely a large hole in the back axle and a tape measure!

Barry and Mike press new solid tyres onto the rear wheels with an original hydraulic solid-tyre press rescued from a garage in Luton, which at one time specialized in a fleet of World War One Thornycroft J lorries for its haulage business.

were there any drawings available – but I did have a tape measure! With the help of Jim Rochester, a traction engine enthusiast who had just retired from his business as a gear cutter (and had a shed with some equipment in his back garden), we managed to solve the problem. The X type (and 'RAF type') had a double-reduction, bevel-driven back axle, and we found that the two intermediate small spur gears and the differential from the 'RAF type' could be made to fit inside the X2's axle gearbox (as Leyland called it). This meant making a new crown wheel and bevel pinion from scratch. We cut the axle end off an 'RAF-type' torque tube and fabricated a new axle end, including the housing, to take two new bearings. The time then came to put it together, and it all fitted perfectly, with exactly the right tolerances: thank you, Jim!

The Tyres

New solid tyres were bought from Dunlop (ouch!): fortunately these were still available at the time (120 × 720mm rim at the front, and 120 × 850mm rim at the back). However, Dunlop only made a 160mm width of 850mm diameter tyre, and so each of the four rear tyres had to have 40mm (1½in) machined off the side of the tyres and bands to make them fit – another nightmare! It is not easy to find someone with a lathe big enough to turn 40in (100cm) or so, and who can also machine rubber to the right standard and get the smooth finish.

The Oil Reservoir Box

Leicester Museum very kindly lent me the oil reservoir box from their 1911 Leyland ST Tower Wagon, which I was then able to copy, making patterns and having a new aluminium box cast. This is mounted on the driver's side of the dashboard, and oil is fed from the box down to each main bearing by gravity, through three copper pipes. The big

'The Porcupine': the back mudguards are made out of laminated birch ply, and it took thirty-two sash cramps to hold it all together.

ends are then fed with oil from the main bearings, through holes drilled in the crankshaft. The engine has a dry sump, with oil being pumped straight back to the oil box on the dash. The oil capacity of the engine is therefore only one gallon.

The Water Pump

The Leyland Museum also helped by lending me the water pump from the Carter Paterson X type for me to copy. However, it turned out that it would be prohibitively expensive to have the patterns made, and I ended up by using an 'RAF-type' water pump, turned round on its side with pipes made to fit. There is another story here – in fact there is a story attached to nearly every aspect of the preservation of these older vehicles. When I started to dismantle the X.35hp engine, there was something about the water pump that just did not feel right. As I undid the nuts and bolts holding it on, a piece broke off it, and I discovered that the whole pump was made out of a solid lump of wood! Having thought about it for a while, I realized that this was latterly a display engine – perhaps the water pump had been lost at some time and so somebody had carved one out of wood to make the engine look right. Well, nearly right! By a remarkable coincidence (yes, another one!) a fellow enthusiast, David Bryant, who usually comes to our annual Open Day and barbecue, and who used to live locally, called in by chance one Sunday morning, soon after my 'wooden water pump discovery'. David used to call from time to time for an update on restoration progress, usually on a Sunday morning in his immaculate red MGA sports car; sitting beside him on the passenger seat was always his faithful Labrador, called Monty – probably the best behaved dog I have ever had the pleasure to meet. He used to sit patiently in the MGA, with no restraint, waiting for the time for him to leave, and the journey home.

David Bryant coincidentally spent his time at Leyland, in particular in the engineering apprentices' department. On seeing the wooden water pump, he

The crew pause for some relaxation during the final push to get the bus ready in time for the Brighton Run. From left to right: Mike, Neil, Ricky, Steve, Vic and Yours Truly.

With only a few weeks to go, the body is mounted on the chassis but with the upper deck yet to be made.

laughed out loud and said 'You are never going to believe this!', and he told me the story. When he was at Leyland, the apprentices were given the job of restoring the 1910 Carter Paterson Leyland X2, and also the Class F steam wagon that came back from Australia. The Carter Paterson X type had been to many local rallies, fetes and carnivals, but the drivers always complained that it did not run very

well and overheated. David was delegated to investigate the problem, and when he removed the water pump he found that it also had been carved from a solid lump of wood. Word soon got around, and one of the pattern makers in the foundry came up with the answer. When the Carter Paterson was first restored it was found that the water pump had been severely damaged by corrosion, and as it was thought that

The luxurious interior of the Tilling body, designed to entice passengers off horse buses and onto the motor bus.

A close-up of the front bulkhead with the original mahogany panel proclaiming 'Thomas Tilling – Makers and Job Masters'.

the lorry would be used for display purposes only, he copied the shape of it by carving a piece of wood and bolting it on. No wonder the engine overheated, as the water could not circulate at all! A solution had to be found, and one bright spark remembered that there was a similar engine used for display purposes – that would certainly not need a water pump that worked, so 'why don't we swop the water pumps?' Well, that was all right, until Mike Sutcliffe got his hands on it!

Outward Appearance

There is no doubt in my mind that these early buses are probably the most complicated restorations of all road-going vehicles – hence the challenge! A very wide range of skills is necessary to complete all the tasks, nearly all of which we tackle ourselves, and many of which relate to trades and skills that have now died out. But as said earlier, if a job has been done before, it can be done again – you just need to be persistent and totally committed to completing it.

These first generation buses were so different from what followed after 1910. As I continued my research into them, it became apparent that the makers of these vehicles were very proud of the new machines that they were producing, and went to enormous lengths to make them the best on the road. This

is evidenced by the very elaborate paintwork with bright colours (originating from the horse-bus days), plenty of gold leaf, and ornate lining-out on virtually every panel or body part that they considered to look bare. A major task facing the restorer is that there are no colour pictures/photographs of these vehicles, and all details about the colours must be gleaned from what scant bits of information survive, newspaper reports and suchlike, and by close examination of black and white photographs with a large magnifying glass. Such examination sometimes produces some almost unbelievable results – and also many more questions. Who would ever think of making a wrought-iron 'gate' to fill in the space under the stairs (another little challenge for our restoration team!). There is sign writing everywhere, particularly the destinations on boards carried on the exterior, but also inside where it talks about 'No Smoking or Spitting'; 'Wet Mackintoshes Must Be Removed Before Entering This Omnibus'; 'Beware Of Pickpockets – Both Male And Female', and it even tells you that 'Small Dogs Must Be Carried On Laps'!

The Interior

The green-upholstered seats in the lower saloon are buttoned and covered with a cotton velvet material. The lower saloon is lit with four

acetylene gas lamps – yet another nightmare! Fortunately I found a 1906 advert in *Commercial Motor* for the 'Ross Patent Inside Lamp – the only inside lamp that won't burn the ceiling'. Three telephone calls to the Patent Office Library located the original 1905 patents, which produced the drawings and detailed description. We then fabricated the brass pipework and lamp holder, made and silver-soldered the complicated brass parts of the shade together, and filed long eccentric slots in the spring-loaded globe holders: all very time-consuming. Having obtained acetylene burners, the worst was yet to come – I then prepared drawings to have graphite moulds carved by hand, into which new 'pineapple-shaped' glass globes could be blown. This work was delegated to the Nazeing Glass Works from Epping, who were extremely helpful. They even had 'Ross Patent' cast into the globes in order to be as authentic as possible. Each globe cost £6 50p to be blown – though I daren't reveal how much the first one with patterns cost! Suffice it to say that the four interior lamps ended up costing more than the radiator!

As already said, the first generation bus bodies were quite small and fairly narrow; however, they were much bigger than a horse bus. Many of the early ones had curtains with bobble-edged fringes at the windows, although these generally did not last very long in service. A trip to Oxford Street in London managed to secure the bobble-edged fringing (now made in France), and also enabled me to find the manufacturer of the correct type of moquette, the interior saloon colour being green with polished mahogany timber. Procuring the green Muranese patterned glass for the ventilator windows caused yet another problem, as green rolled glass is no longer made, let alone to this pattern. Fortunately someone whom I met on one of the London to Brighton runs had some broken pieces of exactly the right colour in his garden shed, and there was just enough for all of the twenty-one windows – though sadly one cracked after I had put it in, and there is no spare glass left to replace it.

Reverting to the livery, this is partly documented and there were traces of the original colours on the body. The chassis was known to be bright yellow, and from photos it was possible to see that it was lined out in a slightly darker colour – presumed to be orange. There was a conflict of opinion over the bonnet. Studying the early photographs from my collection, it became clear that the bonnet was either Flag Royal Blue with red edges, or red with black edges, outside the gold lining. The former appears to be the most likely, although the red edges led to red bonnets later in Central's life, when LGOC 'B types' were introduced into the Central fleet. Inside the bus it was nice to be able to use the original mahogany bulkhead panel, proclaiming the words in gold leaf 'T. Tilling Limited, Makers and Job Masters' – the terminology was quite quaint in those days!

Restoration Starts in Earnest

Having stored the remains for several years, the London Central, Leyland X2 had its turn after the Wellingborough Leyland double decker, restoration starting in earnest in January 1992. We completely dismantled the original

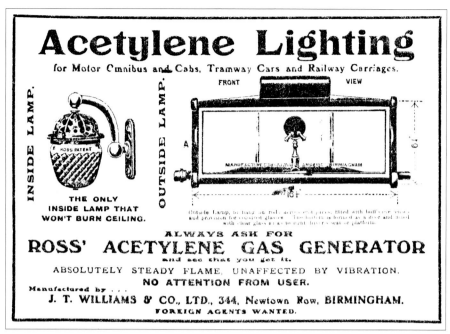

ABOVE: *The original advertisement in a March 1907 issue of* The Commercial Motor *for the Ross Acetylene Gas Lamp – 'The Only Inside Lamp that won't Burn the Ceiling'.*

LEFT: *Pat gives a helping hand sewing the curtains for the lower deck. (Note the original Leyland Motors Ltd wooden yard rule used for measuring upholstery.)*

body, cutting it right down the middle and removing the bulkheads. We then made a new ash frame, grafting on various bits of the original body as we went along. In addition, all the ironwork brackets, straps and fittings, including the bulkhead fire-screen panel, were sandblasted, painted and screwed on. This process had to be completed within five months, as, just

to complicate matters, I moved house in June of that year to Valley Forge. The X type was therefore 'put on ice' for just over a year before I was able to continue, this time in a nice new purpose-built garage, big enough to house two double deckers. As much as possible of the original bodywork has been retained, even though parts are a little bit 'grotty'; but a new platform and

RIGHT: *A close-up of the exhaust side of the engine showing the gravity-fed oil pipes to the main crankshaft bearings, with 'T'-head engine with dual ignition. The four sparking plugs on the exhaust side are powered by trembler coils for starting, with the four on the induction side being connected to the Bosch high-tension magneto.*

BELOW: *The driving compartment is totally open to the elements, and it could not have been pleasant driving on the London streets in the middle of winter. Note the alternately stained Colombian pine roof-boards and acetylene-powered lanterns.*

BELOW RIGHT: *The controls, with central throttle pedal and gate quadrant for the 'change speed lever'. The wooden trembler coil box containing four 4-volt coils, sits on the dash panel next to the aluminium engine-oil reservoir.*

staircase and upper deck have had to be made.

The engine appeared to be in a reasonable condition, although it had at one time been stripped down and put back together with the timing completely out of sequence and many nuts and bolts loose. Possibly it could have been used in Leyland's Apprentice School at some time. Neither of the two camshafts (twin-cam engines are not a new idea!) had been put back in the right position, and with no manual, we had to calculate the correct positions to assemble them in, in order to obtain the correct degree of valve overlap – not an easy job, but we must have got it about right.

As everything had been dismantled, we had to check every nut and bolt, and also found that No. 1 cylinder had been badly scored at some time. This had to be sleeved and bored back to the size of the cast-iron pistons, which I wanted to retain in order to preserve the original handling of the engine. New valves had to be made, and the big ends and main bearings have all been re-white-metalled, and then laboriously scraped in. The engine has exposed valves on each side of its 'T' head, which are driven by the two camshafts, driven in turn from timing gears at the front. These timing gears have fibre inserts for supposed quiet running, but they are quite noisy. This led to Leyland producing spring-loaded double helical timing gears for the 'S' series of engines; these were also fitted to the 'RAF type'. There are four cylinders cast in pairs, with blind cylinder heads – again, nothing is new! The valves are therefore removed by unscrewing valve caps, which sit on top of the blocks. Each of these eight valve caps, four on each side, carries a sparking plug, the inlet side of the engine being ignited by sparks from the trembler coils and tower distributor, the exhaust side being ignited by the Bosch high tension magneto.

These engines were very prone to icing up on the induction side of the engine. Consequently the inlet manifold is water-heated, and also the carburettor has two chambers for hot

The first trip onto the road for a test run, standing beside Valley Forge.

BELOW: *A helping hand on the way to the start of the London to Brighton Run. The 1908 Leyland X2 looks like a toy compared with the low-loader (I suppose that is just what it is!).*

water – so there are copper pipes everywhere! Even the air intake to the carburettor is fed by a massive copper pipe that goes right over the top of the engine to the exhaust manifold in order to suck in hot air. When testing the bus on the road, its performance was awful to start with, with the petrol vaporizing badly, even in cold weather. This was overcome by turning off all the taps and preventing water from heating the petrol vapour intake – presumably the petrol in those days was nowhere near as combustible as today's four star.

For cooling, the three-blade fan is situated on the front end of the crankshaft, hence the need for the lower position of the radiator, with the starting handle going right through the centre of the radiator.

According to an article in *Motor Traction*, when the X2 superseded the X in 1908, it stated that the maximum engine revs were only 670rpm, and although I haven't tested it with a tachometer, I would presume this gives a speed of about 12mph (19km/h) (the legal limit at the time). The bus travels very comfortably at about 22mph (35km/h), and I never attempt to push it above 25mph (40km/h) as this could cause severe damage; but it was certainly capable of breaking the speed limit of the time.

The First Major Outing for the Leyland X2

Apart from a few test runs, the first major outing for the Leyland X2 was the 1996 London to Brighton Run, which it completed faultlessly, taking the trophy for the outright Concours winner, among other prizes. The following year it was the runner-up in the Concours, and it has won many other awards, including the Transport Trust Preservationist of the Year Award, and the Eastbourne Historic Vehicle Club Awards. The restoration work was finished just in time to take the bus back to Leyland for the 100 Years of Leyland (1896–1996) celebrations, where it led a procession of preserved Leylands through the town centre of Leyland. It has also appeared in a number of films,

Pat and Mike with the trophies following the successful completion of the 1996 Brighton Run.

including *The Wings of the Dove* with Helena Bonham-Carter, *Fairy Tale – A True Story* with Peter O'Toole, and *Cider with Rosie* with David Troughton and Juliet Stevenson. It has been featured on the TV programme *Top Gear* in 1996, and has recently appeared again on the Discovery Channel. In 2000, the Leyland X2 was depicted on the special issue of Royal Mail postage stamps to commemorate buses through the ages. The bus is taxed and insured for road use, and is 'on the button' (or should I say, 'on the handle') all the time. It is fun just to go for a ride in it on the spur of the moment, and it is

Filming for the TV programme Top Gear *in 1996.*

ABOVE: *An interesting line-up of preserved buses in October 1999 in London Transport's Stockwell Garage, famous for its concrete roof structure. The London Central X2 is about to lead a procession through the streets of London to commemorate '100 Years of the Motor Bus in the Capital'.*

RIGHT: *A study of rear ends: the X2 with its wrought-iron gate stands next to Barry Weatherhead's London General K type, next is the London Transport Museum's S type, and then the Cobham Bus Museum's Dennis.*

a regular performer at our Valley Forge Open Days. It is very satisfying to be able to use the oldest surviving British-built motor bus on a regular basis, and to give people the opportunity to hear the sounds it makes, to see it moving and, of course, to have a ride on it.

	Specification – Leyland X2 Straight
Operator	London Central Motor Omnibus Co., No. 14, registered LN 7270, new June 1908
Model	Leyland X2 Straight (meaning straight frame, 38in (96.5cm) wide, as opposed to a 'joggled' frame (38in increasing to 43in (109.2cm)); 3–4 ton chassis
Chassis No.	X2.64. (This was the number used to license the vehicle, as the original number could not be found at the time. The chassis number of the Carter Paterson X2 Straight that donated the wheels was X264/???)
Engine	Four-cylinder, 35/40hp, Class X, built by Leyland, No. X114 (two pairs of cylinders with blind 'T' heads and twin camshafts)
Body	New 1906 and built by Thomas Tilling Ltd, thirty-four seats (eighteen outside, sixteen inside)
Length	23ft 5in (7.14m) (including starting handle)
Width	6ft 8in (2.03m)
Height	12ft 7in (3.84m)
Weight	4 ton 12cwt 1qtr (4,686kg)

CHAPTER FIVE

The Barnsley & District 'Combination Car' of 1913

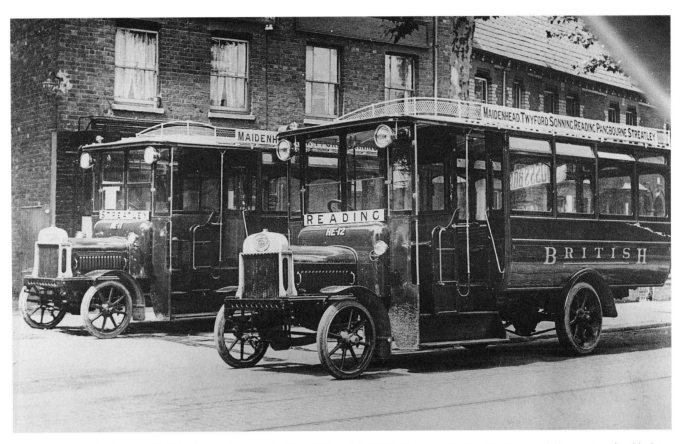

The only photograph I have of HE 12 is after transfer to the Reading Division of the British Automobile Traction Co. However, the bus was transferred back to Barnsley & District fifteen months later, in 1916.

Leyland Motors – Rapid Expansion

In the last chapter we looked at the first petrol vehicles made by the Lancashire Steam Motor Co., later Leyland Motors, and these were generally heavier models. A smaller range was introduced early in 1908, with a new worm-driven back axle. Dennis had pioneered the 'live' worm axle, and in fact by coincidence their very first worm-driven axle on a bus was fitted to the 1905 Dennis delivered to the New London & Suburban Omnibus Co. as their letter 'B' (*see* previous chapter). The worm-drive axle had the benefit of a quieter operation, rather than the continual whine or hum of the bevel drive with its straight cut gear wheels.

The new Leyland axle was given the Class letter 'T', intended for a carrying capacity of 2–2½ tons (1,016-1,524kg), and was to be the first of a new design of axle for Leyland, which would become very common for smaller vehicles and passenger models. The Class T was initially powered by a two-cylinder engine offered in two sizes: 18hp and 25hp. It is presumed that these had single pairs of cylinders taken from the X and U ranges, on smaller crankcases, and they therefore had much shorter bonnets. They can be distinguished by the number of bonnet louvres: eight for the smaller, and eleven or twelve for the larger engine. It was also possible to use the larger X.35hp engine in this lightweight chassis, which then became the Class XT (i.e. an X engine in a T chassis). This latter vehicle had the normal bonnet length for an X engine, but initially had the fluted radiator that had previously been seen on the Class Y2. Only a few of these Ts were made with the two-cylinder

engine before the Class S was developed in 1909.

Initially the S range had been designed with an even lighter-weight back axle, together with the new 'L'-head engine, for use as mail vans in Leyland Motors' own fleet. Although these were successful, not many were built, with Leyland concentrating on the heavier-weight chassis. The important thing about the S type was its newly designed 'L'-head engine, first built in two sizes, 24hp and 30hp, both using the same aluminium crankcase, but with different cylinder-block sizes, still cast in pairs. The smaller engine had four cylinders of 4in bore × 5in stroke (4.1 litres), whereas the 30hp was 4½in × 5in (5.2 litres). Later designs (Mark 2)

TOP: *The first worm-driven axle used with a bus was on this Dennis, operated for a short time by Ben Richardson's company The New London Suburban Omnibus Co. Ltd, letter 'B'.*

ABOVE: *The Class T.25hp, two-cylinder, 2 ton, utilized the new 'T' worm-driven back axle and one block of two cylinders from the Class U 50hp engine. Note the Yorkshire and Leyland steam wagons standing outside the extension to the original North Works at Leyland. (BCVM Archive)*

CK 449 was a Class S van for Charnley's 'Celebrated Biscuits', built in 1910. It had the new 'L'-head engine that changed Leyland's fortunes. (BCVM Archive)

of these engines resulted in the S2.24hp and 30hp engines in 1911, followed by S3.24hp and 30hp variants in 1912. It is the S3.30hp engine that is fitted to both my Barnsley & District Leyland single decker and the Wellingborough Motor Omnibus Co. double decker, both built in 1913, and this engine remained in production virtually unchanged right up to 1927, when the smaller models were replaced by the Leyland Badger. As with all the other Leyland engines up to the mid-1920s, they had non-detachable cylinder heads, enormous fly wheels, cast-iron pistons and a very long stroke – in short, they were exceedingly good engines, whose design is the principal reason why so many have survived until today. They had tremendous torque, and it is easy to pull away in top gear from 4 or 5mph (7 or 8km/h)!

Leyland's Fortunes Improve

The success of this engine changed the fortunes of Leyland Motors. In the four years from 1905 to 1909 Leyland's production had been steady, at a total of just over fifty vehicles a year. This included a general decline in steam wagon numbers, offset by growing numbers of petrol-driven lorries and buses, the merger with Coulthard in 1907 having made no noticeable difference to the numbers produced. It was a different story in 1910, with 110 vehicles produced, double the previous output, and assisted by extensions to the factory. Output in 1911 was 189 vehicles, followed by 330 in 1912; 390 in 1913; and a further 270 in just over seven months in 1914, up to the outbreak of war. Much of the additional output was due to increases in sales of chassis for bus work, and further details on the numbers produced, chassis and engine number series, Lancashire registration notes and many more technical details can be found in the second issue of *The Leyland Society Journal*, July 2000. The Class S chassis numbers had reached 610 by the outbreak of war, and a large proportion of these were fitted with the Class T 2–2½ ton back axle, thereby becoming model ST, as in the case of my Barnsley & District and

Wellingborough buses. The full classification included details of the engine, and in both cases they were therefore S3.30.T (in other words, a third generation S-type engine of 30hp, and Class T worm-driven rear axle).

To complete the story on Leyland petrol-model developments up to 1914, it should be noted that the Class

R referred to the axle for the railcar, and an enormous six-cylinder 160hp engine (based on the S range) was developed for a railcar delivered to South Africa. A few petrol trams were built, notably four for Morecambe and a pair for Parahyba in Brazil.

The Class Q for payloads of 15cwt and 1 ton was introduced in 1911, but

The British Electric Traction Group experimented with petrol buses for the second time in 1911 with this Brush-bodied Leyland, FK 311, for Worcestershire Electric Traction. It carried the S-type engine and had the Class T 2–2½ ton back axle, thereby becoming model ST. It was the direct forerunner of the twenty Barnsley & District buses. (Brush)

The Class Q 15cwt/1 ton with Aster engine was the smallest Leyland in the range – about twenty-five were built from 1911 to 1914. B 4393 was new to the Darwen Industrial Co-operative Society. (BCVM Archive)

was not really a success, with only about twenty-five being built up to August 1914. These were odd little trucks and vans (plus one ambulance), and were fitted with Aster engines, with a choice of a 12–16hp for the 15cwt chassis and a 16–20hp engine for the one-tonner. This was Leyland's attempt to get a foothold in the lighter end of the market, but the price was probably uncompetitive compared with the products of Albion, Lacre and Dennis. None is known to have survived but, as mentioned in the previous paragraph, I have two bonnets, one for each size of engine, that were found under the floorboards of the Leyland drawing office when the factory was demolished! Whatever should I do with these? They are so attractive, complete with their double lining-out, but they are no use whatsoever to anyone!

Barnsley & District Electric Traction Co. Ltd and their No. 5

Between April 1913 and March 1914, Barnsley & District bought twenty Leyland S3.30.T chassis, and had them fitted with twenty-seven and twenty-eight seater bodies by Brush of Loughborough. These were numbers 1 to 20 in the fleet, registered HE 8–12, HE 45–49, HE 68–77, and they had unusual bodies: following tramcar practice, they had open bench seats at the front, with an enclosed saloon at the back; in tramcar parlance these would be described as 'combination cars' (or 'room and kitchen' cars).

Demise of the Tramcar

Barnsley & District Electric Traction was a subsidiary of the British Electric Traction Co., and BET were large operators of tramcars throughout the country. Realizing the potential for the motor bus, the BET Group, through their subsidiary Brush, the British Electrical Engineering Co., the makers of tramcars based in Loughborough, had two attempts at making complete motor buses: the first was in 1904, followed by a handful of Brush B types in 1906/07. These latter vehicles were only moderately successful, and it was decided that in future chassis should be purchased from other manufacturers, with the majority of bodies being supplied by Brush. The first experimental vehicle was therefore the Leyland model S2.30.T purchased for the Worcestershire Electric Traction Co. in December 1911, and this was followed by similar 'combination car'-bodied vehicles for the same operator, and one for Deal & District Motor Services. Apart from the seven Leyland double deckers for Aldershot & District Traction Co. and two chars-a-banc, all of the BET Group Leyland buses followed this pattern up to 1914, when a new model, the Leyland S4.36.T3 was introduced; but more about that later (*see* the chapter on my L&NWR char-a-bancs).

The BET Group grew to be one of the largest operators in the country, gradually replacing its trams with

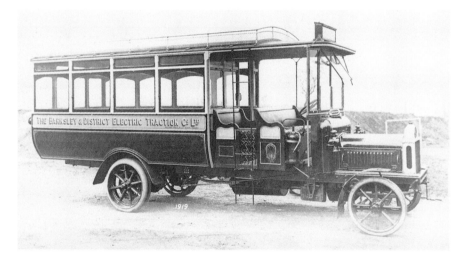

LEFT: *One of the first batch of five, HE 8–12, at the Brush Works when new. Note the large fire extinguisher and offside ladder to the luggage rack. (Brush)*

HE 10, when new in service with Barnsley & District Electric Traction Co. Ltd. (Yorkshire Traction Co.)

motor buses and expanding bus operation through its many subsidiary companies. Barnsley & District was one of these, and changed its name in January 1929 to Yorkshire Traction Co. Ltd; it remained as such until March 1968 when BET sold out to the Transport Holding Company, which in turn passed to the National Bus Company in January 1969.

The Importance of HE 12

My Barnsley & District bus, HE 12, therefore represents a very important chapter in the development of the British motor bus, purchased by the biggest tramway operator in the country in the knowledge that the modern motor bus would change the face of their operations, bringing about the death of the tramcar.

These twenty Barnsley & District Leylands had long and eventful careers, many of them being passed on to other BET/BAT (British Automobile Traction group) subsidiaries, including Potteries Electric Traction

bus until 1924, after which it was converted to a breakdown lorry and saw a further six years' service – a very long time for a vehicle of that age. How it then got to Newark is a mystery.

It is interesting to note that the entry in the *Register of Motor Cars* of the Barnsley vehicle licensing office gives the Barnsley & District Electric Traction Co. Ltd address as Sheffield Road, Barnsley. HE 12 was a 'single-deck motor coach, dark and light green, relieved in white, with the name of the firm upon it'. It was a 'public conveyance', the unladen weight 4 ton 0cwt 3qtr, with front axle weight 1.10.1 and back axle weight 2.10.2. These details are held in the Sheffield City Council Archives under reference SYCRO 176/L1/1, and an extract from the *Register of Motor Cars* is shown below. The Barnsley & District livery changed after World War One to maroon, later with white around the window pillars, before changing again to the more familiar red and cream of the Yorkshire Traction Company.

Rescue and Restoration

Apart from one or two rare examples, such as the 1910 Carter Paterson, Leyland X type lorry, the preservation movement did not get under way until the late 1950s. At that time there were some real gems to be found, and one or two early preservationists, such as Jack Sparshatt, did a good job in collecting what had survived, usually in a reasonably complete state, and not requiring a great deal of dedicated restoration work. After a further twenty-five years had elapsed, by the late 1970s/early 1980s, when Barry Weatherhead and I spent nearly every weekend bringing vehicle remains home, there was very little left dating from the 1920s or before, and what remained was hardly worth having. By that time most of the bus bodies that had been converted to sheds or living accommodation had been demolished, or had almost totally decayed. There were virtually no complete chassis, and a dwindling

Index Mark and Number on Identification Plates. (1)	Full Name of Owner, and Postal Address of his usual Residence. (2)	Description or Type of Car. (3)	Type and Colour of Body of Car. (4)	Weight Unladen. (5)	Whether intended for (6)			Date of Registration. (7)	If Cancelled, Date of Cancellation. (8)
					(a) Private Use.	(b) Use for Trade Purposes.	(c) Use as a Public Conveyance.		
HE 12	The Barnsley and District Electric Traction Co. Ld. Sheffield Road Barnsley	Single Deck Motor Coach Leyland chassis	Single Deck Motor Coach Dark and Light Green relieved in white with the name of the firm upon it.	4 0 0	1.10.1		4.0.3	Public Conveyance 30th April 1913	Transferred 7th Augt 1915
do	Transferred to Barnsley The Barnsley Coy & District Electric Traction t. ld. Barnsley	15th November 1916		2.10.2					

Extract from the Register of Motor Cars *for Barnsley C.B.C. for 1913.*

Co., and Peterborough Electric Traction Co. The first five, HE 8–12, went to the Reading operations of The British Automobile Traction Co. (a BET subsidiary), which went on to become the Thames Valley Traction Co. Ltd. – thereby doubling my interest in preserving this bus! My bus, HE 12, being one of these five, passed to BAT on 7 August 1915 after overhaul by Birch Bros. Just over a year later, on 15 November 1916, HE 12, together with sisters HE 8 and 9, were sold back to Barnsley & District. HE 12 ran as a

The chassis number plate of HE 12, showing chassis no. S253/1020. (The 253rd Class S produced, and 1,020th Leyland produced.)

number of solid-tyred trailers used by farmers, usually devoid of any running units such as engine, gearbox, radiator, controls or even the contents of the back axle. If the back axle of the vehicle had been worm-driven, the phosphor-bronze worm wheel would have been weighed in long ago in order to buy a few pints of beer or a hundred Woodbines.

A Chassis Discovered

It was therefore remarkable when, in April 1997, a further twenty years on, a friend of mine (Mick Giles, who is restoring an early 1920s Dennis char-a-bancs) telephoned one evening to say that a solid-tyred chassis had been found near Newark. Apparently it was inside a chalet bungalow that was being demolished, the plans being to

replace it with a brick-built farmhouse, next to Southwell Racecourse, Newark. After pulling off some of the side panels of the chalet, a solid-tyred wheel was revealed, to the amazement of the owner of the property. Further demolition work showed that the whole of the floor of the main part of the house rested on timbers supported by the chassis frame.

ABOVE LEFT AND ABOVE: *Two views of the chalet bungalow on the outskirts of Southwell Racecourse, near Newark, in which also resided my Barnsley & District 1913 Leyland.*

Demolition work now reveals the chassis frame (left) and wheels (above), on which sits a large wooden framework that supported the floorboards of the chalet.

The original springs, axles and wheels were all there, but had been totally enclosed by further rooms, and verandas on each side.

What was it? The owners were friendly with people in the steam/traction engine world and word soon got about, but nobody who came to see it could identify it. Word then got to Mick who went to have a look, but there were no identification marks on it. He described it to me over the telephone, and when he said 'There are some holes in the front cross-member' my ears pricked up, and I could not wait to go and have a look for myself. Another interesting feature was that it had a joggled frame, 38in (96.5cm) wide at the front, and 43in (109.2cm) wide behind the driver. This *had* to be a Leyland, and a very early one at that!

The next day I found myself in Newark – what a surprise! And I instantly recognized the chassis: it was clearly an S type with the early Class T back axle. However, not only had all the running units been taken, as usual, but the worm had gone from the back axle. Very fortunately, however, the phosphor-bronze worm wheel remained intact, as it must have been virtually impossible to remove without dismantling the back axle. This was one of the early Class T axles made in three parts, with the two axle tubes carrying the half shafts being bolted to the central axle gearbox, and all supported by an adjustable tie-rod underneath.

On further examining its mortal remains, it became clear that the vehicle in its operating life was very worn and had been badly neglected. There was an enormous amount of play in the spring shackles, and the front wheel bearings were so worn that each front wheel could be wobbled about 2in (5cm) sideways! Further evidence of abuse was that the bolt holes supporting the engine mountings had worn oval and had clearly chattered away so much that the chassis frame around the bolt holes had been reduced to about 1⁄16in (2mm) thick! Still, as has been said many times before, nothing is impossible,

and this machine just *had* to be saved and brought back to life!

The owner wanted to see it go to a good home, and surely there was none better than mine! After a quick haggle we settled on a price, I paid the deposit, and returned home. On arriving back, I instantly phoned my friend Bill Newens, who has a wagon with a very useful Hiab crane on the back; and thus the following day he also found himself in Newark.

The chassis comes home to Valley Forge, thanks to the careful handling of Bill Newens and his lorry with Hiab crane.

The Chassis Arrives at Valley Forge

The next Saturday was spent measuring all aspects of the chassis and scrutinizing it for numbers. Fortunately the original chassis number could be read at the front nearside corner of the frame, which sent me scurrying back up to the house as fast as I could, to go through my records. Yes, found it! It was Barnsley & District No. 5, HE 12. Not only that, it was one of the five S3.30.T buses that were transferred to British Automobile Traction at Reading, the forerunners of the Thames Valley Traction Co. – what an amazing find!

The construction of the chassis is very similar to my Leyland X2, with the same early type of tubular cross-members, and 'D'-shaped ends to the holes in the front cross-member. The three-part back axle is bolted together, and it has a virtually straight front axle that has its king pins inside the front wheels, on the centre line of the wheel, rather than a forked end to the axle with the king pin holding a stub axle. This earlier method of pivoting the wheel seems to me to be a lot more efficient than the later type, and makes the steering very light compared with the 'RAF types'. It does, however, rely on a very large and narrow bearing around the inside of the hub, and possibly these were expensive to manufacture (and therefore replace?). Finding the correct S3.30hp engine was no problem – I already had three and a half in stock, from previous adventures. Also in stock were the correct gearbox, pedal shaft, steering column and box (robbed from another chassis), scuttle and scuttle supports, and many other bits and pieces.

A posed photograph showing what the vehicle may look like, using parts from other vehicles, including yet another bonnet that was found underneath the floorboards of the Leyland drawing office when it was demolished. This photograph was taken in October 1997, some time before restoration work started.

The Barnsley & District chassis, now sandblasted and in primer, is totally dismantled down to every nut and bolt. It was found to be in an amazingly worn and neglected condition after a very hard life in service. A ball race in the back axle had disintegrated and the loose ball bearings broke most of the teeth on the worm wheel.

I still have the patterns for the Wellingborough radiator, and have commenced making a radiator from scratch (again!). I have also made a bonnet using the Wellingborough's bonnet as a pattern. Tyres are going to be a problem as Dunlop no longer make solid tyres, and in any event the fronts are an odd (and very early) size, being 670mm rim diameter × 110mm wide. I have, however, been fortunate enough to find two solid front tyres intended for a Foden steam wagon, and although these are 160mm wide, they can be machined

down to fit the Barnsley & District. As with most of these early commercials, the hind wheels are bigger than the front, and in this case are 771mm with twin rubbers – I have yet to find these, which may be a problem. An even bigger problem is going to be the torque tube, propshaft and worm for the back axle – there seems to be a bit of *déjà vu* here! Still, I am a firm believer that problems do not exist – they are all opportunities! And I am sure there will be someone that will come to my rescue somewhere.

The body for this bus, originally built by Brush of Loughborough, is going to be difficult, as this is the first restoration where I have nothing at all to go from, other than photographs and the knowledge that I have built up over the years. With all the other vehicles I have at least had the remains to work from, but this one is going to have to be a new body from scratch. I have already started, but it is early days yet, and the completed vehicle will not see the road again until about 2005 – so watch this space!

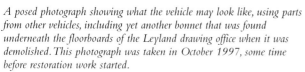

	Specification – Leyland S3.30.T
Operator	Barnsley & District Electric Traction Co., No. 5, registered HE 12 on 30 April 1913
Model	Leyland S3.30.T
Chassis No.	S253/1020
Engine	Four-cylinder, 30hp Class S3, built by Leyland, No. E11031 (29/9/22, and identical to its original engine)
Body	Brush, 'Combination Car', with twenty-seven seats and front entrance to the rear saloon
Length	Approx. 24ft 6in (7.5m) (including starting handle)
Width	7ft 2in (2.18m)
Height	10ft 1in (3.08m)
Weight	4 ton 0cwt 3qtr (4,102kg)

CHAPTER SIX

The Wellingborough, Leyland S3.30.T, of 1913

On Brighton seafront, having just completed the run in May 1990, the Wellingborough S3.30.T gets a final polish prior to the judging.

Leyland Motors, Rebuilds and Fire Engines

As less than three months separate the dates new of the Barnsley & District and Wellingborough buses, there is little to catch up on in the development of vehicles produced by Leyland Motors. By 1913 the Class S had leapt ahead of the Class X, with almost twice as many vehicles being produced, such was the success of this model. After its introduction in the

latter part of 1909, for a period of about a year or so, Leyland offered a service rebuilding other makes of chassis and installing the new S-type engines. This frequently included re-framing the chassis, and at the end of the day, one wonders whether many of these conversions were financially viable. Work on the rebuilds then stopped, as they were no doubt taking up too much time and space in the factory at a time when volume production was rapidly growing.

The Leyland Fire Engine

One area that has so far not been covered is the Leyland fire engine. The first machine was built for the Dublin Fire Department in December 1909, and it combined the U.50hp 'T'-head engine with the lightweight Class T worm-driven back axle. This made a formidable vehicle, and speeds of around 60mph (100km/h) were attained. Following this, developments were fairly slow with the second appliance, built in November 1910 for

B 5517 was a Leyland-bodied covered char-a-bancs on an S3.30.V chassis (with Class 'V' back axle). (Alan Lambert collection)

Sheffield City Fire Department, and which now included a massive six-cylinder, 80hp version of the S-type 'L'-head engine. The engine was designated U.80hp, and formed the basis for a number of larger fire engines. By 1911–12 a smaller, four-cylinder, 55hp version had been built for London County Council Fire Brigade, using the same cylinder blocks but only two pairs, and this, together with the U.80hp, had become the mainstay of fire-engine production. By 1913 the slightly heavier Class V 3-ton back axle was being used, and around the second quarter of 1914 the low-slung X-type radiator gave way to a more pleasing and modern radiator that sat mainly above the frame. This radiator was to last until the end of the FE1, FE2 and FE3 fire-engine production in 1931. A

The second Dublin Leyland fire engine, RI 2080 with U55hp engine, no doubt being guarded in 'the troubles'. (BCVM Archive)

booklet detailing the history of Leyland fire-engine production is currently in the course of preparation by The Leyland Society, and it is hoped that this will be ready shortly, if not before the publication of this book.

As there is little else to describe regarding the development of Leyland models at this time, I will proceed to outline the more specific details about my Wellingborough bus.

The Wellingborough Motor Omnibus Co. Ltd and its Letter 'H'

You will recall from the chapter on my London Central, Leyland X2 of 1908, that the New Central fleet of Leylands was absorbed into The London General Omnibus Co. fleet in 1913. At the time, the fleet consisted mainly of 'second generation' buses built on Leyland S2.30.T and S3.30.T chassis. Not much is known about the builders of the bodies except that some were built by Brush of Loughborough, some possibly by Birch Bros, and others by a fairly obscure firm called Cremmen. The New Central operations in Bedfordshire also went with the business to London General, but there is a mystery surrounding the fate of the balance of the order for 100 Leyland buses.

No doubt thinking of the future, Ben Richardson looked a little further afield to Northamptonshire. His attention was drawn to the Wellingborough area when a driver and conductor from the Bedford Depot of the New Central Omnibus Co. hired a bus one weekend when they were off duty, and used it to very successfully ply for hire around Wellingborough. After similar hires had been made by the crew on several occasions, arrangements were made for an official of the company, travelling on a motor cycle, to follow the bus to find out what they were up to. This led Ben Richardson to consider the possibilities of further expansion, and accordingly on a Saturday late in 1912 a bus was sent with a driver and conductor to Wellingborough to operate a circular service from Wellingborough

London County Council had the first fire engines with the new radiator that lasted well into the 1920s. LH 8819 was an 'escape van', built in 1914.

The Irthlingborough headquarters of the Wellingborough Motor Omnibus Co.

Twelve years ago when my Wellingborough bus revisited, most of the buildings remained.

via Finedon, Irthlingborough, Higham Ferrers and Rushden, and back to Wellingborough. The service operated from about 10 o'clock in the morning until about 11 o'clock at night, at which time the bus was parked in the yard of the Cambridge Hotel (later The Leather Bottle), Cambridge Street, Wellingborough, and the crew stayed overnight at the hotel, returning to Bedford the next day. For a number of weeks the same procedure was followed, and then Mr Richardson sent a second vehicle to Wellingborough to work the same route but in the reverse direction.

The Wellingborough Motor Omnibus Co. Ltd

Shortly after the New Central Omnibus Co. was leased to London General from 1 January 1913, Ben Richardson relinquished his position with the company; he was paid £5,750 compensation for loss of office, and this enabled him to concentrate his efforts on new ventures. Together with some local Wellingborough businessmen, he formed The Wellingborough Motor Omnibus Co. Ltd, being incorporated on 3 May 1913 and with a nominal capital of £10,000. A prospectus was issued, but the response was poor, in that local people only applied for 1,954 of the 7,500 shares offered.

Concurrent with this, Ben Richardson was involved in the formation of another company, and on 14 May 1913, the United Counties Omnibus Company Ltd was formed, with its headquarters in Westminster. Amongst the original fourteen shareholders of this company were Henry Spurrier Jnr and Henry Spurrier Snr, managing director and chairman respectively of Leyland Motors Ltd, and William Benjamin Richardson. This company did not operate buses, but immediately invested £4,000 in shares of the Wellingborough Motor Omnibus Co. Shortly afterwards, United Counties Omnibus Co. was put into voluntary liquidation and wound up, and the assets of the company in the form of shares in Wellingborough MOC were divided amongst the shareholders.

Now what was called 'The London Syndicate' controlled the company. It can therefore be seen that there were very close connections between the Wellingborough company and Leyland Motors.

It was this syndicate that supplied the Leyland ST buses to Wellingborough MOC (possibly some of the balance of the order for 100 buses?), and this probably explains why the buses were registered in London. The first vehicles arrived complete with their Birch(?) and Dodson bodies by May

Letter 'H', my bus, photographed in service when new.

1913. The buses were not numbered as such, their stock 'numbers' reverting back to letters, the same practice as had been seen with the New London & Suburban Company back in 1905. By July 1913 the letters had reached 'H' with my bus, registered LF 9967. It carried a thirty-six-seater double-decker body with open stairs, almost certainly built by Birch Bros. Most double deckers seat 34 but two extra seats had been fitted on the offside of the upper deck, so there were five pairs on each side, giving a capacity of twenty seats outside, over sixteen seats inside. These buses all had the S3.30hp

engine, combined with the Class T worm-driven back axle, and were an instant success, many of them achieving very long lives indeed.

A few of the buses were requisitioned by the War Department in World War One, but the twelve remaining buses, including some single deckers, were re-numbered in the 'A' class in 1919, becoming A1–A12. Many were rebuilt, with the new lower radiator generally fitted to the C-type 3-tonner after the war, and with a new bonnet this modernized

their appearance significantly. During September 1921 the company, being under-capitalized but quite profitable, was reformed into the United Counties Omnibus & Road Transport Co. Ltd, and this new company took over the ownership of the vehicles; by now these comprised seventeen of the 'A' class, nine 'S'-class rebuilt Subsidy 'RAF' types, together with fourteen 'B'-class Leyland 36hp double deckers, many of which had bodies built by the operator. (The fifteenth 'B' class was yet to come: B15 was the 'Charabus' – but that story is yet to be told, later in this book.)

TOP: *Letter 'M', another S3.30.T, with its enormous registration number painted on the scuttle, outside The Bull Hotel at Irthlingborough in June 1914.*

ABOVE: *Letter 'N', LH 8721, came to grief in January 1916. This photograph helped immensely with the detail of the underside of the chassis and body! Note the very wide ceiling boards.*

LF 9967

LF 9967 had become stock No. A3. It lasted with its original body until April 1925, when it was rebodied with a Dodson twenty-seater saloon body that gave it a further lease of life, being re-registered RP 977 at the same time; like this it lasted until March 1930. The original Birch Bros body off LF 9967 was sold and became a shed in the grounds of Wellingborough Sewage Works, where it remained, out in the open, for the next fifty-three years. Its ultimate salvation was due to the fact that the body could be seen by passengers on the nearby mainline railway, as will be seen in the next part of the Wellingborough ST's story.

Rescue and Restoration

It was back in 1975 when I first saw a photograph of the body of my

Photographed one frosty winter's morning by Roger Warwick in the grounds of Wellingborough Sewage Works, the remains of the 1913 Wellingborough body, built by Birch Bros, awaits its rescue and subsequent restoration.

The same frosty morning: the front bulkhead, still in remarkably good condition, shows the outline of the position of the seat cushions.

Wellingborough bus: it appeared in *Old Motor News*, a periodical vintage vehicle news update connected with Prince Marshall's *Old Motor* magazine. At that time I lived in Wiltshire, and it wasn't until 1977 after a house move to Bedfordshire that I mentioned the body to other members of the HCVS Chiltern Branch, and we decided to go and have a look. Four of us, including Barry Weatherhead and myself, jumped into my car one Friday evening and off we went to Wellingborough in search of the sewage works. We soon managed to sniff it out, but wherever was the body? We knew it was visible from the railway line, but that was over the far side of the grounds of the sewage works. Fortunately, however, there was a small concrete road that seemed to lead in the right direction, though it disappeared through a lot of undergrowth and vegetation; nevertheless with great trepidation we set off along it. It seemed to go on for some distance before it opened at a clearing with four houses, a gap between the middle two leading to an overgrown field. We were also now next to the railway line. Dusk was beginning to fall so we had to be quick – over the fence and into the field, and sure enough at the side of the field, under some trees, lay 'the body'. What an interesting find! It was clearly pre-World War One, and instantly recognizable as one of the bodies from the Wellingborough Motor Omnibus Company, ST types. It even had a notice on the inside front bulkhead informing passengers that 'Complaints had to be addressed to the Manager at The Garage, Irthlingborough'. It was now getting dark and so there was nothing more we could do except wait and contact the Anglian Water Authority, who owned the premises.

I returned to work the following Monday morning to be confronted by the transport manager who informed me that he had had a telephone call from the police and they wanted to talk to me. I racked my brains trying to recall any misdemeanours that I might have committed, but my sense of curiosity overcame my fear and I made the telephone call. They asked of my whereabouts the previous Friday

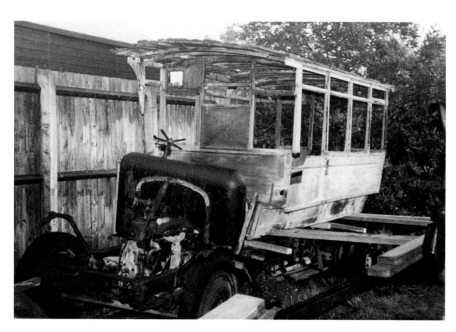

The body is mounted on a suitable Leyland chassis with S3.30hp engine.

evening, as they had had a report of four youths leaping out of a car between some houses in Northamptonshire and acting suspiciously. They had traced me through the registration number of my company car. I explained what we had been up to, finding the remains of a decomposing body in the woods, and they took quite a bit of convincing!

A price of £5 (including VAT) was agreed with Anglian Water, a cheque was sent, and off we went to recover the body. Again, Barry initially purchased this body, but it became mine soon after, when Barry and I exchanged a number of his Leyland items for my share in AEC Y types, White & Poppe engines, and so on, and so forth.

Finding a Chassis

Next an appropriate chassis needed to be found as there were no running units; but several years went by. However, in 1986 the remains of an early Leyland lorry became available. It had the correct S3.30hp engine, the correct gearbox and controls, but the later T4 version of the worm-driven back axle. It also had a longer wheelbase and frame. On checking the vehicle's chassis number I realized that it was one that I had seen some eleven years earlier whilst living in Wiltshire. It lay in an orchard in a place with the rather odd name of Middlezoy near Westonzoyland in Somerset. What a small world! The chassis was available and, although on 36 × 6 pneumatics, I later discovered that it had originally been a char-a-bancs registered in Carmarthenshire in South Wales, which had ended up with Greenslades of Exeter. The body had then been removed and a lorry body fitted (the usual story!).

On getting the chassis back home, I shortened the wheelbase by redrilling the bolt holes for the rear spring hangers and moving the axle forwards some 13in (33cm). We cut the propshaft in half, sleeved and welded it, the brake rods were shortened – and we were 'in business'. I already had another ex-farm trailer chassis and

wheels 'in stock'(as you do!), made from a 1919 model A-type 2-ton Leyland, and this provided the solid-tyred wheels. Its T4 back axle was devoid of worm wheel and differential, but these parts from my newly acquired chassis fitted perfectly – all I had to do then was to have two new half shafts made out of hardened steel, and we were ready to roll.

The chassis was not in bad condition at all, although it originally looked dreadfully rusty. I had it sandblasted, and then we dismantled it completely, every nut and bolt. After, we carefully put it back together again, refurbishing anything that was necessary; this included skimming the back brake drums and having new brake linings, and the same was done with the cardan shaft brake at the back of the gearbox.

The Radiator and Bonnet

I did not have a radiator, and knew of only one of this model that survived at the time: the 1911 Leicester City Tramways Tower Wagon, preserved in the Leicester Museum. I went to the museum to take measurements and many photographs, with a view to making patterns to have castings

made for my radiator. However, when I was there, the curator asked if I could help repair the Tower Wagon's radiator, as it leaked badly. This was too good to be true, and I left with the Tower Wagon's radiator in the boot of my car. It meant that I could make the original radiator tanks into patterns from which to have new ones cast for both the museum and myself. I made a completely new core for the museum, as had been requested, and repaired the old core to go in my Wellingborough bus. This couldn't have worked out better, and I now have half of an original radiator!

Next came a remarkable stroke of luck: on one of my many trips to the British Commercial Vehicle Museum at Leyland, carrying out research on these very early Leylands, I visited a local scrapyard near Leyland. The owner was preparing to have an auction sale, and in the middle of his yard was a Rolls Royce Merlin engine, possibly out of a Spitfire, and painted yellow. Much of the yard had been cleared, but as usual I had a good poke about and, lo and behold, in the corner of a shed was a Leyland bonnet, in almost 'as new' condition but rather dirty. It had its original double brass

A 'chassis-up' restoration – the chassis progresses well, with a new body floor frame beside. Note the bonnet just ready to go on (found under the floorboards of the Leyland drawing office, and absolutely original).

The body, now mounted on the chassis, has new side framework, but retains the original front bulkhead, roof members and so on.

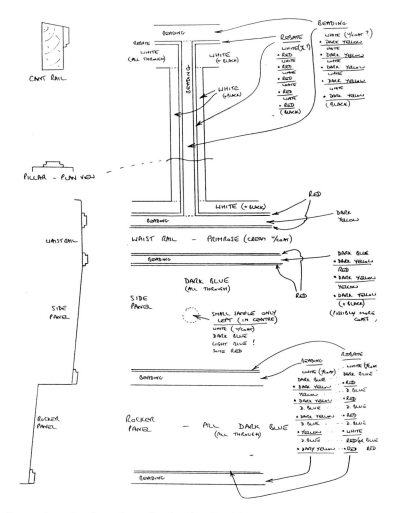

This diagram shows the colours of paint found on the sides of the Wellingborough body. With a magnifying glass it could clearly be seen that the vehicle had been painted five times during its working life, and this close inspection gave valuable information relating to the colour scheme.

hinge down the centre, brass handles and edging strips, and I recognized it instantly as a bonnet from a pre-World War One vehicle with 30hp engine. £10 exchanged hands, and I took it home and put it on the Wellingborough chassis: it fitted absolutely perfectly and with no adjustment needed whatsoever – the 'Sutcliffe luck'!

Restoring the Body

The Wellingborough body, although looking very rough, was amazingly sound. The floor had rotted badly, however, and a new ash frame had to be made. Most of the original, highly polished ceiling boards were salvageable, and on expert advice I was informed that they were made from a special Russian redwood. Not having a clue where this could be obtained, I managed to find some Douglas fir to repair the damaged pieces on the offside, and these matched quite well. The steel platform bearers were still there, although they had been cut off short, so these had to be extended. We made a new platform and staircase, as well as the whole of the upper deck with seats. The staircase was not at all easy as it was very difficult to measure the true dimensions – the back of the body is shaped like an old-fashioned three-penny bit both horizontally and vertically, in true horse-bus fashion.

The lights for the vehicle posed quite a problem. The side lamps are conventional oil lamps, but the headlamps and rear tail lamp are aluminium, and are powered by acetylene. These were eventually found at various trips to Beaulieu Autojumble, and are now all 'piped-up'. The pipework must also accommodate three acetylene lanterns that illuminate the ends of the lower saloon, two at the front and one at the back; these include a 'bull's eye' in each, which doubles up as an additional side/tail lamp. The original lamps were still there on the body, but had to have quite a lot of refurbishment to get them back into pristine condition, and it was not easy to find domed solid glass 'bull's eyes' in both clear (for the front) and red (for the rear).

Restoring the Paintwork

When researching the colour scheme for the bus there were conflicting views, but I was convinced that the livery changed during the long lifetime of the bus in service. There was 'evidence' of paintwork still on the body, although most of this had come off. The remaining flakes were examined under a magnifying glass, and it could be seen that the bus had been painted four times during its life. However, what about the primrose yellow band beneath the windows? What was the colour of the bonnet? Was there a red band around the front canopy cant rail? What were the seats like? An elderly gentleman called Ted Gafney remembered the buses in the early 1920s, and he helped me a great deal. Also Roger Warwick from Northampton gave me two more names of very old employees of United Counties whom he thought might have been able to help. One of these I was unable to find, and the other, known as 'Titch' Hawes, was initially elusive to trace; but eventually I managed to get his address from the National Bus Company Pension Fund. 'Titch' has proved to be a veritable mine of information, and it is him I particularly have to thank for enabling me to get the colour scheme right.

Finally came the signwriting, and just at the right time, Roger Warwick came up with an absolutely brilliant photograph of my bus, letter 'H'. (Roger published a book entitled *Leylands of the Wellingborough Motor Omnibus Company Limited* a few years ago – an excellent book and one that I found very helpful when carrying out my research for the restoration.) He had come across a large framed picture of the bus, found hanging on the bedroom wall of a house that was being cleared after the elderly occupants had died. Apparently their daughter had died at a young age, and they had virtually sealed up her bedroom, not changing anything since that date, presumably back in the 1920s! But why would a young lady have a large picture of my bus on her wall? I had enlarged part of the photograph to establish the shape of the 'buckles' at the end of the

Ready for the signwriting and some coats of varnish, the Wellingborough is now nearing completion. This was the last restoration that I completed in an open car port (or should I say 'bus port'!)

ABOVE: *The handsome young man stands by letter 'H' before the Great War.*

1991 letter 'H' revisits exactly the same spot at The Green Dragon, Higham Ferrers.

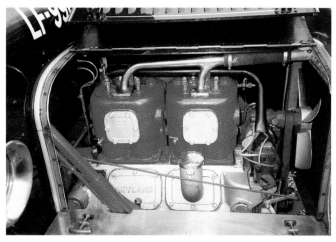

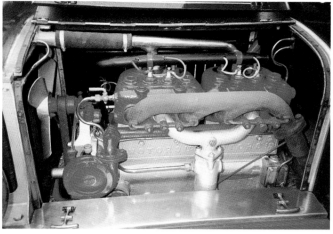

The offside of the S3.30hp engine clearly shows the cylinders cast in pairs.

The nearside of the engine – note the coloured HT leads, a typical Leyland feature so as to avoid getting them mixed up.

ABOVE LEFT: *The lower saloon is quite spartan, reflecting the efforts made with 'second generation' buses to reduce weight as much as possible. Compare this with the interior of the Leyland X2 of 1908.*

ABOVE: *The upper deck contains an additional pair of seats as compared with most thirty-four seaters of the time, the usual configuration being sixteen passengers inside, and eighteen outside (i.e. upstairs!).*

The 'Gaunt for Bikes' advertisement is shown here, together with the acetylene rear lamp. The occasion was the trip around the old routes, and the bus is parked outside the Irthlingborough Garage staff houses, which have an inscription 'WMOC' over the door.

garter on the side of the bus, pronouncing the name 'WELLING-BOROUGH'. At the time I had just got together with Pat, and I showed her the photograph, saying that I was puzzled why the picture had so obviously been treasured, having been carefully framed and hung on the wall – and she immediately said, 'It's not the bus that the young lady was interested in, it's that handsome young conductor standing beside it!' One can only speculate as to what happened – perhaps he went off to war in 1914, never to return? Who knows?

Letter 'H' Takes to the Road

Having finished the restoration just in time for the 1991 Brighton Run, I took it to the local scrapyard to weigh it (not weigh it in!): it was 3 tons 19cwt 3qtr 18lb (4,059kg). Although the finish of this bus is quite Spartan, it is clearly heavier than the earlier London versions that were even lighter at just under 3 tons 10cwt (3,556kg).

Shortly after a very successful Brighton Run, attended again in full period costume, Pat and I took the bus back to Northamptonshire to drive it over all its old routes, and to photograph it in the same locations as in the many pictures I have of the bus when it was new and in service; Roger Warwick acted as navigator. When we were parked outside the George & Dragon at Raunds, an old boy of about eighty saw us and came over: evidently he couldn't believe his eyes, having seen the advertisement panel underneath the staircase advertising 'Gaunt – For Bikes, Repairs & Accessories, High Street, Raunds': the shop had closed decades ago, but he had clear reminiscences of the bicycle he had bought at that shop when he was a boy!

Since then the 'Wellingborough' has been on many rallies, including the TransPennine Run which, for a vehicle of this age, is so long that it had to be spread over two days, starting on the Saturday. It has starred in *Fairy Tale – A True Story*, when it carried Peter O'Toole, and in more recent years has been on display in the British Commercial Vehicle Museum at Leyland.

A rather bleak view on top of Saddleworth Moor in Yorkshire whilst en route back from the Historic Commercial Vehicle Society's TransPennine Run.

BELOW: *The Wellingborough comes head-to-head with a bus from the previous generation, the 1908 Leyland X2, the occasion being one of the Valley Forge 'Crank-Ups'.*

Specification – The Wellingborough, Leyland S3.30.T	
Operator	Wellingborough Motor OC, Letter 'H', registered LF 9967, new July 1913
Model	Leyland S3.30.T
Chassis No.	S209/954
Engine	Four-cylinder, 30hp, Class S3, built by Leyland, No.12749
Body	Birch Brothers, 36 seats (20 outside, 16 inside)
Length	22ft 8½in (6.92m) (including starting handle)
Width	7ft 0in (2.14m)
Height	12ft 4½in (3.78m)
Weight	3tons, 19cwt, 3qtr, 18lb (4,059kg) (4tons, 0cwt, 0qtr painted on the chassis)

LEYLAND PRODUCTION   1896 – 1930
MAIN MODEL TYPES AND APPROXIMATE NUMBERS PRODUCED

Year	Total	Steam	1-1½ Ton	2-3 Ton	3-4 Ton	5-6 Ton	Fire Eng.	Low Level Passenger		Other
1896 to 1904	135	B etc 134	Z 1							
1905	49	B/G/H 31		Y/Y2 18						
1906	61	H 35		Y2 15	X 11					
1907	53	H 36			X 17					
1908	50	H 27		T/XT 5	X/X2 18					
1909 (note 1)	53	H 14		T/XT 12	X2 29	W 12	UT 1			
1910 (")	110	H 14	S + XT/ST 43		X2 52	W 7	U.80 1			Tram 2
1911 (")	189	H/F 18	S/S2 + ST/SV 70		X2 76	W 21	U.80 2			Tram/R-car 2; Q 1
1912 (")	330	H/F 27	S2/S3 + ST/SV 155		X3 91	W 27	U/U.80 9			Tram 2; Q 9
1913	390	H/F 34	S3 + ST/SV 195		X3/X4 105	W 33	U/U.80 12			Tram 1; Q 10
to Aug. 1914 (Total to 8/14 1690)	270	F 34	S3 + ST/SV 150		X4 45	W 15	U/U.80/FEU4 31			Q 5
Sep-Dec 1914	377	-	Subs B [Total 375]		Subs A	-	FEU4/X4V4 2?			
1915	1187	F 7?	Subs B [Total 1185]		Subs A	-	FEU4 2?			
1916	1643	F 4?	IMT 11+		Subs A 1610-	-	FEU4 12+			
1917	1515	-	IMT 45		Subs A 1463		FEU4 7			
1918	1437	-	IMT 17		Subs A 1401		FEU4 19?			
1919 (note 2)	1279	F2 12	IMT 24	A/C etc 43	G to O 1184	P/Q (incl in 4 ton)	FEU4 14?			ex WD est 120?
1920 (")	1545	F2 56	IMT ?	A/C 490	G to O 980	P/Q (incl in 4 ton)	FEU4 19			ex WD est 500?
1921 (")	655	F2 48	D ?	A/C 255	G2 to G7 263	P/Q 57+	FEU4 32			RAF est1000?
1922 (")	624	F2 21?	D ?	A/C 284	G2 to G7 196	P/Q 80	FEU4 43			RAF c539?
1923 (")	856	F2 5?	Z 33	A/C 314	GH/SG/LB 389	P/PH/Q/QH 93	FE1-3 21			RAF 495
1924 (")	1293	F2 5?	Z 89	A/C 552	GH/SG/LB 472	PH/QH/SQ 141	FE1-3 34			RAF 389
1925 (")	1734	F2 1?	Z 29	A/C 834	GH/SG/LB 626	PH/QH/SQ 203	FE1-3 26		LG1 15	RAF 386
1926	1960	F2 2?	LA (2 ton) 60	A/C 631	GH/SG/LB 456	PH/QH/SQ 282	FE1-3 22	LC/LSC 455	LG/LSP 52	-
9m to Sept 1927	1701	-	LA 8	A/C 357	GH 286	PH/QH/SQ 324	FE1-3 14	LC/LSC 684	LSP 28	-
to Sept. 1927/28	3448	-	-	A/C 441	GH 394	PH/QH/SQ 509	FE1-3 25	PLC/PLSC 1548	TD1/TS1-2 531	-
1928/29	3329	-	-	-	GH 345	PH/QH/SQ 520	FE1-3 21	PLSC/LT1 866	TD1/TS1-2 1106	T Goods 471
1929/30	3274	-	-	-	GH 107	PH/QH/SQ 190	FE1-3 12	LT1-2/LTB 565	TD1/TS1-2 1324	T Goods 1076

Notes - 1. Rebuilt vehicles using S and X frames are not counted in the totals of chassis built for the year.
2. Rebuilt ex-WD lorries (later described as Reconditioned ex-RAF lorries) are not included in the totals built for the year.

CHAPTER SEVEN

The L&NWR, Leyland S4.36.T3, 'Torpedo' Char-a-bancs, of 1914

The elegant lines of the Leyland 'Torpedo' body are shown well here, photographed just prior to the start of the year 2000 London to Brighton Run.

Leyland Motors, up to and into World War One

In an earlier chapter we saw how the Class ST vehicles developed. In addition to the New Central Omnibus Co., the London & North Western Railway and East Surrey Traction Co. were early takers of the model. This was followed by the British Electric Traction Group through their subsidiary, Worcester Electric Traction Co., and although the BET and BAT (British Automobile Traction) initially took small quantities of Leylands, they were clearly impressed by the Leyland's quality and were looking ahead

to develop the model further. Aldershot & District Traction Co. (another BAT company) took seven S2.30.T double deckers in 1912–13, and the twenty S3.30.T single deckers went to Barnsley & District Electric Traction, as already mentioned. In the meantime, the London & North Western Railway took further deliveries of both double and single deckers.

Improvements to the Single Decker

While all this was going on, Leyland were developing a new single-decker chassis, designed for bus work, and almost certainly looking for orders

from the BET Group. There were three main alterations from the STs that had been built so far: first a new, enlarged class engine was introduced, designated S4. Initially there were two variants: the S4A for 35hp, with 4½in bore; and the S4B, a slightly larger variation for 36hp with 4⅝in bore (the S4A can virtually be ignored, as few, if any, were made). The next modification was the back axle. Electric steel furnaces were now in operation, and it was possible to cast a one-piece axle with enough strength, rather than making it in three sections bolted together with a tie rod underneath. The new worm-drive axle (for quieter running) was slightly larger, able to take 3 tons (3,048kg), and it was designated Class T3. This newly designed chassis was therefore classified S4.36.T3.

The third, and probably the most interesting alteration, was the gearbox. This had four forward speeds, but was of the double helical type, being a very early design of this type of gearbox. Leyland Motors were clearly at the forefront of technology at the time. The gearbox, probably classified as 'S8', had the advantage of quietness, compared to the straight-toothed conventional gearboxes that were quite noisy, particularly in the lower gears. It was clearly aimed at the London market, where the Metropolitan Police, who licensed London's buses, were very keen to reduce noise levels; but of course that market had virtually vanished overnight with the absorption of the New Central Omnibus Co. into London General! However, the BET Group, through British Automobile Traction (BAT), were also keen on this new design and ordered a batch of fifty S4.36.T3 chassis fitted with the helical gearbox. They were to be delivered in 1914, going to the fleets of Worcestershire Electric Traction (later to become Worcestershire Motor Transport), Kidderminster &

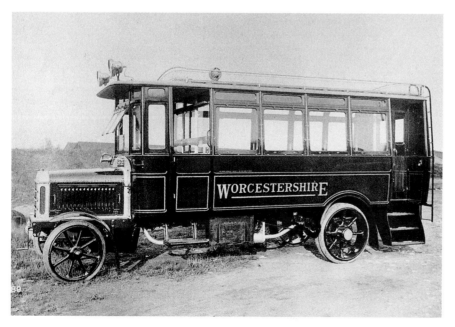

TOP: *One of the first S4.36.T3 chassis for the BET Group, loaded onto a railway wagon ready for dispatch to the Brush Works at Loughborough for its body. (BCVM Archive)*

ABOVE: *A look inside the S8 helical gearbox. Leyland Motors were ahead of their time for technology in 1914.*

LEFT: *Most of the BET S4.36.T3s had Brush saloon bodies, as did FK 539 for Worcestershire. (Brush)*

District Electric Light & Traction Co., Deal & District Motor Services, South Wales Transport Co., and BAT, North Devon. The delivery of these last fifty buses may have been frustrated by the outbreak of war at the beginning of August 1914, as I can only account for forty-nine.

Also in 1914 a few other operators looked at the S4.36.T3 with great interest, notably the London & North Western Railway Company and Edinburgh Corporation, who took six and three respectively, all in July and August 1914. None of these were to operate in public service for very long, as they were all requisitioned by the War Authorities – more of that later.

Other Leyland Petrol Vehicles

While we are in 1914, it is worth just having a look at what other Leyland petrol vehicles were being made at the time. For instance, the Class Q 15cwt/1ton was being built in very small quantities, with production coming to an end with World War One. The Class S range, apart from the developments that we have already looked at, was progressing strongly on another front – that being the War Office subsidy scheme. Leyland Motors were the only British manufacturer to get approval from the War Office in 1912 for both the War Office Subsidy Class A 3-ton and the Subsidy B 30cwt chassis. These had S-type engines married up to Class V 3-ton back axles, the Subsidy A having the S3.30hp engine and the Subsidy B the smaller S3.24hp engine. Both of these models went on from success to success with War Office orders, and in particular the Subsidy Class A that was further developed – more of that later.

The X type had also been modified and upgraded in late 1913, with the new X4.40hp version of the 'L'-head engine to become the X4.40.X2. In 1914 the back axle was modernized, culminating in the X4.40.X4 which had a single piece 'electric steel' cast back axle, still double-reduction bevel-driven. The 5/6-ton range followed suit, usually with the same X4.40hp engine, but now with the Class W3 'electric steel' back axle (this axle continued well into the 1920s on the heavier goods models of 5 to 6 tons).

In the few years prior to World War One there had been flirtation with the idea of producing overtype chassis in order to save space and maximize on carrying capacity. Usually based on

the 5/6 ton range, and sometimes 8-tonners, these featured a driving position situated over the bonnet, with the driver perched right up in the air – quite ungainly looking machines. A few lighter-weight overtypes were built on SV chassis for use as dustcarts in Liverpool, but apart from these, and a few more built around 1922–23, no others were built.

By August 1914 the standard fire engines were the FE.U4.55hp with the four-cylinder engine, and the FE.U.80hp with the six-cylinder engine. London County Council Fire Brigade were in the process of taking delivery of a large batch of FE.04.55hp machines with V4 back axles, and the new radiator, when war broke out and some were never delivered, being

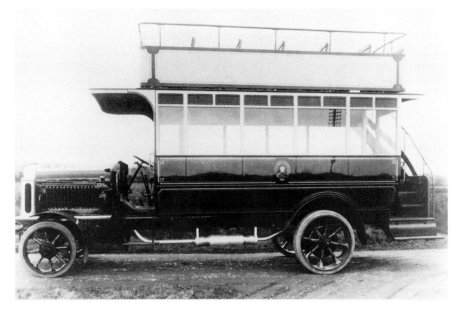

The final development of the X type was the X4.40.X2. No. 5, B 5771 was new in March 1914 to Todmorden Corporation. It was fitted with a Leyland-built 'Eastbourne-type', forty-three-seater body, with all lower deck seats facing forward. It is the design of this body that was copied for my Phoenix-bodied Leyland G of 1921 – more on that in a later chapter. (BCVM Archive)

Inside the Leyland works in 1913, with a thirty-two-seater char-a-bancs body being built, identical to those for the L&NWR. An enlargement of this photograph was very useful to get the right construction for the seat backs and tip-up seats and upholstery. (BCVM Archive).

ABOVE: *Immediately after World War One, char-a-bancs production took off in earnest in the Leyland Works. This batch was almost certainly for the fleet of White Rose, Rhyl. (BCVM Archive)*

BELOW: *On the open road in 1919 is this Leyland-built char-a-bancs on an 'RAF-type' chassis. Note the maker's transfer on the windscreen, identical to the two that I found.*

requisitioned by the War Office and fitted with lorry bodies.

This therefore completes the picture of Leyland petrol-driven vehicle production when war broke out. Steam wagons were still being produced, with production of these and fire engines being moved to Chorley Works. The current steam-wagon model at the time was the Class F, of which approximately eighty were built, the last ones being completed during the early years of the war. When steam-wagon production was recommenced in 1919 the model became the F2, of which 150 were built up to the end of production of steam wagons by Leyland in 1926.

The L&NWR and their Number 59, CC 1087

Most of the railway companies saw the benefit of operating buses on feeder services to their railways. They also saw a major threat in rural areas as the motor bus became a more reliable and cheaper alternative to rail transport. Several railway companies, and in particular the Great Western Railway, bought large numbers of buses and dominated some areas of the country.

By the late 1920s the companies realized that the existing bus operators were more efficient, and decided to buy into those companies, either as co-owners with the British Automobile Traction group or Tilling group, or as sole owners. They then merged their own bus services with the operators taken over. In addition to these company operations, the railway companies entered into joint operations with four municipal bus operators, including Todmorden Joint Omnibus Committee, as will be seen later.

The L&NWR first experimented with mechanically propelled road vehicles for the delivery of parcels with a Daimler van; this ran from November 1898 to February 1899, but it was decided that 'The time had not arrived for the adoption of motor vans'. A further experiment took place in 1903, but it was not until 1905 that the 'Premier Line' took the plunge and decided to purchase twenty vehicles for goods and passenger operations by road. The goods operation included the purchase of two steel-tyred Foden steam wagons, for service in Birmingham and Holywell in Flintshire, whereas Milnes-Daimler 24hp buses were purchased to initiate the bus services in North Wales. A year later services were started around Watford in Hertfordshire, again with Milnes-Daimler buses, all bearing the standard carriage colours of 'dark plum and spilt milk', and carrying the company's elaborate coat of arms.

Pre-World War One Development

The L&NWR bus operations continued to grow steadily mainly in these two areas, and from 1910 with the addition of buses made by Commer and Leyland. These initially carried bodies by Christopher Dodson, but from 1911 the L&NWR made most of their own bodies in their works at Wolverton (now part of Milton Keynes). Some Daimlers, model CC and CD (based on a similar design to the LGOC B type, and with Daimler sleeve-valve engines) were introduced

in 1913/14. Later in 1914, eight Leyland chassis were ordered for service in North Wales, but only six were actually delivered due to the war. Leyland Motors were awarded the contract to build the bodies, three being thirty-two-seat 'Torpedo' chars-a-bancs, and three with saloon bus bodies, all being fitted to the S4.36.T3 chassis. (The name 'torpedo' was used extensively at this time, particularly relating to touring cars and chars-a-bancs that were long and sleek-looking.) The charas were registered locally in North Wales

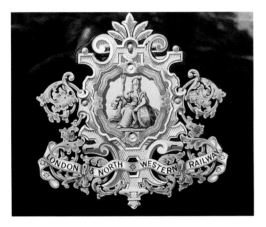

ABOVE: *The L&NWR coat of arms as shown in this eighty-year-old original transfer, which I applied to the sides and rear of my preserved char-a-bancs.*

RIGHT: *LC 5405 was typical of the early Milnes-Daimler buses run by the L&NWR. It was No. 7 in the fleet run between Watford Station and Croxley. (L&NWR Society)*

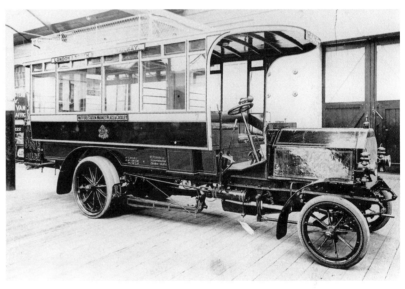

BELOW: *The first of the three 1914 chars-a-bancs was No. 59, photographed when new in July 1914. I was fortunate to find this picture of my vehicle. (BCVM Archive)*

and included my char-a-bancs, No. 59 in the L&NWR fleet, and registered CC 1087. It was delivered and entered service on 14 July 1914, three weeks before war was declared, and ran on a new service from Colwyn Bay Railway Station to Rhos Pier. This service was initiated to convey the wealthy cotton barons from their large mansions on the North Wales coast to the 'Club Train' on which they proceeded to Manchester for a day's work. They returned in the evening. This was surely not a very viable operation, but no doubt the cotton barons had a lot of clout with the top brass of the L&NWR! The service did not last long, however, as in March 1915 all six of the Leylands delivered only eight months previously were commandeered by the War Office.

L&NWR Bus Operations during the War

Little is known about No. 59's war exploits, except that it was sold off with other war-surplus Leylands from the Slough Dump around January 1920. It became a builder's lorry, and was re-registered XA 8086. After a long and gruelling life (as evidenced by the state of the vehicle when restoration commenced), the Leyland was laid up in a garage building in south London.

The story of the recovery of CC 1087 is related later in this chapter, but what happened to the L&NWR bus operations? With the continuing

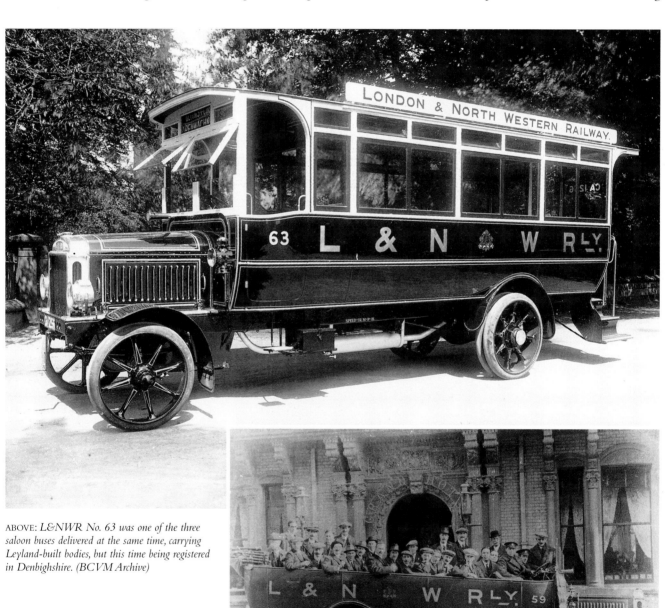

ABOVE: *L&NWR No. 63 was one of the three saloon buses delivered at the same time, carrying Leyland-built bodies, but this time being registered in Denbighshire. (BCVM Archive)*

My Leyland chara stands outside The Grand Hotel (but where?) after having been requisitioned by the War Department – note the towing hooks front and back. It was possibly carrying new recruits ready for the war effort.

call-up of staff, and with the possibility of more vehicles being requisitioned, the L&NWR Officers' Conference of 13 April 1915 decided that, at the end of that week 17 April, nearly all the bus services should be withdrawn (apart from a few workmens' journeys and the services at Boxmoor and Tring, the latter continuing to be operated throughout the remainder of the Great War). As the majority of the remaining L&NWR buses were therefore out of work, the bodies were removed, and lorry or parcel van bodies were fitted. The old bus bodies were stored during the war years, after which they were sold. With this much

reduced service, three Thornycroft J's were added in 1921–22, but the L&NWR bus service would diminish further owing to the mistaken policy that 'The railway was for running trains on rails, not motor vehicles on roads'. The Thornycrofts and possibly three Daimlers did, however, last into LMS days following the railway grouping of 1923.

The history of the London & North Western Railway's interest in road vehicles, and particularly bus operations, is well told in John Cummings' book *Railway Motor Buses and Bus Services in the British Isles 1902–1933*, Vol. 1.

Rescuing the Mortal Remains of XA 8086

I purchased the mortal remains of XA 8086 from Bob Bennett in June 1980, but the story goes back further than this. Bob had found the builder's lorry in a garage in south London, somewhere near Peckham. It was in a very sorry state indeed – some gypsies had beaten him to it and removed anything that was brass or aluminium. The off-side hubcap had gone, the carburettor, radiator and bonnet – in fact anything they could get their hands on. They had even smashed both cylinder blocks of its original S4B engine in order to extract the four small brass priming cocks situated on top of the cylinders. What vandals! (The phosphor-bronze worm wheel had, however, amazingly survived the attack.)

It was felt that the remains of the lorry were still worth saving, particularly as the site was to be redeveloped and the building demolished. However, there was a large pile of rubble preventing the doors being opened, so Bob and his colleagues set about totally dismantling the chassis and extricating it bit by bit out through a window – wheels, engine, axles, gearbox – the lot! The only part that would not go out in one piece was the chassis frame, which was cut in half at each end.

When I first saw it, it was in Bob's yard on pallets under a tarpaulin. By then he had sold all four wheels and the front axle to a man in South Wales who intended to convert a restored lorry from pneumatics to solids, although I've never been able to trace this vehicle. The other rear hubcap was now in use as a door-stop, and there didn't seem much likelihood of what was left ever being restored. However, *nothing* is impossible! I brought the bits home and kept them together in the hope that one day they might be useful, even if just for spares.

I managed to identify the chassis as being one of the three L&NWR chars-a-bancs, and with the help of John Cummings, the expert on railway buses, learned a bit about its history with the L&NWR. I had always

The dismantled chassis of XA 8086 in Bob Bennett's yard, waiting for a new home.

CK 3090 was a Leyland G 36hp new in March 1919 with Leyland char-a-bancs body. It was one of the first post-war chars-a-bancs to be built.

The body from CK 3090 can just be seen protruding from the bushes.

When I got the body home it totally collapsed; here it is sitting on the 'Florence Nightingale' Leyland G chassis.

One of the lifting eyes fixed around the floor framework.

wanted to restore a char-a-bancs, and at one time thought of building a body on my 1919 Karrier WDS; but that would not have been authentic, it would have had no 'pedigree' – it would not have been right.

Many years passed until one day I had a telephone call from Peter Dawson, the then manager of the museum at Leyland, to say that they had had a visitor who had found a Leyland char-a-bancs body near Preston. The body had been new in March 1919 on a Leyland G chassis to a firm in Preston, and was virtually identical to the L&NWR 'Torpedo' chara, even down to the earlier design with a sloping floor. It had a detachable body with lifting eyes, which could be lifted off the chassis, so a lorry body could be fitted for general haulage work during the week, and the chara body for weekends or special outings. The char-a-bancs body had remained hanging high up in the roof of a garage long after the lorry had been disposed of, and the owners wanted to find a good home for it. It had been lowered down from the roof and put outside, and the word had been put around the steam fraternity. But unfortunately there were no takers, and as time went by, the chara had started to decompose. Nor did Peter have the address, and this was very, very frustrating – however could I find out where it was?

About three years later Peter phoned me again to say the same man had been into the museum again, and this time he had his address. A few days later the remains of the 'Torpedo' char-a-bancs body arrived at Valley Forge; by this time most of the nearside and the rear had collapsed, and it was in a very sorry state indeed. It would, however, give me many original Leyland fittings, dimensions, the shapes of the curves of the body, and full details of its construction. This was vital to the restoration of the L&NWR char-a-bancs, as only a few parts of its original body floor remained. In the meantime, however, I had applied to the DVLA at Swansea, who very helpfully re-allocated the original registration number to the vehicle: CC 1087.

All the chassis components except the engine gathered together ready for assembly.

Yet another front portion of a Leyland chassis, this time a model G5, once owned by Wood Bros of Blackpool, FR 4660. This was found at Graveley, Hertfordshire, and provided the scuttle and front wheels.

Restoration Begins

After returning from Brighton with the London Central Leyland X2 in May 1996, I had a week's break from restoration work (from Saturday to Saturday!); then I assembled all the chassis parts for the L&NWR chara in my garage ready to start rebuilding it. I already had the correct wheels and front axle in stock: the back wheels came from a model C-type Leyland that Stephen Hubbuck had recovered from Cornwall (the model C had the same T3 worm-driven back axle); and the front axle and chassis front cross-member, again exactly the correct specification, came from the front half of a chassis that Mike Jones of Ruthin had found for me in North Wales. It had originally been a model SG7 of J. D. Hendry, of Coatbridge in Scotland, registered VA 2649. As I have said, these were exactly right, and they even carried the same part numbers as were applicable to my L&NWR chara.

Finding an Engine

The engine was a potential problem with its smashed cylinder blocks. I did, however, know of a 1929 Leyland QH6 6-tonner that had originally been a tanker of Shell Mex. It was owned by a man in Cornwall, and at some stage it had been fitted with an S4.36hp engine built in 1914 (engine No. S4/49 – only fifteen numbers away from my engine, which was S4/64!). I already had a spare 1929 Ricardo head engine (E36HP/2) and in very good condition, so I approached the man in Cornwall to see if he would let me exchange the engines. Unfortunately he was in the process of selling the lorry, and this would only have complicated matters. However, once the deal had gone through I approached the new owner, who was in Yorkshire, and he kindly agreed to do the swop. So Mike Street and I went up to Yorkshire for two days and exchanged the engines, which did both owners a good turn!

Finding a Radiator

When you reach the chapter on the Chocolate Express, Leyland LB5, you will see a reference to the radiator that came from Blackburn following an advert in *Exchange & Mart*. This radiator was perfect for the L&NWR 'Torpedo' char-a-bancs – it was even the early model with cast-iron sides, which was fitted to the S4.36.T3. It held water and all I had to do was to replace the front row of tubes and gills to make it look more presentable. The filler cap was badly worn and had to be repaired, and fitted with the royal coat of arms 'By Appointment' badge. There are still a number of these badges in circulation, albeit at

ridiculously high prices, but I have now managed to secure enough of them to fit to all my restored Leylands that carried them from new.

The Restoration of the Body

This was perhaps the most complicated restoration that I have achieved (apart from the front end of the White Rose SG7). It is full of compound curves not only for the steel panels, but for the ash framework, around the doors, the doors themselves, and of course each seat frame. This proved to be very difficult, and the more complex timbers had to be carved out of the solid by hand: this was done by Mike Street, who is now an expert at this sort of task!

Although I had one door latch that came from the front door of the char-a-bancs body found in the brewery in Lancashire, I needed five matching latches, all left-hand, for the five doors. I was very lucky to find a set at the

ABOVE: *Mike Street examines the 1914 S4.36hp engine, about to be removed from the later Leyland QH6.*

ABOVE: *The ash framework on the nearside is very complicated with all the doors, which, without all the original steel bracing, would severely weaken the structure.*

RIGHT: *Looking down into the seats, showing one of the two hinged tip-up seats where there is no door because of the wheel arch.*

The chara is taking shape two years into the restoration, but with the most complicated part of the body yet to do – the front curved panels including the shaped driver's door.

Beaulieu Autojumble, where I managed to purchase a box full of them – there were seven altogether and when I laid them all out, I found that six were left-hand and one was right-hand. This was absolutely perfect: five nearside ones for the char-a-bancs, and a matching pair for the front doors of the White Rose, Leyland SG7 – the Sutcliffe luck strikes again! Also at Beaulieu I found a hand-operated windscreen wiper, designed for an open vehicle, and a large one at that. The wiper screws on to the top of the glass of the windscreen and has a wiper blade each side, because with the hood down, a quick shower will wet both sides of the windscreen! Turning to the windscreen frame, I did of course have the windscreen, that also came from the brewery; but amazingly enough I came across the remains of another Leyland chara windscreen on one of my expeditions – I think it may have come from Mr Mills at Chesterfield (more of him later). These windscreens provided all the hinges, knurled knobs and handles that I required, which was

exceedingly useful. They also carried, of course, the Leyland maker's transfer which, although not good enough to use, gave me an exact example to copy, and this has now been reproduced not only on the L&NWR char-a-bancs but also the White Rose, Leyland SG7.

All four of the lifting eyes from the original char-a-bancs body have been fixed in the appropriate positions underneath the second row seats and the sixth row. To lift the body off the chassis, the seat cushions would have to be removed, which is quite easy, and the lifting hooks would go straight onto the eyes. However, it was not an easy job to connect the front of the body to the shaped dash panel, and so I fixed these fairly permanently (the body could be removed, if desired, but it would severely damage the paintwork at the front end, when nuts and bolts were undone).

The Paintwork

Within the last three months of finishing the restoration came the paintwork, and this proved to be an absolute

nightmare! Every time I manage to find a supplier of old-fashioned coach-paint, when I come to the next restoration I find that the manufacturer has stopped producing it! This is generally due to the fact that it is a dying market. Because the L&NWR chara is a railway vehicle, there are plenty of model makers making models of L&NWR carriages, and it was fairly easy to determine the exact colour for the 'dark plum' (almost an aubergine colour). The first paint manufacturer whom I contacted said they could match the colour, but I would need to take a minimum order of 200 litres (they must have thought I had a whole fleet of chars-a-bancs to paint!). I did, however, find a firm in Manchester who mixed the colour very precisely – in fact they got it spot on. When brush painting, however, it is necessary to flat each coat with wet and dry before applying the next, and in particular prior to the yacht-varnish final coat. *But*, and it was a very big but, being such a dark colour, as soon as you rubbed away the surface, even with 1200 grit paper, the pigment was damaged and went a funny sort of brown colour in strong sunlight. Not being satisfied with the results, I ended up by painting the final coat about three times. And having applied all the gold leaf, transfers and signwriting, I remember the sun came out and shone on the gleaming new paintwork, only to show some more brown patches. There was only a week to go before the London to Brighton Run, but being a perfectionist I wanted to paint it yet again; but Pat said '*No!*' and sense prevailed! (She doesn't often say '*No!*' and she was right!)

You may like to know that, before finding a modern paint manufacturer, we very seriously considered actually making the paint from scratch ourselves, in the same way that the L&NWR did back in the nineteenth and early twentieth centuries. This was to be done in conjunction with the L&NWR Picnic Saloon Trust, who had been restoring an 1886 six-wheeled picnic saloon carriage. Readers may be interested to see the paint

Preparation:	Eight coats of priming, filling, etc.
1st Coat:	Lead Colour (afterwards stop and face with pumice stone)
2nd Coat:	Body Brown, ground in the paint mill as follows:

Drop Black	10lb
Indian Red	9½lb
Liquid Dryers	2lb
Sugar of Lead	1lb
Linseed Oil	6 pints

3rd Coat:	Carmine Lake, ground in the paint mill as follows:

Lake Powder	2lb
Sugar of Lead	8oz
Linseed Oil	3 pints

After grinding, 1 pint of Liquid Driers and ½ pint White Spirit added

4th Coat:	Varnish Colour, made up as follows:

Carmine Lake (as above)	3lb
Varnish	2 pints

After lining and lettering has been carried out, four coats of varnish to be applied. All paint to be applied at the rate of not more than one coat per day, and two days to be allowed between each coat of varnish. The varnish to contain no gold size.

specifications for the Carmine Lake (deep plum) portion of carriages, below waist level (note, there are sixteen coats!): *see* box left.

The Carmine Lake colour uses cochineal as its basis. Cochineal comes from beetles' blood and provides a very intense deep red colour. These beetles come from Brazil. Through an L&NWR Society friend we even went as far as making enquiries with the Brazilian embassy to see if there was any way of sourcing such vast quantities of beetles, but it all came to no avail and proved too difficult – just imagine how many millions of beetles one would have to rear (on a beetle farm?) to paint a whole train of L&NWR carriages! It must have been a terribly messy job treading on them all to squeeze the blood out!

Next came the gold leaf, and also the transfers – the L&NWR coat of arms, which is exceedingly complicated. When I bought the second Leicester Tower Wagon chassis, the owner, knowing that I was planning to restore the L&NWR chars-a-bancs, gave me two L&NWR coat-of-arms transfers. I did, however, need three – one for each side and one for the back of the chara. But after carrying out further research, and with the help of John Cummings,

I discovered that the transfers I had were slightly too big, being locomotive transfers rather than railway carriage-size transfers. I was lucky, however, to find a railway buff in Birmingham who not only had a few of the smaller transfers, but was prepared to exchange my two larger ones and sell me two more, so that I would have three, plus a spare. Being delighted with my find, I started to apply the first transfer, only to have it tear in half when I pulled off the backing paper, which was very firmly fixed. What a disaster, and what a waste! Having learned from this, I applied the next transfer with the transfer varnish a little bit wetter and more tacky, and I delayed the removal of the backing paper. This worked perfectly, and the next three went on with no problem – thank goodness!

Restoring the Upholstery

As one would imagine, the upholstery of a char-a-bancs is an absolutely enormous job – can you imagine making from scratch seven five-seater settees, two having hinged tip-up centre seats? I was very fortunate in that Geoff Golding on the Isle of Wight has the remains of a 1922 Leyland C-type char-a-bancs, that had been converted to a lorry. He discovered that the front driver's seat cushion had been taken out of the lorry at the end of its life, and put in a local café. Fortunately for us he managed to acquire the cushion from the owner of the café, partly dismantled it to send me samples, and did some very detailed drawings as to its construction: thank you Geoff! It matched exactly with official pictures of Leyland chars-a-bancs being made in the factory, with the doors open, and enabled me to copy the construction of the seats in every last detail.

I prepared full working drawings, had the seat spring bases (for the seat backs also) made at Wade Springs in Nottingham, and then a local vehicle enthusiast, John Hearne, upholstered them – and he made an excellent job of them. The backs are especially complicated as they are all pleated, including around the inside corners of each seat, and also including the two small

Some of the detail of the paintwork – the lining-out consists of a broad band of yellow edged in white, with a smaller white line inside. The same colours are applied to each bonnet louvre. Note also the Leyland 'By Appointment' coat of arms on the filler cap, and the legal lettering: 'L.W. Horne, Sup't of the Line, Euston Station'.

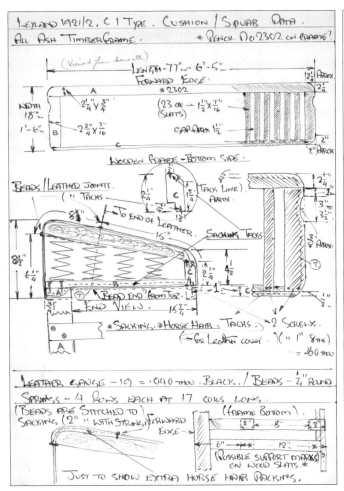

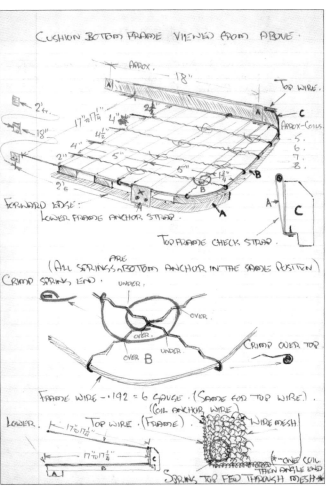

Geoff Golding's drawings of the Leyland char-a-bancs seat cushion that he found in a café on the Isle of Wight.

An interior view showing the pleated seat upholstery and the two gangway tip-up seats.

Steve Elliott fits the bonnet centre double hinge, again from one of the 'spare' bonnets!

tip-up seats that enable passengers to reach rows five and seven, where there are no side doors. I was able to match the colour of the leather cloth exactly with specimens of the original from the Preston body, and I used a modern equivalent PVC that looked virtually identical, this being fastened down with thousands of brass 'daisy' nails. The only problem with the latter was that they were all shiny brass and looked totally out of place. So first I had to 'distress' every one of them individually, which involved hammering them into planks of wood, in rows like regimented soldiers. I then sprayed them with etch-primer mixed with a bit of matt black cellulose paint, which gave them a rather dirty, tarnished brass look. They were then removed and individually held against my buffing wheel to remove some of the paint on the high spots. This worked a treat, but what a tediously boring job – almost as bad as threading 21,850 radiator gills!

Restoring the Hood Frame and Side Screens

The hood frame was made out of steam-bent ash, each hoop having to be made in three sections and spliced due to their enormous length. The whole hood is held taut by two leather straps with buckles that are fastened to the front mudguards (these were a second wedding anniversary present (leather) from Pat). As it turned out, the sewing of the double-duck canvas for the hood was a relatively easy job, because I found a sail-maker who had a heavy-duty industrial sewing machine. The most difficult part of this was making the two rather ugly, but necessary, side screens, which go the whole length of the vehicle, and which include a number of rectangular celluloid windows. When the side screens are in position, (which is very rare because they look so ugly!) they are extremely dangerous in that they prevent the doors being opened for a quick escape from the vehicle for passengers in an emergency.

When I was at a recent rally, an old gentleman came up to me and told me that he nearly lost his life in one of these 'Torpedo' char-a-bancs during the 1920s. It was being used as a school bus, and as it was raining, the side screens had been fitted. But the vehicle broke down, having developed a carburettor problem, with the carburettor dripping petrol onto the floor. Rather carelessly the driver, who had been smoking and should have known better, inadvertently threw the cigarette end into the gutter, and the inevitable happened: the flames apparently set fire to the char-a-bancs, and along with many of his colleagues, the boy was rescued through the side of the vehicle by a thoughtful pedestrian tearing at the side screens!

Restoration Complete: CC 1087 Takes to the Road

Again, the L&NWR chara restoration was finished through burning the midnight oil in the week before the London to Brighton Run. I slept in it on the back seat at Battersea on the night before, and it was quite cosy with all the side screens in place. The next day it performed faultlessly, where we

LEFT: *Making the double duck hood outside 'North Works', our upper garage at Valley Forge.*

BELOW: *The L&NWR chara with my colour co-ordinated Rover car, GUY 3, and the very ugly side screens in place.*

SOME CLOSE-UP DETAIL OF THE CHAR-A-BANCS:

ABOVE: *Water tank for the water-cooled foot brake, and to the right of it is the oil 'tell-tale': when the knob is up there is oil pressure.*

RIGHT: *A detail of the hind wheel.*

Hackney licence plates issued by the various Police Watch Committees in the towns where it plied for hire.

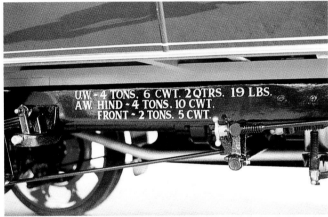

The unladen and axle weights – note the reluctance to move away from the horse.

jointly won the class award with Fraser Clayton and his immaculate Leyland Cheetah. We also won several other prizes, including the outright winner of the Concours d'Elegance.

The year 2000 was a very busy year for the char-a-bancs, travelling to rallies all over the country, including the L&NWR Railway Centre at Quainton near Aylesbury, the Leyland Society annual gathering at Wroughton in Wiltshire (followed by a trip to Leyland in the pouring rain the following year), Woburn, Stockwood Park in Luton, Showbus, and so on. We also took it on a surprise visit to the Milton Keynes Museum of Rural Life at Wolverton for the annual general meeting of the London & North Western Railway Society. Nobody knew it was going to be there and it caused quite a stir, as the amazed L&NWR enthusiasts arrived.

One story that I have heard several times is that char-a-bancs bodies, because of their inherent weakness of construction and flexibility, are prone to the doors all jamming closed, or flying open, depending on the unevenness of the ground on which it is standing: this is absolutely true, and on a couple of occasions when the doors have jammed shut the passengers have had to climb over the seats to reach a door that will open, or even over the sides. We have also had occasions when the more portly passenger has not been able to get onto the char-a-bancs because of the small doorways. This has caused much embarrassment – in fact we were at one time to lead a procession carrying the mayoress, but there was no way that her large mass would go through the aperture, and she had to take second best and ride in Chitty-Chitty-Bang-Bang instead!

The following year, 2001, Pat and I took the chara to the Llandudno Festival, back to its home territory, and re-enacted its journey from Colwyn Bay Railway Station to Rhos Pier Point, the route on which it was originally used when it transported the cotton barons to and from their mansions for a day's work in Manchester. Rhos Pier fell into the sea in a gale many years ago, and all that remains now is the toll

RIGHT: *This rear view, before the licence plates were fixed, shows the 6in (15cm) slope of the seats (and floor).*

BELOW: *The L&NWR chara re-visits Conwy Castle.*

Specification – Leyland S4.36.T3	
Operator	London & North Western Railway, No. 59, registered CC 1087, new July 1914 (re-registered XA 8086 on disposal by War Office and reverted to CC 1087, 8/95)
Model	Leyland S4.36.T3
Chassis No.	S568/1687
Engine	Four-cylinder, 36hp, Class S4, built by Leyland, No. S4/49
Body	Leyland 'Torpedo' char-a-bancs, seating thirty-two
Length	24ft 1in (7.34m) (including starting handle, and with hood up)
Width	7ft 7in (2.31m)
Height	8ft 8in (2.64m) (with hood up, 7ft 6in (2.29m) with hood down)
Weight	4 tons 6cwt 2qtr 19lb (4,402.7kg)

BELOW: *Hood down – ready for the summer sunshine.*

booth at Rhos Pier Point, though this has now been converted into a café. We went for a cup of tea in the café, and the owner, who had renovated it some time ago, came running out with a wooden box under his arm. It was of a dark polished wood and was sign-written 'L&NWR – Please Take One'. This was clearly a leaflet or timetable dispensing box that he had found among rubbish in the derelict toll booth prior to its renovation. What an amazing find! A lengthy (very) discussion took place on the best and most appropriate future for the little wooden box, and then after a short haggle it was brought home, to be kept at all times with the L&NWR char-a-bancs – a really fitting ending for the little box, and this chapter!

CHAPTER EIGHT

The Todmorden No. 14, Leyland G, of 1921

The 1921 Leyland G returned to Todmorden in 1984, seen here in the company of the preserved PD2/1 now owned by David Powell. Standing next to me in the centre is Teddy Metcalfe, the former general manager of Todmorden JOC; he was in the same class at Todmorden Grammar School as my father. Marc (my eldest son) and Matthew (middle son), then only nine, also posed for the camera together with, on the right, Dennis O'Neill, of the Todmorden Antiquarian Society. Dennis has unearthed a massive amount of early information on the bus operation in Todmorden.

Leyland War Office Subsidy Models

Picking up the story from August 1914, apart from a handful of fire engines, steam wagons and a few other oddities, production was concentrated on the War Office Subsidy A and B lorries. Soon into the war the Subsidy B 30cwt was uprated with the 30hp engine to become Class S3.30.V4. Similarly the Subsidy A 3-ton was uprated to include the S4.36hp engine, but also its carrying capacity was increased by switching to the X4 back axle from the X-type range, becoming the S4.36.X4. Despite this it was still called a 3-tonner – both this and the Subsidy B with its V4 3-ton axle were grossly over-engineered for their purpose, although no doubt the military authorities knew that the lorries were likely to be heavily overloaded, and compensated for this!

From 1916, production was mainly Subsidy A models, but a few other lorries were built, in particular some for

Pause for a fag! The earlier 30cwt War Office machines were based on the S engine with 'T' back axle. B 2399 was built early in 1912 before the Subsidy models were available.

Leyland were the only manufacturer to gain approval for the Subsidy A (3 ton) and Subsidy B (30cwt) machines for the War Office in May 1912. Their 1914 brochure proudly relates their success, with orders from the War Office. It also shows a U.55.V fire engine for Southport.

Standard WO Subsidy Model, Class A, Type 5000

In April 1916 it was decided that only standard models should be built, in order to maximize volume production. The then current design for the 3-ton War Office model was frozen, to be called the 'Standard WO Subsidy model, Class A, Type 5000': what a mouthful! The 'type 5000' merely relates to the fact that a new chassis number series was started at 5000 for these standard models, but also some of the major component part classifications gained a '5' at the same time; for instance, the S4B 36hp engine became S5 (I know of no physical change to this engine, which continued with a bore and stroke of 4⅝in × 6in). The rear axle became Spec. No. B.A. X/5, but strangely enough the four-speed gearbox (heavy) remained Spec. No. G.B. X/4. Very often there appears to have been no logic in the way Leyland allocated their classification numbers and letters – it just seems to have been what was 'a good idea at the time': but it makes life for us historians very difficult indeed. Wouldn't it be nice to be able to go back to those days, have a good look around the factory and inspect the records, and be able to talk to some of the engineers and ask hundreds of questions: if only!

The War Office Subsidy model Class A, type 5000, continued almost unchanged through to the end of the war, with the majority of the production being switched from the Army Service Corps to the Royal Flying Corps, later Royal Air Force (therein lies another story to be told!). There were a few exceptions to the standard model, including some extra-long wheelbase chassis used for carrying aircraft.

Post-War Model Range

At the end of the Great War, and with normal production yet to come back on stream, the two larger models were re-classified as model G for the standard wheelbase, and model I for the long-wheelbase version. These fitted into a new model range that was first set out in catalogue No. 17 dated

service in India; these were designated IMT (standing for Indian Mechanical Transport). They were based on the Class S 2/2½-ton chassis, but had the Class V, 3-ton back axle and S5 36hp engine (more of this engine later). They were also fitted with very spindly-looking disc wheels of enormous diameter, both front and rears being of 881mm tyre size.

The standard War Office Subsidy Model, Class A, Type 5000; these two were assembled by the Lancashire and Yorkshire Railway at their Newton Heath Carriage & Wagon Works, near Manchester. (Alan Lambert collection)

An early 1919 picture of a White Rose Leyland G, DM 1317, being completed. The S5.36hp engine can be seen – also the similarity with my Todmorden G, the Leyland body being copied by the Sutcliffe Brothers (Phoenix Cabinet & Joinery Co.). There is also a similarity with the signwriting – see the chapter on the White Rose SG7! (BCVM Archive)

1 January 1919, and full details of the range and how it developed are set out in my article in the first issue of *The Leyland Society Journal*, dated July 1999. It is too complicated to go into all the detail here, but the model range could be summarized as follows:

Models A and B
Two-tonners with the S3.24hp engine, and a new development of the worm-driven 'T' axle known as T4.

Models C, E, F
Formed the 3-ton range, mainly with S3.30hp engines and the heavier T3 type worm-driven rear axle.

Model D
Replaced the IMT chassis (just re-designated).

Models G, H, I, and J
All 4-tonners with the S5.36hp engine and high radiators similar to the War Office Subsidy A. The H and J were intended to be passenger versions of the G and I, with the T3 worm-driven back axle instead of the X5 bevel axle.

Models K, L, M, N and O
Were originally intended to replace the G, H, I and J; they had the new low radiator and low bonnet line with S19/5 36hp engine and with one extra model, the 'O' with longer wheelbase.

Models P and Q
The 5- and 6-tonners, again with the low radiator and the W19/3 double-reduction bevel back axle (the '19' meaning the 1919 version of the W3). These initially had the pre-war X4 40/50hp engine, now re-designated X19/4 40/48hp.

The Model G continued to be produced, though in very small numbers because there were so many rebuilt Subsidy models flooding onto the market; and by 1921/22 this had almost killed off the demand for new lorries. A G2 version was brought out briefly, with low-type radiator, but in 1923 the high-type radiator came back, albeit in a revised design, when the model became GH2 (the 'H' being for high bonnet/radiator). This model continued in production right

This Model C, XX 2623, with equal-sized wheels and Leyland cab, was probably chassis no. 35354, new to Kia-Ora Ltd, London SE1, in February 1925.

The 4- to 6-ton models of the 1918–1920 period can be recognized by the extra-long bonnet with eighteen louvres (instead of sixteen); this meant that the larger X4 40/50hp engine could be fitted. With bevel-drive back axle, this Model M for Brookes Brothers, Rhyl (probably DM 734 or DM 1800) was one of ten Leyland chars-a-bancs bought for the 1920 season. Henry Spurrier the second, keen to establish a Leyland stronghold in North Wales, is reputed to have told the Brookes Brothers that they needn't pay for the chars-a-bancs until the end of the season, when they could afford to pay! (BCVM Archive)

up to 1930 and sold in quite large numbers, particularly when the supply of rebuilt RAF types had dried up.

The Todmorden G, with chassis No. 9961, was one of the few that were built in 1921 for the Todmorden Corporation in June of that year.

Todmorden Corporation, and their No. 14

Todmorden is a small town with a population of about 15–20,000 in the heart of the Pennines and on the border of West Yorkshire and Lancashire. In fact it is now wholly in Yorkshire, though its postal address is still Lancashire. The Borough of Todmorden came into being near the end of the nineteenth century, and it was planned that an electric tramway should be installed along the three main valleys, which meet at the centre of Todmorden. This tramway was not to be, however, possibly because of the heavy investment needed in the permanent way; so the local horse-bus operator, the Todmorden Carriage Co., had a temporary reprieve from intense competition.

Todmorden's First Buses

One of Todmorden Corporation's claims to fame is that it was the second municipality in Great Britain to operate the motor bus in a serious way (the first was Eastbourne). Late in 1906 the Corporation placed an order for two Critchley-Norris double-deck buses

with Crossley 40hp engines. These chassis were made at Bamber Bridge, Lancashire (near Leyland), between 1905 and 1907. Mr J. S. Critchley was a director of the Daimler Company, and he had also been with Crossley. Mr Norris was works manager at Peter Pilkingtons, Steam Hammer Makers at Bamber Bridge. Closely following the two Critchley-Norris buses that entered service in December 1906, were two Leyland 'U types', numbered 3 and 4, delivered in January and February 1907 respectively. All four buses had bodies built by UECC at the Dick Kerr Works, Preston (builders of tramcars). The chassis

of the two Leylands cost £610 each, and No. 4 was probably the first Leyland to have a pressed-steel frame. They were the first Leylands to have the larger Class U 50hp engine, in a Class X chassis. However, the increased power of the 50hp cylinder blocks on the standard X-type crankcase caused problems, mainly arising from weak conrods. In September 1907 their engines were removed and replaced by Aster 46P 40hp engines at a cost of £240 each, after which the Leyland engines were rebuilt, and later re-used.

A Ryknield 40/50hp bus arrived in July 1907 (No. 5), followed by some second-hand purchases in 1909 and

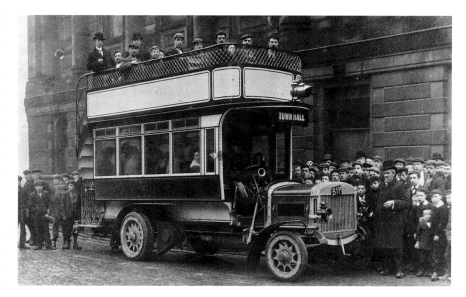

Todmorden's first bus, a Critchley-Norris with Crossley 40hp engine delivered in December 1906. The body was by the United Electric Car Co. (Dick Kerr Works), Preston, and was identical to Todmorden's first two Leylands. Note the fluted radiator designed by Critchley of Daimler fame.

1915, bringing more Critchley-Nor-rises into the fleet and a further Leyland. At the end of the day, Todmorden Corporation probably operated most of the Critchley-Norris production!

The second-hand Leyland was acquired in November 1909 from J. Roberts (Rossendale Divison Carriage Co. Ltd) of Bacup, and was of particular interest. Registered AP

The prototype Birch-bodied Leyland Class X, AP 2015, new in April 1906 and purchased second-hand. (Illustrated in Chapter 4.) When this photograph was taken it had received the slightly later radiator and an extended front end to take the longer Aster engine. It is uncertain what the celebrations were for, but they would have been between November 1909 and the outbreak of World War One.

2015 and carrying a Birch Bros O18/16RO body, it was in fact the first prototype Leyland X type dating from April 1906. It had original-ly been purchased new by a Mr W. Ellis of Hassocks, Sussex, and ran 'By Appointment to the London, Brighton & South Coast Railway' on a service from Hurst to Hassocks. The body was finished in 'natural wood' – in other words, varnished – and was invoiced by Birch Bros on 12 April 1906 to W. Ellis at a cost of £142. For some unexplained reason the Hurst–Hassocks service only lasted for two months, and the bus was returned to Birch Bros, being advertised for sale in March 1907. A buyer was eventually found around January 1908 – a Mr J. Roberts – and the X type returned to Lancashire, where it, too, was fitted with an Aster engine. This engine was clearly too large for the chassis, which had to be extended and fitted with a longer bonnet, in April 1909. The further history of this vehicle with Todmorden Corporation is exceedingly complicated and very interesting, but unfortunately too lengthy to include here (yet another story to be told one day!).

In these early days, buses did not last very long; they were not very reliable, and technology had not advanced enough at that stage. Operators lived from crisis to crisis, having to make new parts to keep vehicles on the road, and probably had to work with staff who did not have enough technical knowledge about motor vehicles and were happier riding horses! Todmorden Corporation struggled on with its elderly buses and, being Yorkshiremen, did not feel inclined to dip into the brass in their pockets to fork out for new vehicle replacements. Consequently the buses were rebuilt, and rebuilt again, with a major programme of purchasing chassis frames and engines in the period 1912 to 1915, transferring over the gearboxes, axles and wheels and bodies (this all sounds vaguely familiar!).

New Buses for Todmorden

The next new Leyland was purchased in 1913, No. 8 in the fleet, being the latest Class X3.40hp, and its double-deck body was one of two purchased second-hand from Leyland, having originally been fitted to a vehicle owned by the Peverell Road Car Co. of Plymouth, being new at the end of 1909. The Peverell company had failed

B 5628 was No. 8 in the Todmorden fleet. A 1913 Class X3.40hp, it had a second-hand body purchased from the Peverell Road Car Co. of Plymouth. It was the first of Todmorden's buses to be impressed by the War Office and sent to Bulford Camp. Note the torsion bar on the rear axle.

financially following a series of fatal accidents with its buses. Next, in March 1914 came a new No. 5, a Leyland X4.40hp (still with X2 back axle) but fitted with a new style of Leyland-built double-deck body, seating forty-three (twenty-three outside, twenty inside). This bus cost £715 and had the wider 'Eastbourne' type of body with all seats facing forward, and did not have the tram-style rocker panels in order to accomplish this.

The War Effort

In September 1914 the War Office, from their Manchester office, directed that this newest Leyland be impressed and delivered to Bulford Camp, Salisbury Plain, to be fitted with a lorry

BELOW: *Todmorden, No. 9, CW 1948, was a rebuilt Subsidy G-type Leyland that carried the 'Eastbourne-type' body, previously on No. 5, the X4.40.X2 that had also been requisitioned by the War Office (see the first part of Chapter 7). It was this body that was copied for the Phoenix body on my No. 14.*

RIGHT: *In 1921 there were relatively few routes in Todmorden, the system not yet having been fully developed. It is interesting to see that there were reductions in fares to encourage more people to use the buses.*

BELOW: *A sample of Todmorden Joint Omnibus Co. tickets, albeit from a later period.*

TODMORDEN

Reductions of Fares.

Bacup to Sharneyford.   Bacup to Newkin.
and Intermediate Stages.

From SUNDAY, 14th OCTOBER, 1921,
Fares will be Reduced as follows :-

	Old Fare	New Fare
Bacup to Sharneyford School	2d	1½d
„ „ G. & H. Pit	2½d	2d
„ „ Borough Boundary	3d	2½d
Co-op. Store to Sharneyford School	1½d	1d
„ „ „ G. & H. Pit	2d	1½d
„ „ „ Borough Boundary	2½d	2d
Sharneyford School to „	1½d	1d
Bacup to Northern School	2d	1½d
„ „ Weir Hotel	2½d	2d
„ „ Doal's Chapel	3d	2½d
„ „ Newkin	3½d	3d
Meadows Mill to Weir Hotel	2d	1½d
„ „ „ Doal's Chapel	2½d	2d
„ „ „ Newkin	3d	2½d
Weir Hotel „ „	1½d	1d

The Stage point at Weir Co-op. Stores will be changed to
Weir Hotel.

Millwood, Todmorden,   JAMES WILD,
10th October, 1921   Engineer and Manager.

body and go to war. They had no doubt inspected the Leyland production records, but Todmorden Corporation tried to be clever, and sent their older No. 8 to Bulford Camp instead! The impressment authorities were clearly not impressed, and the following month the chassis of No. 5 was ordered to be despatched to Salisbury Plain. Todmorden Corporation had therefore lost its only two half-decent buses!

They were now desperate for new vehicles, but the whole of Leyland's production was being directed to the war effort. In December 1915 the

Corporation was lucky enough to be able to purchase a new Straker-Squire model CO5. This was followed in April 1918 by a 1916 Karrier WDS (War Department Subvention) chassis with lorry body. It had carried a thirty-two-seater char-a-bancs body at one stage, named 'The Princess'. The Corporation therefore struggled through the war with patched-up vehicles, and some buses even ran on town gas, the gas bags being bought from Taylor & Ross of Nottingham (Nottingham seems to have been the centre for the production of gas bags for use on buses in World War One!).

In 1919, after the end of hostilities, it was difficult to obtain new buses, but Todmorden were able to purchase three new G types through Oswald Tillotson at Burnley (Nos 10, 11 and 12, No. 12 being nicknamed 'The Dirty Dozen'). These were followed by three more vehicles via Oswald Tillotson in 1920. No. 9 was a rebuilt Subsidy chassis, but its delayed delivery caused Todmorden Corporation and Oswald Tillotson to fall out with one another. The other two were new G1 chassis, with bodies built by Central Aircraft of Kilburn, London NW6. Three second-hand Leyland N chassis were also purchased from Northern General Transport Co. in that year; they were fitted with double-decker bodies.

1921 was a very important year, because in June No. 14 arrived, a Leyland G, registered C 2367. This must have been one of the last re-issued registrations prior to the system changing in 1921. It was fitted with a temporary second-hand body while a new body was being built across the road from the Millwood Depot in Todmorden, by the Sutcliffe Brothers, who traded as Phoenix Cabinet & Joinery Co. This was a forty-three-seater body built along the lines of the Eastbourne type originally fitted to No. 5 in 1914, and which now sat on the rebuilt Subsidy chassis as No. 9 in the fleet. No. 14 had a double reduction bevel rear axle, which Todmorden Corporation preferred due to the hilly nature of the terrain. It had the standard S5 36/40hp engine and high radiator/bonnet line, despite having been sometimes described as a G2. It had originally been intended that the corporation build No. 14 from spare parts, but Leyland persuaded Todmorden to buy a new chassis, and purchased various spares from the corporation in part exchange. The bus had a fairly uneventful life with Todmorden, being withdrawn in August 1928 and replaced by a Leyland Titan TD1, also numbered 14 in Todmorden's usual 'gap-filling' way. It was sold, with others, from Todmorden in October 1928 to A. Brittain Ltd of London N7, and became a box van, fitted with an oil engine. This must have been a very early oil engine, as it was withdrawn in March 1930, being sold to Cook (Dealer), London SW8; it was last licensed in March 1940. No. 14's body, together with a second body from another Todmorden double decker (built by Leyland), found its way to a farm near Navestock in Essex. The two bodies were placed at the edge of a field, still complete with their upper decks and staircases, though the lower deck seats were removed so that the bodies could be used as sleeping accommodation for temporary farm labourers during the summer harvest months. (The story of these bodies is continued below.)

Todmorden Corporation continued to buy more Leylands, some with Phoenix bodies, throughout the 1920s, and it is interesting to study the models purchased, as they follow closely to the history of Leyland production. Todmorden Corporation became a very profitable operator and expanded considerably in the early 1920s, with a very modern fleet. By 1932 all of their Leyland 'RAF'-type derived vehicles had been replaced, even the Leviathans, and none of the fleet of thirty-six buses was more than five years old. By that time the corporation had sold 50 per cent of the undertaking to the London Midland & Scottish Railway Company, on 1 January 1931 – and this leads us nicely to the Leyland Tiger TS6 described later in this book.

The crews stand proudly by the backs of two Leyland-bodied Leylands, No. 4 being a bonneted G2, and No. 23 a side-type SG4. On the right is the solid tyre press, a water press similar to the one that Barry Weatherhead and I rescued from a garage in Luton.

Rescue of the Todmorden Leyland G

Earlier in the book I have related the story about the find of the Todmorden Leyland G. When living in Brentwood, Essex, a fellow member of the Historic Commercial Vehicle Society called and told me of a couple of early 1920s ex-Todmorden Corporation bus bodies in a hedge, on a farm not more than 5 miles (8km) away. After a lot of hard work, the body was found and rescued, and taken to our new house in Wiltshire.

Not far away I discovered the remains of a Leyland G chassis in a very sorry state, having once carried a water tank for the farm. The engine, radiator, gearbox, change-speed quadrant and lever (gear lever), steering column and all other running units had vanished years ago. The front spoked wheels were original and of a smaller diameter than the rear, being 720mm, but the back axle had acquired some earlier disc Leyland Subsidy-type wheels, but of the correct size (881mm) – all on solids, of course. The steering box, drop arm and track rod were fortunately still intact, but the springs had all collapsed. I went back to collect these remains, and the farmer could not understand why I wanted such a lot of old junk: he didn't want anything for it, and would have nothing to do with me, but just said 'Take it, take it!' (sounds familiar!)

Finding the Other Parts

Now, where was I to get the rest of the bits? Well, it's absolutely amazing just what you can turn up if you are persistent. The correct spoked hind wheels (as they frequently called them), a S5.36/40hp engine, a gearbox, the remains of an 'RAF-type' bonnet, petrol tank and scuttle (all acutely infested with tin worm) were found by Richard Peskett under bramble bushes in Percy Volkes' scrapyard near Billinghurst, Sussex, where they had been since 1938. The low-lying ground was very wet, and water

The Phoenix body was well and truly in the hedge, and wielding an axe, I set about its rescue!

Viewed from inside the hedge, the body looked remarkably intact (note the front of the upper deck and handrail leaning against the body).

On returning home after the rescue I sketched the bus, as I could imagine it running again – and it did, ten years later!

LEFT: *Not one of the better corners! The roof, rear pillars and floor frame were all kept intact (note the steel strap inserted in the pillar on the left) and re-used.*

BELOW: *Picking up the body to carry it about fifty yards.*

ABOVE: *Safely back at home, in Wiltshire, and ready for restoration work to begin.*

LEFT: *Squeezing the body into the removals van.*

The correct Leyland G-type chassis but with the wrong rear wheels and no mechanical parts. It had carried a water tank on the farm.

The S5.36hp engine after it had been dragged from the lake.

The gearbox with cardan shaft brake nestles among the briars.

Bonnet remains and skeleton of the petrol tank – all useful patterns, and of course brass fittings.

The rear axle with correct spoked wheels, once completely overgrown, has been pulled out of the nettles.

had submerged the engine at times. Nevertheless I hired a pick-up, and Bob Hearn came with me to help collect the treasure.

A newly reconditioned radiator was found in the back of a garage in Cumberland, and I heard of it quite by chance. But what a long way – in the end I met the owner at the junction of the M4 and M5 near Bristol, parted with a few notes, and it was mine. The magneto came from a scrapyard in Newbury, the scuttle (in better condition than the other), steering and pedal shaft from Surrey, and, thanks to the late Prince Marshall, the staircase was found in someone's

greenhouse: it had reputedly originally been fitted to a London 'Pirate' Straker Squire.

The wood-rimmed brass, five-spoke steering wheel was another remarkable find. Quite by chance I was looking at some elderly vehicles in a barn in Norfolk, and just happened to mention that I still needed a brass five-spoke steering wheel for the Todmorden Leyland. The owner disappeared for a while, and came back clutching the brass centre portion of a wheel: 'Something like that?' he questioned. 'Yes, I suppose so,' I said, at the time not knowing exactly what a Leyland wheel looked like. However, I noticed

the number 699A cast into the back of one of the spokes and immediately remembered the number from the Leyland parts lists that I had been studying not so long ago. Would he part with it? The initial answer was 'No', but the persistence of the young Sutcliffe was to win in the end, and I felt that it was well worth the £10.

On the way back home, I visited a man called Mr Mills at Chesterfield – Chesterfield being *nearly* on the way back from Norfolk to Bedfordshire! Mr Mills was ending his days as a haulage contractor, having recently operated a number of Albion eight-wheelers. His operating days, and probably his father's too, went right back to the early days, and he had sheds *full* of really interesting goodies: there were magnetos, lamps and bulb horns everywhere, though one or two enthusiasts and dealers had got there before me, and there was not a lot left. I bought some magnetos from him and opened the car boot to put them in, and Mr Mills saw my steering-wheel centre. 'Just a minute,' he said, and now *he* disappeared. Ten minutes later, after much rummaging in one of his sheds, he came back with a five-spoke brass steering wheel, though this one was absolutely complete, with the five wooden segments on each side. 'Look, I've got one of

those, too!' he said, as he compared it with my brass centre. 'We used to have an old Leyland X-type char-a-bancs that we broke up for spares.' On enquiring what else might be left of this char-a-bancs, the answer was unfortunately 'not much', but after a brief discussion the steering wheel changed hands for £5. It is now on the Todmorden G. Mr Mills did, however, disappear again and came back with the char-a-bancs windscreen which he kindly gave me!

Restoration Begins

It was not until March 1980 that restoration began seriously; in the

meantime we had moved house again to Studham, a village near Whipsnade in Bedfordshire. I was fortunate enough to find a local man, Nick Downes, who was an experienced joiner who taught joinery and lived locally, and I managed to persuade him to help me with the woodwork as and when I came across difficult bits (most of it!). Moreover, for the first two years all the work was done under a scaffolding frame with plastic sheets draped over – not really ideal! The biggest problem initially was where to start, because clearly, to be a proper restoration job, all the sound timber, or timber still in reasonable condition, had to be retained. In fact it would have been much quicker to have built a new replacement body, but that would not have been the same.

Thus everything that could be used has been kept. The sides, or what was left of them, were in a very poor state, and the cant rails, light rails, waist rails and all but three of the pillars had to be replaced. Fortunately I had had the foresight to purchase three ash trees, already cut into planks, and had seasoned them in readiness for the job. The original roof sticks, complete with all ceiling boards, were all in good condition, and were then strapped up to a scaffolding structure built over the

Part No. 699A – one five brass-spoked steering wheel with wooden rim, now in place.

BELOW LEFT: *The frame-work takes shape, still under the awful poly-thene shelter.*

BELOW RIGHT: *Now panelled, the body could be glazed.*

top of the body, so the roof could be suspended while the pillars were removed and the floor repaired. New pillars were put in where necessary, and all the side rails. The rails around the front and rear canopies were made by laminating strips of ash round large chipboard formers.

The front bulkhead was made of oak with inlaid mahogany, and was in virtually perfect 'as used' condition. Also, nearly all the steel hoops supporting and tying the side pillars to the floor and roof were still intact. A small part of the ceiling boards had to be repaired by letting in some Colombian pine, and parts of the side interior oak panelling were repaired. But restoration of the rear bulkhead was abruptly brought to an end when a nest of blue tits was found within the body framework; once they had left the nest, work re-commenced.

The 'nightmare come true': the better remains of the upper deck, set out in position on my drive; all the steelwork (stantions, straps and brackets) has been re-used, as have some of the timbers, and the rest proved invaluable for patterns.

Restoring the Interior Fitments

It was not long before all the exterior panels were on, the windows reglazed and interior completed. Now it was looking more like a vehicle again! The upper opening vent windows and bulkhead windows are in yellow hammered glass, half of which are original. However, as this type of glass has not been made for some time, I had to go on the scrounge to find something suitable for the missing panes. Eventually I found someone in Chertsey with a conservatory that was made from coloured glass. I knocked on the door, and stated my case, but even after pleading with the owner, I was told politely to 'Go away'. Not to be dissuaded, the next time I was in Chertsey I went to see the gentleman again, and managed to persuade him to let me exchange the larger sheets of yellow glass for another colour – so it *was* worth persisting!

The remains of the upper deck and staircase, most of which had to be dug up from the ground surrounding where the body had stood, were then laid out on my drive – one friend described it as a 'nightmare come true'. All but one of the steel side stanchions had survived, also for the staircase, as

had many parts of the seats and seat supports, and the decency board supports were also intact. There were enough bits of seats (very rotten) to take precise measurements to make new ones, and within only three months, the decency boards (upper deck side panels – to prevent young boys from peering up the skirts of the opposite sex on the upper deck!), handrail and upper deck seats were in place and being painted and varnished.

It was interesting to find the remains of one of the upper deck lamps buried at the hedge site in Essex. It's remarkable just how many bits were actually exhumed, and it was certainly worthwhile spending some time at the site carrying out an archaeological dig. By another coincidence I found a similar lamp for sale at a Beaulieu Autojumble, and on enquiring, discovered that the owner had bought it for his boat from a ship's chandlers in Norfolk. After a few phone calls and a few days, the upper deck sported not one, but two lamps!

The staircase needed a little alteration to fit, and a new banner (the banner is the decency board on the staircase – it would certainly not be adequate for mini-skirts!). In the area

of the rear platform, the biggest shock was when I was trying to procure a length of brass handrail of an unusual size: it cost a staggering £1 per inch run, and that was in 1983! Fortunately not too much was needed and I was exceedingly careful when it came to putting a bend in it. Throughout the restoration great care was taken to get the bus absolutely as it was when running in service. Prince Marshall, who by then lived at Berkhamsted, used to visit regularly to inspect the progress on the Leyland G, and to offer advice. What a great pity he died so young – he did so much to promote bus preservation in the early days.

Restoring the Engine

With my S5.36hp engine of 6.6 litres capacity, I was very lucky. It came with most accessories still attached to it, though many were broken or damaged. It had, however, stood for thirty-six years in the scrapyard, and clearly water had at times submerged the engine completely, since when I started to dismantle it, I discovered that it was absolutely full of silt and rubbish. When I removed the sump I couldn't even see the crankshaft, and all this hardened silt had to be dug out with a screwdriver first. When one could see what was inside, the big ends were undone from the crankshaft, but the conrods would not budge. I removed the crankshaft and inserted a scaffold pole through the big ends, that were done up again. Two 6-ton hydraulic jacks were then placed at strategic points under the scaffold pole, and a massive amount of pressure was applied. One wonders if the conrods are now even longer? This was, of course, after many gallons of diesel, Plus Gas and WD40 had been wasted trying to free the pistons, but without any success. More pressure was applied, and something had to give: first the scaffold pole bent into a V-shape, and then there was a loud bang: the piston had moved about 1/64in (0.4mm to younger readers). More pressure was applied, and then 'bang'. This process continued for a long, long, long time until all four cast-iron pistons were out.

The 4⅝in bores were surprisingly good. In fact the engine, after a very thorough clean, was so good that it all went back together again virtually untouched, except for new valve guides and valve springs, the latter having completely rusted away. I also had to grind the valves in, but that was about it – which was amazing! These Leylands were really well made.

Restoring the Chassis

The chassis was soon reassembled after a good sand-blasting and painting, with the engine, correct wheels and new solid tyres from Dunlop (ouch, again!), and it was now ready to receive the body. The chassis restoration only took about nine months to complete. How much quicker and easier it must be to restore a lorry with a platform body. The body was restored separately while conveniently standing on another 'RAF-type' Leyland chassis. (In fact it's surprising how much one can find in spares. I started out by looking for just one complete Leyland chassis to complete the Todmorden Leyland, but obsession took over, and…!)

Remounting the Body – and Under Way!

Now came the time to put the body back on the chassis, after all those years. It just so happened that it was my turn to have our local vehicle club committee meeting at my house (what a coincidence!), and the meeting in fact started with the last item on the agenda: 'Any other business' – and the job was soon done!

September 1983 was a great test – a tow up the road behind Nick's Land Rover, into third gear, clutch up and guess what – I was actually driving it!

Clouds of black smoke soon engulfed the area, and about 300yds later, at a steady half mile per hour, it had consumed nearly 2½ gallons of petrol. I know these engines are thirsty, 4–6mpg (56l/100km) being the norm, but at the rate of 15 gallons to a mile it gets a bit expensive! Anyway, after some investigating and harsh words at the Zenith 42 DEF carburettor, I remembered that I had not put the main jet back in the carburettor and the petrol was being sucked up through a ¼in hole – well, you can't win them all!

The Final Details

Finally came the paintwork. It was all hand-painted, and I lost count of the number of empty paint and varnish tins, and the wads of wet and dry. There was no less than 750ft – ⅐ of a mile! (230m) – of lining-out to be done, much of it in gold leaf (none of this pin-striping rubbish!), as well as the signwriting and final coats of varnish. Many of the northern municipalities took so much pride in the liveries of their buses that they were very elaborately painted, and rarely carried any advertisements. Fortunately I had previously purchased some of the Todmorden coat of arms from Butchers, the transfer people, and a very helpful man at Crich Tramway Museum let me have some

ABOVE: *The S5.36hp engine, now restored.*

RIGHT: *A momentous moment: remounting the body on the restored chassis.*

The Todmorden coat of arms: an original transfer surrounded by a hand-painted garter.

The driver's controls, also showing a close-up of the intricate lining-out.

A mock-up of the original road-fund licence carried by the Todmorden G. All my vehicles carry period licences, and on one occasion a policeman chided me that the tax disc was out of date! (The proper one is always close to hand!).

'acorn and oak leaf' transfers for the corners of the lining-out.

When the vehicle was built the windscreen was an optional extra, as was the CAV lighting set, which cost an extra £60 when new. This included electric conversions to the oil side and tail lamps, a practice common in the 1920s and even later. One other interesting point is the oil 'tell-tale' on the dash panel, a crude form of oil gauge: when the pressure builds up, a knob on the top of the 'tell-tale' rises, thus communicating with the driver that there is oil there; it then lets the oil dribble down all over his passenger's feet!

When standing on tick-over the engine revolves very slowly, due to its heavy flywheel, cast-iron pistons and very long stroke, and the most prominent noise one can hear is the 'clack-clack-clack' coming from the joint in the 2in flat leather fan belt.

Restoration Completed

The restoration of the Todmorden Leyland G was completed in May 1984, just in time for the London to Brighton Run; with the usual last-minute panic, I was still painting it on the Saturday morning prior to driving it down to London for the start. At the time of writing the bus has completed the run several times, and it has also been back to Todmorden several times, completing the Trans-

Pennine Run twice. Having finished the restoration to a very high standard and taken it to various rallies, it is very gratifying to discuss the vehicle and the restoration with everyone who derives pleasure from seeing it. After several seasons' rallying, it has been on display in the Bradford Museum for a while, and more recently at the Manchester Museum of Transport, as the limited space at Valley Forge means I cannot keep the bus here at present.

At the start of the Brighton Run. Note the tram-like rear panel.

Parked at Copperas House, Todmorden, with what used to be my grandfather's mill in the background.

Leading the procession from Todmorden to Halifax, commemorating transport in 1987.

Specification – The 1921 Todmorden Leyland G	
Operator	Todmorden Corporation, No. 14 C 2367, new June 1921
Model	Leyland G
Chassis No.	9961
Engine	4-cylinder, 36hp, Model S5, built by Leyland, No. 21485 (ex re-conditioned RAF type)
Body	Phoenix/Todmorden Corp'n, with 43 seats (23 outside, 20 inside)
Length	23ft 10in (7.27m) (including starting handle)
Width	7ft 4in (2.24m)
Height	12ft 4⅛in (3.78m)
Weight	4 tons 18cwt 3qtr (5,016.5kg)

Fun at the local village fête at Kensworth near Dunstable.

BELOW: *A trip to Belgium for the 1986 UITP Bus & Coach Show took the Todmorden G on the* Herald of Free Enterprise, *only weeks before the boat sank: what might have happened!*

The Todmorden G was the first of what I would call my serious restorations, of which there were more to come, and all Leylands. It has a number of family connections for me, and in particular, of course, the bus comes from Todmorden, the town that holds so many happy memories for me.

Rules and Regulations up to 1930

The size and weight of commercial vehicles has always been affected by the laws governing these matters. Nowadays a much more uniform approach is taken, with regulations not only covering the whole of the country, but Europe as well. However, in the early days there were separate rules for London, these being dictated by the Metropolitan Police.

As will be seen by the details below, the Metropolitan Police were always more stringent and not only with dimensions. From about 1909, maybe earlier, buses had to be fitted with engine undertrays and gearbox undertrays to catch a large part of the oil and grease being dropped on the streets of London. Soon afterwards it became a Metropolitan Police regulation that buses had to have 'silent' gearboxes. This lead to AECs being fitted with chains in the gearboxes and Leylands with double helical gears, as shown in the chapter on my London & North Western Railway char-a-bancs (the same S8 helical gearbox was fitted to the Leyland 'London Bus' LBs).

The Metropolitan Police were at times exceedingly backward in their thinking, thereby obstructing the development of the motor bus. Examples include the ban on covered top double deckers in the mid-1920s, despite the fact that the London General NS was built with a dropped frame and was designed to carry a roof. The use of headlamps in the central area was prohibited up to the early 1930s and windscreens were considered to be dangerous and therefore not allowed right up to about 1931. Even the driver's-side windows on the early LGOC B types were considered to be an obstruction to the driver's visibility/hand signals and had to be removed. This is why many of the front-side pillars, windows and side panels were rather crudely cut off either side of the driver on some of the earlier B types. Later vehicles were built without side windows/panels.

One odd little Metropolitan Police stipulation in the early 1920s was for a small pruning saw to be carried above the driver's head. The purpose for this was to enable the crew to cut through the life-guards on the side of the bus to reach any pedestrian who had been unfortunate enough to be run over by the bus and end up underneath it! (A saw of this type is fitted on my Chocolate Express bus.)

In other areas of the country the regulations were more relaxed, even though the local Police Watch Committees were initially responsible for licensing buses. These Watch Committees issued their own licensing plates which were carried on the back of buses, prior to the 1930 Road Traffic Act, which set up Traffic Areas to regulate bus services.

Up to the mid-1920s the national size limitations, or recommendations, could be altered by special dispensation and the most extreme example of this was Barton's 'Long Tom', which ran in Nottinghamshire. 'Long Tom' was a Daimler Y type from World War One, which was rebuilt in 1923 and extended to the enormous size of 36ft 6in long and 7ft 2in wide (11.12 × 2.19m). It seated sixty-six passengers, with a further standing room for about forty more! Nottingham Corporation did not like the size of the bus and as a gesture the seating capacity was reduced to fifty-six; in this form the bus ran until March 1929. Not surprisingly there are a number of amusing tales arising from 'Long Tom': knocking cyclists off their bikes with the rear overhang; becoming grounded over the local hump-back bridge with its wheels suspended in mid-air; rear seat cushions being flung onto the floor at the back of the bus; and so on!

Surely the longest bus of its time was 'Long Tom', a rebuilt and extended Daimler Y type, at 36ft 6in (11.12m) long.

Despite these oddities the regulations settled down with the Heavy Motor Car (Amendment) Order of 1927 and most of the anomalies disappeared once the vehicles were withdrawn.

Set out below are some of the more important changes relating to weights, sizes and speeds of larger vehicles. The details are not comprehensive, but are designed to give an idea of the restrictions put on the development of early commercial vehicles.

continued overleaf

Rules and Regulations up to 1930 *continued*

1896 Locomotives on Highways Act (the 'Red Flag' Act): Removed the most stringent of the regulations in respect of road vehicles up to 3 tons unladen (4 tons with trailer).

1903 Motor Car Act: Raised the speed limit for vehicles up to 3 tons to 20mph (30km/h)

1905 Heavy Motor Car Order of 1904: Defined 'Heavy Motor Car' as a motor car exceeding 2 tons unladen, and required the laden weight of each axle to be registered. Maximum unladen weight 5 tons (6½ tons with trailer) as from 1 March 1905, with max. speed of 12mph (19km/h) provided all wheels fitted with rubber tyres. Maximum width 7ft 2in (2.2m) up to UW 3 tons, 7ft 6in (2.3m) above 3 tons. (No maximum length specified.)

January 1906 Metropolitan Police Regulations: Max. length 23ft (7m), max. width 7ft 2in (2.2m), wheelbase not over 14ft 6in (4.4m).

August 1909, Metropolitan Area: Max. UW 3 tons 10cwt, or max. laden weight 6 tons (back axle 4 tons, front 2 tons).

1919 Ministry of Transport: Formed under Sir Eric Geddes, to bring order to public transport generally, but particularly in London with dialogue thereafter between MoT and Metropolitan Police Authority.

1920 Metropolitan Area: Max. length now 25ft (7.5m) (exclusive of starting handle or hood when lowered), width still 7ft 2in (2.2m), max. laden weight 8 tons (back axle 5 tons, front axle 3 tons max. loading).

By 1924, Metropolitan Area: Length limit now 27ft 6in (8.4m), max. laden weight 8 tons 10cwt, calculated as vehicle full of fuel, or oil and water, plus 140lb (63kg) for each seat provided, plus driver and conductor.

15 August 1927, Heavy Motor Car (Amendment) Order 1927

ABBREVIATED TABLE OF REQUIREMENTS FOR RUBBER-TYRED VEHICLES.

Maxima	*UW* tons	*Laden* tons	*Axle weight* tons	*Speed* mph (km/h)	*Length* ft in (m)	*Turning* circle (ft)	*Width* ft in (m)
Goods: Four-wheeled	7¼	12	8	12 (19)	27 6 (8.4)	...	7 6 (2.3)
Four-wheel + trailer	9¾	22	8	5 (8)	26 0 (8)	...	7 6
			(trailer 6½)				
Flexible six-wheeled	9¾	18½	8	12 (19)	33 0 (10)	...	7 6
			(trailing wheels 6½)				
Rigid six-wheeled	10	19	7½	12	30 0 (9)	...	7 6
Passenger: Four-wheeled							
Limit suggested by MoT	...	9	5½	12	26 0 (8)	60	7 6
Four-wheeled							
Legal limit authorized by order	...	9	5½	12	27 6 (8.4)	66	7 6
Rigid six-wheeled	...	12	4½	12	30 0 (9)	66	7 6
London Bus	...	8½	5	12	25 0 (7.6)	60	7 2 (2.2)

(Note the differences between the MoT's suggestions and the authorized regulations – probably the reason for the various Leyland Tiger and Lion model lengths in the 1927–31 period.)

Overhang: Seven twenty-fourths of overall length (starting handle and projection of hood when down are not included in length). In rigid six-wheelers of the one steering-axle type, this is measured to a point 4in (10cm) behind the centre of a straight line joining the centre points of the rear and middle axles; in six-wheelers in which two axles are steered, to the centre of the fixed axle.

Ground Clearance: 10in (25cm) minimum.

Number Plates: White letters and figures on black background to be (as before) 3½in (8.8cm) high, ⅝in (1.5cm) broad lettering.

1 October 1928 Heavy Motor Car (Amendment) Order 1928: Speed limit raised to 20mph (32km/h) for vehicles fitted wholly with pneumatic tyres (still 12mph (19km/h) for solid rubber tyres, and 8mph (13km/h) for metal tyres). All articulated vehicles still 12mph.

Road Traffic Act, 1930: The speed limit for passenger vehicles carrying more than seven passengers (exclusive of driver and with all wheels fitted with pneumatic tyres) was increased to 30mph (48km/h). Goods vehicles remained at 20mph (32km/h), or 16mph (25.7km/h) with 'soft or elastic tyres', but 30mph (48km/h) was allowed for heavy motor cars constructed or adapted for the conveyance of horses and their attendants. An extra 6in (15cm) width was allowed for vehicles converted from solids to pneumatics.

CHAPTER NINE

The 'Charabus', Leyland G7, of 1921

What better use to put 'The Charabus' to, than to drive to the Register Office with your family and friends – 3 September 1994, Pat and Mike's wedding.

Leyland Motors in 1921

In the first few years after the Great War, it took the Leyland model range a little while to settle down. Initially there were vehicle shortages and large order books, together with high inflation and rapidly increasing vehicle prices. Production levels had been at about 1,500 vehicles per annum in the last three years of the war, with a peak of 1,643 lorries and fire engines in 1916. 1919 saw a sharp drop in military orders, but even so 1,279 chassis were built. With the pent-up demand caused by the war, particularly for passenger chassis, production in 1920 increased to approximately 1,550 chassis. But then came the crash, with three

years of real hardship, which nearly caused the end of Leyland Motors. 1921 saw Leyland production of new chassis drop to less than half of that level, with only about 650 new vehicles built, followed by 624 in 1922. Then in 1923 production rose to 856 new chassis – not a huge increase, but a step in the right direction. To add to these figures were of course the reconditioned 'RAF types', but these were being renovated at a loss to Leyland in order to protect the reputation of the company's products. The detailed figures of Leyland production (*see* table on page 86) tell the story – one can see that the depression in the early 1920s was very severe, but it was followed by steady growth until the PLSC Lion got

into full swing, followed by the Titan and Tiger, which changed Leyland's fortunes.

Reverting to 1921, the 4-ton range of models classified as G, I, K, L, M, N and O were replaced by the G2, G4 and G6 double-reduction bevel-driven chassis, with differing wheelbase lengths, aimed primarily at goods work, and the G3, G5 and G7 with the same wheelbases respectively and worm-driven back axles aimed at passenger work. These models continued until the late 1920s, albeit with higher bonnet lines and radiators generally from 1923.

In a desperate attempt to win orders and to have something 'different' to sell, experiments were carried

LEFT: *Two apparently similar buses for G. Edwards, South Normanton, Derbyshire: AL 6841, photographed in January 1922, at first glance appears to be a G6 (with X5 bevel-drive axle), and Leyland 'Edinburgh-type' body. However, the eighteen louvres give it away as being an earlier chassis, probably an 'O' type, new in March 1920 with a char-a-bancs body and now re-bodied. (BCVM Archive)*

BELOW: *Sister bus R 8400, with sixteen bonnet louvres and later front wheels, carries a rather angular English Electric twenty-six-seat body new in April 1922. It has the T3 worm-drive axle, and is probably model G5 (though the Leyland sales records say G7). The railway, or rather tramway, lines are outside the Dick Kerr Works at Preston. The G. Edwards & Holmes Ltd company went into liquidation on 1 April 1924! (EEC)*

LEFT: *Quite a rarity are these two model 'R' tippers, new in April 1923 to the Westminster Wharfage Co. Ltd, SW1. Built to take 8 tons (8,140kg), they were really a QH6 ('H' for 'high radiator'), with heavier springs and rear wheels. Note the hub-odometer on the lorry behind XN 4636.*

out again with an 'over-type' driving position. Simultaneously the 'side-type' was introduced (what we would normally regard now as forward control). AEC were among the first, if not *the* first, to adopt the driving position by the side of the engine, with the K

Cumberland Motor Services purchased this side-type in July 1923: No. 17 (re-numbered 37 before entering service), AO 9103, a model SG6 (bevel-axle) with forty-seat body. (BCVM Archive)

type for the London General Omnibus Company. This prompted Leyland to build side types from 1922 onwards, originally designating them as 'Specials', based on existing models. This was most illogical, as the side-type needed the 43in (109cm) wide frame, as opposed to the 38in (96cm) frame that was now standard, the wider frame not having been used for some time. The steering box was turned upside down and mounted in a forward position, and the engine and gearbox mountings had to be wider, as did the front and back axles. The pedal controls were totally different, and bonnets and bonnet boards had to be redesigned. They were hardly, therefore, variations from the standard model. By 1923 this was recognized, and separate designations were given, for example SG7, SG9, SG11 and SQ2 (the 'S' standing for 'side-type').

Turning to the G7, the chassis model for the Charabus, it is interesting to note that this was very similar to the S4.36.T3 of 1914, although the latter had a 43in (109cm) frame: in fact it was a direct descendant of that model, the other major alteration being the use of the standard X4 straight-toothed gearbox instead of the S8 helical box. The wheelbase of the G7 was slightly longer, at 15ft 10in (4.8m), and it used the same back axle, the T3 worm-driven axle.

The 'Charabus' is Shown at Olympia

Christopher Dodson was a well known coachbuilder from Cobbold Road, Willesden, in north-west London. He had been in the coachbuilding business since the horse-bus days, and may well have also built taxi-cab bodies. Although Dodson occasionally built bodies for London General, he was very wary of becoming reliant on the General, with 'all of his eggs in one basket', particularly with the 'stop/go' policy of the Combine's purchasing of buses. He preferred to deal with small orders and, of course, latterly built a large number of bodies for customers outside London, particularly on trolleybus chassis (for example, Wolverhampton and Hastings).

In August 1922 Dodson must have welcomed Arthur Partridge with his Chocolate Express bus with open arms (more of that later): here was a new market for his bodies, which he sold in large numbers to the 'Pirates'. He even arranged finance for their buses to be purchased. However, the writing was on the wall following legislation to remove the 'Pirates' from the streets of London and, with a substantial part of his market disappearing overnight, Dodson closed his business in the early 1930s and retired to the Isle of Wight. This was not an entirely unexpected move, because since October 1921 the Dodson family had been involved in a bus-operating business on the Isle of Wight called Dodson & Campbell Ltd. The venture had prospered almost immediately, and in September 1922 the company was renamed Dodson Brothers Ltd, the owners being Christopher and Frank Dodson. The company adopted the title 'Vectis Bus Company' (vectis in Latin meaning 'area' and a word frequently associated with the Isle of Wight), then changed its name yet again in 1929 to Southern Vectis Omnibus Co. Ltd. This operator was also a ready market for the coach-built products of Dodson in Willesden.

In 1921 Christopher Dodson invented and patented the 'Charabus'.

This design combined the advantages of a completely open char-a-bancs type of vehicle, from which passengers could enjoy the sunshine, together with those of a saloon bus, with electric lighting, for inclement weather or the journey home after a day's trip out. The Charabus also had the advantage of gaining an extra ten 'Jubilee' tip-up seats in the gangway, which could increase the seating capacity of a normal saloon of thirty-two seats to a forty-two-seater (something that would never be allowed today!).

Proud of his new invention, he ordered a Leyland chassis of the maximum size in those days: this was the G7, albeit with normal control. He built his prototype body on the chassis, painted it an all-over 'Eau-de-Nil' livery (light green), and demonstrated it in pride of place on his stand at the Commercial Motor Show, Olympia, in October 1921. It received a good press write-up in *Motor Transport*, *Commercial Motor* magazine and other periodicals of the time, and Dodson waited for the orders to roll in. However, its launch came at a time when there was a slump in demand for vehicles, as we have seen with the Leyland production levels. It was, however, moderately successful, and quite a number of these 'Charabus' bodies were built, particularly for operators who provided excursions and tours at holiday resorts.

The Charabus is Sold to United Counties

After the show the vehicle was nominally sold to a timber merchant called Luck & Andrews of Kettering, but it was immediately re-sold to … wait for it! …William Benjamin Richardson's United Counties Omnibus & Road Transport Co. Ltd, where, having the S19/5.36hp engine, it was numbered B15 in the fleet. Isn't it a small world!

Throughout its existence with United Counties, the 'Charabus' retained its demonstration livery of 'Eau-de-Nil' until it was withdrawn from service in May 1927. During its life with United Counties it was converted into a fixed saloon by adding

ABOVE: *Christopher Dodson's advert announcing the new model 'Charabus' body to be exhibited at the Commercial Vehicle Exhibition at Olympia.*

RIGHT: *An artist kindly drew the interior of the Charabus 'for all weathers', showing how the centre portion of the roof and side could be entirely opened when desired. 'The fore and aft portions of the permanent roof are connected by a beam that houses a roof hood, which is extended to the sides and locked in position.'* (Motor Transport)

*At the Olympia Show with the offside open and the nearside closed. (*The Commercial Motor*)*

FOR ALL WEATHERS.

ash roof struts to each side of the central beam, and then it was boarded in to make a fixed roof. It was probably found, as I have found, that it takes quite an effort to convert it from bus to char-a-bancs: this is done by removing each of the eight side windows – budget locked into position – carrying them round to the storage box at the back of the bus, then undoing the six steel-hinged pillars, folding them down to the waist rail, folding up the six roof stays, then undoing the four wing nuts holding the cant rails in position, then sliding them up to the central beam (which is a two-man job), afterwards affixing them in the folded up position with two catches. This, coupled with the fact that being removable the windows rattle terribly – and the canvas was no doubt prone to tearing – would be a terrible nuisance and much better if it was boarded up! However, being a perfectionist and wanting to have the Charabus presented in its original condition, I have undone it all and put it back as the original, as will be seen shortly.

On withdrawal the body was removed and a new single-decker body was built by UCOC, giving the chassis a new lease of life, lasting until December 1932 when it was sold to Thurston, Northampton (a showman). The 'Charabus' body had in the meantime been sold in September 1928 to a Mr Ingyon of Irthlingborough, for use originally as a static shop, and later a garden shed.

The Charabus, when new, at the Irthlingborough Garage of United Counties. Compare this picture with the one of the garage in the chapter on the 'Wellingborough' bus.

The Charabus stands in Kettering with Mr H. Dean, who used to proudly maintain the bus.

Rescuing the Charabus

It was at a club meeting of the Historic Commercial Vehicle Society back in 1978 that Prince Marshall gave a slide show (we all have a lot to thank that man for). His subject related to his vehicle finds over the years, some of which had been rescued and preserved, but the majority having been lost forever. The discussion came round to an old Dodson body at Irthlingborough, Northants, which had been operated by the United Counties Omnibus Co. It sat behind a shop in Addington Road and the owners,

the Ingyon family, had had the foresight to build a pitched corrugated iron roof on a timber frame over it. It all looked rather intriguing, and with the help of Roger Warwick, *the* expert on United Counties, I managed to locate it in Irthlingborough. On discovering that it was the 'Charabus', formerly stock No. B15 in the United Counties fleet, and knowing that I already had a spare Leyland chassis available, it just had to be saved.

Mrs Ingyon shared our enthusiasm, and yes, I could have it! A couple of weeks later I went to arrange to collect

the body, only to be told: 'Not yet – I am too sentimentally attached to it!' Some time went by and I tried again, only to be told 'Not yet!' and 'It creates a nice windbreak for the house.' I telephoned and wrote to her several times, and while trying to avoid becoming a nuisance, kept in contact; but the answer was always 'Not yet'.

In the meantime, while searching for goodies at one of the Alexandra Palace Autojumbles, I came across a set of CAV 'F'-type bell-shaped brass headlamps, instantly recognizing them as being identical to those in the picture

The shed, or rather 'windbreak'. (Roger Warwick)

of the 'Charabus'; and seeing that they were in perfect condition, I bought them. Well, if nothing else, I had a set of nice lamps (funnily enough I have done the same since with headlamps for a PLSC Lion, and although I would *very* much like a Lion – where do you stop?).

Four years later at another HCVS meeting, a colleague told me that he had driven by Mrs Ingyon's house and that a 'For Sale' board had been put up. The following Saturday I went up to Irthlingborough, only to find that Mrs Ingyon had moved to a nursing home, and that the new owners of the house had already moved in. I asked about the 'old shed', and was told that it was a nuisance, and they wanted to get rid of it – in fact they had planned to set fire to it the following weekend. Good! – I'm in with a chance, I thought. On hearing of my interest I could see their eyes light up, and could read the thought going through their mind 'It's got to be worth loads o' money' – how ridiculous! After an extremely long haggle I discovered they wanted a caravan, and as a colleague of mine had an old caravan for sale, a deal was agreed whereby I bought it and we swopped the caravan for the Charabus body.

The Problems of Recovery

The next task was to recover it – not easy! Firstly, it was plumbed in for water, gas and mains electricity, and all of these had to be disconnected. On close examination of the floor at the front offside, it was found to be particularly rotten, and I learned that it was at this point that a bathtub had been installed at one time. Mr Ingyon had apparently been sent into the garden shed every time he wanted to have a bath, and the reason for the rot was undoubtedly that he used to splash an awful lot. The gas pipe turned out to be 'live', full of town gas to start with, before natural gas came through. It had to be capped and we had to jack the body up over the end of the pipe, which was all rather difficult. The cap turned out to be too big to go through the hole in the floor, so it had to be removed and replaced with my handkerchief stuffed inside the pipe until the body was high enough to clear it – quite a tricky exercise. One spark and it would have gone up in flames.

We had to demolish a brick wall that was joined to an outside toilet, which could not be demolished, so we had to jack up the body and, with the help of planks sandwiching scaffold poles, rolled it back several feet to miss the outside loo – this was achieved with the help of a Tirfor winch that, attached to the towbar of my car with the brakes hard on, enabled us to move the 'Charabus' the few feet. The Tirfor also came in useful for winching out of the ground two bushes that stood in the path of the Charabus – great fun for my 12-year old son Marc. After this the body could be winched sideways, again on scaffold poles, planks and RSJs, onto a lorry to bring it back home. It turned out to be a very full day's work, and I am grateful to my colleagues for all their assistance.

Restoring the Charabus

Having recovered the body and brought it safely home, it then had to wait in the queue; the Todmorden Leyland G double decker was at that time 50 per cent restored, and that had to be finished before work could start on the 'Charabus'. However, unfortunately for the 'Charabus', almost exactly as the Todmorden bus was completed and taken to Brighton for the first time, the remains of the 'Chocolate Express' turned up, and that jumped the queue. In the meantime, however, my cabinet-maker friend, Nick Downes, had moved out of the area and gone to live in Shropshire, setting up a workshop there. He had an empty barn at his property, and so the answer was obvious – I loaded the 'Charabus' body onto a lorry and sent it off to Shropshire – he wasn't going to get away that easily!

Although some of the framework on the sides and front had to be replaced, virtually all the rest of the body is absolutely original, including the mahogany-framed side windows, which amazingly survived. The aluminium side panels were carefully rubbed down, to reveal the original colour and signwriting. The colour scheme of this bus was clearly built to 'catch the eye': as had already been said, some of these older buses were turned out in very bright liveries indeed. What a shame that all the photographs of them are in black and white.

LEFT: *Removing the cladding and roof structure that had remarkably protected the body.*

BELOW LEFT: *Winching the Charabus sideways onto the lorry. The corner glass window had been removed beforehand for safety.*

BELOW: *The directions to the Shenley chassis in Prince Marshall's handwriting on his* Old Motor Magazine *letterhead. The bus preservation movement owes a lot to this man, whom most would agree was best described as a 'very likeable rogue'.*

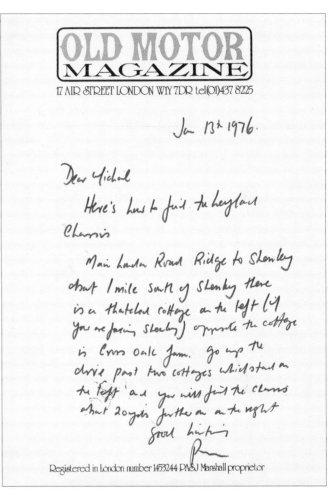

Finding the Chassis

The first chassis that I found for the Charabus was in fact a rebuilt RAF type that had been converted to a farm trailer; it had no running units. It was located at Shenley in Hertfordshire, and the late Prince Marshall gave me directions as to how to find it. A deal was struck with the farmer, and the chassis came home. However, it was missing a lot of bits, including

The rebuilt RAF type converted to a farm trailer waits for collection in the Shenley farmyard.

ABOVE: *Lifting the South Wales GH6 onto the recovery lorry.*

LEFT: *The front springs were just a bit too rusty to use!*

BELOW: *Welding the chassis frames together, having cut out the rotten sections.*

the differential gears from the back axle, although I was ultimately able to use the rear wheels and some other parts from this chassis.

Soon afterwards a Leyland GH6 chassis with the correct wheelbase length (15ft 10in (4.8m)), though with bevel-driven back axle, was found in Henry Scarratt's showman's yard in South Wales. It was in an absolutely terrible state – in fact the front 5ft (1.5m) of the frame was so bad that it had rusted right through. Fortunately I had previously rescued the remains of a Leyland 'I'-type chassis that had an identical front end, which I then grafted onto the South Wales chassis. The 'I' type had come from a field in Barnet, and had originally supported a box van body, being of the type that Maples and Waring & Gillow used to operate (there is yet another story attached to this). Most of the running units had been removed, but the owner had convert-ed the box van body into a static car-avan, where he lived for many years. He had found it rather unsettling when the weather was stormy as the vehicle was rocked by the high winds, so his answer to this was to bury the wheels and axles in concrete – in fact the concrete was so deep that it came above the hub caps in places. He thought that this would solve the problem, but unfortunately it didn't, because what he failed to realize was that the chassis still sat on its original springs, and it was these that caused the movement! The concrete made it far from easy to recover the chassis, as we had to attack the ground around it with sledge hammers and picks before we could even move it. Why do we do it?

Finding the Engine

The engine and radiator of the South Wales chassis were of the later high type, the engine also having the detachable Ricardo heads, whereas I needed an S5.36hp engine to be absolutely correct. Amazingly one became available for sale at the Myre-ton Museum near Edinburgh, so the following weekend I planned to pick it up with my car and trailer. Then just before I set off, a colleague from Lancashire telephoned to say that a scrapyard was being cleared in the centre of Blackburn, and that yet another 36hp engine had turned up – it had to be cleared immediately, so off I went on the round trip. When I arrived at the Blackburn scrapyard, there was no one with any machinery to help me lift the second engine onto the trailer, so Marc and I struggled for about two hours on our own, armed with only two bottle jacks, a lump of wood and several old bricks that I found lying around; but it had to be done, and done it was. Then back on the M6 and M1 motorways with this enormous weight of two huge engines behind my car.

The Edinburgh engine was just right. It was the S19/5.36hp model with the fan mounting assembly on top of the timing case in the position associated with the lower type of Leyland radiator, rather than the fan being mounted on the front cylinder block. The Engineering Apprentices Department at the United Counties Omnibus Company took an interest in me restoring the 'Charabus', as it had once belonged to that company, and very kindly offered to renovate the engine for me. It had to be bored and sleeved, but when it was put back together it was found that the cylinder blocks were porous. So it had to be dismantled again, and I took the cylinder blocks to a firm in Coventry where they were dipped in a hot resin-based solution in some sort of vacuum chamber, that sucked the solution into all the holes. I never was quite sure exactly how it was achieved, but the end result was that it worked! Mechanically this engine is the best one in my 'fleet' and starts perfectly, like clockwork, every time. On swinging the handle, all you need is to go past two compressions to give the engine two good sucks of the mixture, and it fires on the third compression. All the other vehicles will start on the second or third swing of the handle, which just goes to show how reliable these early Leylands

The Edinburgh S19/5.36hp engine (at the back) and the E36HP/2 engine from Blackburn come home.

Nick Downes (inside) repairs the ash framework of the 'Charabus' at his home in Shropshire.

The complicated tram-like framework is completed, with the body ready for panelling and glazing.

were – there is no doubt in my mind that the Leyland was the 'Rolls-Royce' of commercial vehicles, and this must be a reason why so many have survived in comparison with other makes.

I didn't have a radiator for the Charabus, but when rescuing one of my four Leyland SQ2 6–7-ton lorries from a showman in Carterton, Oxfordshire, I noticed an almost perfect Leyland PLSC Lion radiator in the yard. With a £10 note it changed hands, and I discovered to my amazement that the core and tube plates of the radiator were of identical dimensions to the G7: all I had to do was make a top and bottom tank and two side standards, and I had a radiator. Fortunately, having recently made patterns to make the radiator for the Chocolate Express, which is identical, this all fell into place.

Finding the Wheels and Tyres

The South Wales chassis had been converted to 38 × 7 pneumatic-tyres on 24in wheels early in its life, and so it needed to be converted back again to solids. Personally, I just don't trust these new-fangled pump-up tyres that are so prone to getting punctures – I'm sure they won't last! Fortunately I had previously rescued farm trailers from Old Welwyn and Shenley, both in Hertfordshire and both based on rebuilt 'RAF-type' chassis. It was therefore possible to swop the back axle, complete with springs from one, and the solid-tyred wheels from the Shenley chassis, which then had to be re-rubbered (ouch yet again!). The front wheels were, however, a problem. The Old Welwyn chassis had had just the right wheels, but I had parted with these before I knew I was going to get the 'Charabus', when I part-exchanged them with Michael Banfield for yet another Leyland S5.36hp engine. At the time I thought that I would not need the wheels, but …. However, all was not lost because on one of my excursions with Barry Weatherhead to Purley Park near Reading, we had found an ex-East Kent Roadcar Co. Daimler 'Y'-type chassis inside a house. The elderly owner needed to demolish the house, so Barry and I offered to do the job for him. The body, which stood on the Daimler Y type, had come from a United Automobile Services Associated Daimler model 415, and it even had a brick-built fireplace in the lower saloon! When we managed to get at it, we discovered that the Y type had been fitted with Leyland solid-tyred front wheels of the 2–3 ton variety. This is all a rather roundabout way of my saying that I found two wheels for the front of the 'Charabus'! This time the 140 × 720mm tyres were not a problem – I had found two in a barn in Somerset, and they had been acquired and put into stock.

Restoring the Paintwork

The removable mahogany-framed windows and interior wooden slats – which made the 'Charabus' body look like the inside of a boat – had been painted with what must have been a hundred coats of paint, or at least it seemed like that. So my Rover car was again loaded with timber so that it poked out of virtually every window, as well as the opening roof and the tailgate, and off I went to Hemel Hempstead to visit 'Mr Strip-It'. They were dipped in a horrible-smelling alkaline solution that removed the paint in a flash, and were immediately ready for sanding, staining and varnishing again. One tip I will mention here, which I did not know at the time, is that you should first paint all the treated wood with vinegar, which is an acid solution to kill off any alkaline residue. This helps stabilize the finished product. All this woodwork of the 'Charabus' is original and carries the scars of a working life – very little had to be replaced.

There was, of course, the day when everything went wrong, when trying to get a top coat of white paint on the roof my eldest son Marc fell off – quite a nasty fall. Then my friend Mike Street dropped a full tin of Bondaprimer on the floor – amazing how it seals concrete! Back to painting the roof – but not for long, as the immersion cylinder in the house flooded, and soaked the ceiling and carpet. Back to finish the white paint, only to find next morning that both of our tabby cats (Meg and Mog) had walked along the whole length of the roof and now had eight white paws!

Mr Dean

While restoring the 'Charabus', Roger Warwick put me on to a man called Mr H. Dean, who was in his eighties and lived at Holland-on-Sea, near Clacton. He had actually worked for United Counties in the 1920s, and produced a photograph of himself standing by the 'Charabus' in Kettering. He had been a fitter, and carried out regular maintenance work on the 'Charabus'. I corresponded with him for quite a long time, and he was renowned for typing letters that could go to ten or eleven sides of foolscap, all most interesting stuff, and he told me all sorts of things about the 'Charabus'. I invited him over to see it shortly after recovering the body, and when he visited, I let him drive the Todmorden Leyland G, which he managed perfectly despite his age. Unfortunately he died before he was able to see the 'Charabus' finished. Incidentally, his father 'Papa Dean' and his brothers all worked together, and knew Ben Richardson very well in the London Central days. There are many stories that I could tell, but they will have to wait for another time. By a strange coincidence, when Pat and I got together, we visited her father at Holland-on-Sea, and I was amazed to discover that he lives in the same road as had Mr Dean, literally just a few doors away!

One of Mr Dean's stories that I will relate is as follows: the one-piece back-axle casting on the T3 worm-driven axles had a weak spot, and where the axle tubes were riveted into the casing (the axle tubes house the half shafts) the rivets were prone to breaking. The rear wheel, with half shaft attached, could therefore come totally detached and fall off – so how on earth could you get the bus back to the garage to repair? Ben Richardson had the answer: the back axle was jacked up, the wheel and half shaft pushed back into place, and then a home-made sort of clamp device was attached over the outside of the wheel, with 'sort of grappling hooks' wedged over the rear spring. Then at least the bus could be towed back to the garage without fear of the wheel falling off; though one could imagine the awful noise it made with the wheel rims rubbing against the contraption – and it probably wrecked a few rear mudguards at the same time! No doubt many experienced fitters of the day would be able to relate all sorts of stories such as these.

Refitting the Interior

Proudly displayed at the front of the body, inside, is the Christopher Dodson maker's plate, stamped with body number 6500 (clearly chosen by Dodson as it was a 'Special' number for a special bus). Next to it are three additional plates, on which, when I removed the cream paint, I found various patent numbers. Instantly contacting the Patents Office Library once again, for the sum of £2.50 I received a full set of drawings that showed all the workings of the 'Charabus' roof and windows. Bearing in mind that it had been rebuilt by United Counties with an enclosed roof, I immediately got to work on rubbing down the cant rails to find evidence of its former days as a convertible roof. Sure enough, many of the original fittings were found, including the original slots that had been filled with lumps of wood, which support the hinged steel roof stays. With these original fittings and, of course, its original windows, I was able to rebuild it exactly as it was when it came out of the Dodson Works.

LEFT: *Mr Dean comes to visit in 1984, just as I was finishing the Tordmorden G. Unfortunately he died before he was able to see the Charabus finished, but he had a go at driving the G.*

BELOW: *The Christopher Dodson body plate with body No. 6500 and patent numbers that proved very useful.*

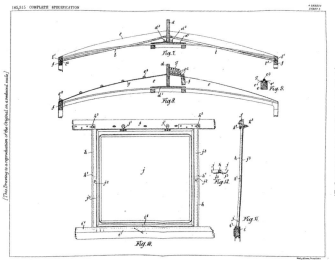

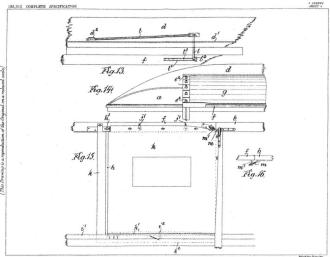

These intricate drawings from the Patents Office Library held the key to how the roof was constructed and enabled it to be rebuilt precisely back to its original condition.

There were no seats left, but part of the interior and the roof were sketched when the bus had been at the Olympia Show for *Motor Transport* magazine, and this gave me enough detail on the shape of the seats to be able to reconstruct a set from scratch. Mr Dean had previously told me precisely how the Jubilee seats were made and hinged, even down to the details of the hinged leather straps that formed the back rests; so these are all now back in place, exactly as it was when it was new.

ABOVE: *The body is mounted onto the chassis in 1987, the usual way – jacks and oil drums!*

BELOW: *Off to Brighton, all dressed in period costume.*

The Charabus Takes to the Road

The first outing in the Charabus was actually the day before the 1989 London to Brighton Run, when, with the usual mad panic, having set the Brighton Run as the deadline to have the vehicle finished, the Jubilee seats were not quite finished. In fact the gun-metal spring mounting brackets were still hot from the foundry when I collected them on the Friday afternoon. All had to be drilled and fitted, removed because the springs did not work (not strong enough), refitted, and were even painted on the Saturday morning whilst actually driving the 'Charabus' down to Crystal Palace for the start of the run. Everything went like clockwork – we all went down to Brighton in period costume, winning

Filming with David Troughton in Gloucestershire for Cider with Rosie.

BELOW: *The Charabus poses in the soft May sunshine, ideal for its Eau-de-Nil livery.*

BOTTOM: *Looking down on the luggage rack with the offside open. Note the Hackney licence plates and tip-up 'Jubilee' seats.*

the first prize for costume; and among other awards, the 'Charabus' was runner-up in the Concours. The following year, 1990, was the first year that Pat came along with me to Brighton, and the 'Charabus' was the outright winner.

It has since been all over the country to rallies, including the Trans-Pennine Run, and it starred in the film *Cider with Rosie*, with David Troughton as its 'driver'. Mike Street acted as 'stand-in' driver, as I refused to shave off my beard!

The 'Charabus' is one of the most sociable of my vehicles as the driver sits in the enclosed saloon with the passengers, rather than being stuck at the front with no windscreen and open to the elements. It is also a very practical and usable vehicle, and although I do not usually 'do' weddings, Pat and I used it to go to the Register Office in September 1994, and we took all the family and close friends with us in the 'Charabus' – a sort of 'modern version' of a country wedding with the bride and groom up front, followed immediately by the relatives and friends. With its attractive Eau-de-Nil livery it is quite an 'eye-catcher', particularly also with its exhaust whistle that makes a rather silly noise!

One other interesting little anecdote occurred when a picture of my Wellingborough bus appeared in the local paper in Northants following its maiden voyage tracing its original routes in Northamptonshire. A telephone call soon followed from the Wellingborough Historical Research Society requesting a visit of their members to see the Wellingborough bus. A date was fixed and a party of twenty-five people turned up to inspect the vehicle with great interest. I took them for a ride around the block, but as I had the gearbox brake of the Wellingborough in bits for repair at the time, I suggested that, as the 'Charabus' came from the same area, they may like to go out in that. Having toured the usual 4-mile route, the passengers were getting out and one lady appeared to be very upset – it turned out to be Mrs Ingyon's daughter, who remembered playing in the shed when she was little. She had seen some initials carved in the leather strap that operates the nearside front door window (railway carriage style): the initials read 'R.I.P', and she exclaimed, 'I remember this!': her father had carved his initials Robert Ingyon, and some wag had added a letter 'P'!

Three pictures show some of the detail of the cab area and 'Jubilee' seats in position. These add a further ten seats, making the bus a forty-two-seater.

Specification – the Leyland G7

Operator	Demonstrator for Christopher Dodson, Willesden, later to United Counties Omnibus & Road Transport Co., No. B15, registered BD 209 October 1921
Model	Leyland G7
Chassis No.	12301
Engine	Four-cylinder, 36hp, Model S5, built by Leyland, No. 15739 (23/3/22)
Body	Dodson 'Charabus' with 32 seats (plus 10 tip-up 'Jubilee' seats), dual entrance
Length	27ft 6in (8.38m) (including starting handle and ladder)
Width	7ft 5in (2.21m)
Height	10ft 3½in (3.14m)
Weight	5 tons 2cwt 3qtr (5,220kg)

CHAPTER TEN

The White Rose, Leyland SG7, of 1923

The White Rose Leyland SG7 waits for the low-loader to take it to the start of the London to Brighton Run, May 2002, the restoration having been completed that day and with wet paint everywhere!

Leyland Motors and their Side-Types

In the comparative 'doldrums' of 1921/22, Leyland Motors were willing to try anything to boost their flagging sales volumes in a difficult market. They had produced the famous 'Leyland Eight' car designed by the legendary Parry Thomas, of which only about eighteen were built, despite their successes in speed trials. At the other end of the scale, Leyland dabbled with the Trojan car, producing several thousand at Ham Works,

Kingston, Surrey, and these helped to fill the factory, which had previously been used for reconditioning the Subsidy 'RAF types'. Further abortive attempts were made at introducing a 30cwt model, although by 1923 this had been replaced by the model Z. The Z was, however, only produced in small numbers, approximately 150 being built in the period 1923 to 1925; it was not successful, as it had a fundamental weakness in the design of its lubrication system. The engine was in fact 'half of a Straight Eight', with one four cylinder block mounted

onto a small crankcase. Little more is known about the technical abilities, or should I say inabilities, of the Z, and more research is needed into this area.

In the meantime Leyland were looking for ways to develop their standard products. As from 1923 a taller radiator was mounted on the 4-ton range, and also the 5–6-ton ranges, with a higher bonnet line, reverting to the dimensions of the 'RAF type' and with the letter 'H' added to their designation (for example GH, PH, QH). It had the narrower radiator, and less room between the

The
Leyland'Eight

The Sporting Four-seater
Wheelbase, 10 ft. 6 in.

ABOVE: *There were only eighteen or so Leyland Eight cars made. This artist's impression appears to be based on the four-seat tourer shown at Olympia in November 1920.*

LEFT: *'Can You Afford to Walk?' was one of the slogans used by Leyland for the Trojan. This light delivery van on the standard 'punt' chassis was registered in Cambridgeshire, ER 2130. It was spartan in the extreme, but they were cheap at £125.*

engine and firewall than had been common on the earlier post-war models (K, L, M, N and O), and all of these inches added together made for a more efficient payload. One exception to the changed radiator and bonnet was of course the London Bus

The Model Z, 30cwt (1,524kg), was not a success, its four-cylinder engine was 'half of a Leyland Eight'. CL 7190 was new to Morgan's Brewery Co. Ltd of Norwich, seen here in the company of a solid-tyred Leyland, possibly a Model A.

This over-type was a Model OQ with 40/48hp engine, a 6-tonner with hydraulic tipper body by Bromilow & Edwards for John Sutcliffe, a coal merchant from Oldham, delivered in July 1921. It was the first post-war over-type built by Leyland. (BCVM Archive)

(the LB series, discussed in the next chapter) and this retained its low radiator to the end in 1927.

The biggest changes in design came with a few more experimental over-types, with the driving position and cab perched right on top of the engine, and of course the side-types. These were the first of the more conventional forward control models produced by Leyland. Todmorden Corporation were at the forefront of these design changes, taking both single- and double-decker versions of

the model G2 Special, followed by SG2s and SG4s (note the even numbers, that denote the double-reduction bevel-driven back axle). Concurrent with this was Leyland's desire to build a maximum capacity bus, which culminated in the SG7.

The SG7

This latter model was an absolutely enormous bus in its time: it was approaching 30ft (9m) long and seated forty passengers, as well as having two entrances. In common with the usual practice of the day, it had two compartments: the front for non-smokers, sometimes seated in more comfort, and which could therefore be regarded as 'First Class'; and the rear saloon, which was the smoking compartment, the seats usually covered in Rexine/leather cloth. Just why it was designated SG7 is a mystery. The 'S' stands for 'side-type', and I suppose the G7 was the longest of the normal control, 4-ton chassis at the time, so this was adopted for the SG7. There were a few SG6 models made, which were identical except that they had the bevel-driven axle as opposed to the SG7's T3 worm-driven axle. Most of the SG7s had full-width cabs, and with their small 11in (28cm) bonnet sticking out at the front like a 'snout', they had a very distinctive and impressive look about them. The first few models had the standard char-a-bancs/bus-shaped dash panel, but for such a long chassis this was clearly too rigid, and it gave way to a less attractive 'floating' dash with a relatively flat front to the cab.

The SG9

A year later came the SG9. This was basically the same as the SG7, except that it now had a more conventional half cab and a revised front axle designed to take the larger 850mm rim-size wheels, which ran on roller bearings. Prior to this the front wheels had been smaller, at 720mm, and ran on plain phosphor bronze bearings, a leftover from the War Office designs. The SG9 was also fitted as standard with the larger S6 40/48hp engine

(frequently referred to as the 'five inch engine' due to its bore size), which it clearly needed due to its weight and carrying capacity.

The SG11

Less than a year after the SG9 was introduced came the SG11, a much more handsome-looking single decker that had lost its 'snout'. On the SG7 and SG9 there was a lot of wasted space behind the engine – approximately 12in (30cm) – so the whole cab was moved forward to be flush with the back of the radiator (why this was not done in the first instance, goodness knows!). This meant that the whole vehicle could be shortened,

ABOVE: *The second side-type bus model was the SG9, of which only a handful were built on pneumatics. Brookes Brothers (White Rose) No. 51, DM 4115, is seen here when new in May 1925. (BCVM Archive)*

RIGHT: *The first rigid six-wheeler Leyland was this SWQ 10-tonner, with trailing (and steering) rear wheels, photographed in June 1926. The lorry appears to have been converted from a standard SQ2 of about June 1925 (London registered and therefore possibly ex-Mickleover Transport). It was converted in Chorley Works and became a Chorley Shop Wagon for Leyland Motors. (BCVM Archive)*

BELOW: *The prototype 'low-type thirty-two-seater bus, Model LC1', seen on 20 August 1925. The body design was clearly influenced by the BET style of body on the SG9s, even down to the short 'snout'. The body looks very high, even beside the tall driver: thank goodness it was redesigned and lowered for this new chassis, which was re-designated the Lion LSC1. (BCVM Archive)*

but it would have a similar carrying capacity (although none was built with as many as forty seats!) and this enabled the bus to comply with the new Ministry of Transport Regulations, that restricted the length of a four-wheeled single decker to 27ft 6in (7m). Here again the SG11 did not last long, because by the end of 1925 the LSC Lion had been introduced. The Lion was a completely new design and of much lighter construction than its earlier 'dinosaur' predecessors. Despite this there were many similarities in the overall look of the vehicle.

A production Lion LSC1 for H.M.S. Catherwood in February 1926, with bodywork of greatly improved proportions. (BCVM Archive)

Lions and Tigers

The Lion, together with the Lioness, Leveret and Leviathan, were to start a new chapter in the story of Leyland buses, in 1925–26, only to be overtaken by yet another major leap forward in 1927 with the introduction of the Tiger, Titan and Titanic, followed shortly afterwards by the 'T' series Lion. These were designed solely as passenger models, and started a totally new phase in bus design that is outside the remit of this book – although, of course, my next restoration, the Todmorden Joint Omnibus Committee Tiger TS6, will take me

into that period, of pneumatic tyres and oil engines: whatever next!

The White Rose Motor Buses and their No. 27

'White Rose' was the trading name for the business run by the Brookes Brothers of Rhyl, and this was used throughout their seventeen years of existence as motor-bus and coach proprietors. Initially the full title had been 'The White Rose Motor Buses', although the odd vehicle carried the word 'Coaches', instead of 'Buses'; but they later adopted the more modern

title of 'White Rose Motor Services'. The White Rose related to the White Rose of Yorkshire, which apparently is where the Brookes family had originated. The bus and coach fleet represented the biggest and most successful part of their business activities, which also included 'haulage contractors, garage proprietors, taxis for hire, motor ambulance, hydraulic press for solid tyres, motor body builders, furniture removers, funerals "completely furnished", contractors to H.M. Government', and last but not least, 'agents for Leyland Motors and all leading makes'.

The Attractions of Rhyl

The Brookes Brothers' business was initially involved in providing sightseeing tours of the district in the early years of the twentieth century. They had several horse-drawn vehicles for hire, including four-horse 'touring cars' – the original type of char-a-bancs from which the name was derived. These 'touring cars' covered quite long distances in the course of a day's tours, and the 'red coaches' became well known in the area. About sixty horses were kept by the Brookes Brothers at their mews in Rhyl, whilst others were stabled in outlying districts to take over the coaches when the first team tired.

John Nickels of Rhyl, who unfortunately died relatively recently, was a keen enthusiast of White Rose and collected a wealth of information; he has helped me enormously with my restoration of the White Rose, Leyland SG7. In a book he described Rhyl as:

> A lively if perhaps brash holiday town at the mouth of the Clwyd, some 30 miles from Chester, it is situated in the former county of Flintshire. It is best known for its good sands, its pier and funfairs, and it is hard to imagine that it was only a small fishing village before its rapid development into a 19th century watering place. The area is full of interest and beauty, with attractions such as Dysarth Falls and Rhuddlan lying inland, and with the modern holiday town of Prestatyn along the coast.

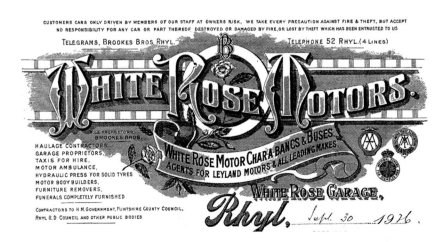

The very attractive White Rose letterhead.

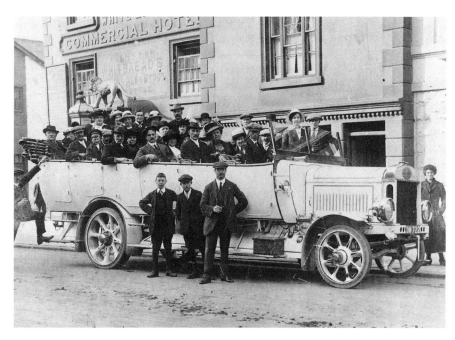

DM 722 was a Leyland X4.40.X4 char-a-bancs with Leyland body; it sat twenty-eight and was built in June 1914. This impressively powerful-looking machine was requisitioned by the War Office only two months later, the chassis being sent to Bulford Camp. The body was retained and mounted on a new chassis immediately after the war.

Early in the century the area was ripe for opening up by enterprising transport services, and in Rhyl there lived the Brookes family who were more enterprising than most.

Early taxis operated by Brookes Brothers were mainly of Fiat manufacture, but in October 1912, right at the end of the season, a Lacre twenty-eight-seat char-a-bancs was purchased, registered DM 472, and this was painted in a white livery. In March and May of the following year came two more twenty-eight-seater chars-a-bancs, but this time they were purchased from Leyland Motors (model X3.40). These were followed in July with a little fourteen-seater char-a-bancs, model S3.30.T, which attracted the name 'Baby White Rose', together with a Leyland S.24 mail van in November 1913. The latter was painted vermilion, and used for the Ruthin to Rhyl mails until May 1920.

White Rose During the War
The three Leyland chars-a-bancs were rebuilt and updated with the latest design of Leyland radiator and bonnets for the 1914 season, when they were joined by two new Leyland X4.40.X4, twenty-eight-seater chars-a-bancs, and two double deckers based on the Leyland S3.30.T chassis. A similar additional char-a-bancs came in August, around the time war was declared. At least six of these vehicles (possibly seven) were requisitioned by the War Department, and this decimated the fleet; the bodies were therefore put into store. The irony here was that an Army camp was very soon established at Kimmel Park, some 4 miles (6.5km) from Rhyl, and transportation was required throughout the war from the camp into Rhyl. This resulted in 1916 in the Brookes Brothers being able to purchase two new S4.36.X4 (Subsidy A) chassis from Leyland, these being just two of the few allowed to be sold for civilian use. The two Leyland double-decker bodies were soon brought out of store and placed on these chassis.

A Period of Major Expansion
After the war came a period of major expansion. In 1919–20 a further Leyland G was added, followed by a thirty-seater, saloon-bodied Leyland O and no fewer than sixteen Leyland chars-a-bancs. It is reputed that the chars-a-bancs were financed by Leyland Motors, with Henry Spurrier telling the Brookes Brothers that they could 'pay for them as soon as they could afford to pay'! This sounds a little far-fetched, but it would certainly be true that Leyland were keen to gain

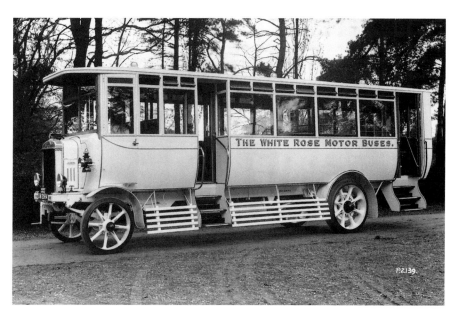

DM 2584, an SG6, No. 28 in the White Rose fleet, was a sister bus to my own SG7. They had been ordered at the same time, and both arrived in May 1923 – seen here before the signwriting had been completed. (BCVM Archive)

a stronghold in such an important area. Most of the chars-a-bancs came complete from Leyland with twenty-three- or twenty-eight-seater bodies, although some were chassis only, with a special wheelbase adjustment in order to fit the best of the char-a-bancs bodies put into store at the beginning of the war. One of the charas was in fact a thirty-eight-seater Leyland O, an enormously long machine with eight rows of seats. This particular vehicle was also used as a removals van, having an interchangeable body.

More eight-seater Fiats were bought, a Vauxhall E, a six-seater Ford and a Daimler T30 eight-seater to augment the private hire/taxi fleet, and some small fourteen- to eighteen-seater Lancia chars-a-bancs were also purchased. Three more Leylands were added in 1922–3, but in May 1923 came two absolute monsters – an order had been placed for two Leyland SG7 saloon buses with forty seats and dual entrance: these materialized as Nos 27/28 DM 2583/84. No. 27 is my SG7, the restoration of which I have recently finished, and No. 28 was an almost identical vehicle, albeit delivered with double-reduction bevel-driven back axle, therefore making it an SG6. White Rose were clearly impressed by this huge number of people that could be crammed into a bus, and ordered yet more, with seven additional SG6s and SG7s arriving by August 1924. (Another five SG9s and one SG11 followed shortly afterwards.)

Two of the SG7s were 'Specials': Nos 34 and 35. These were double deckers with sixty seats, and were similar in appearance to a single decker but with an open-top upper deck added. They were gigantic for their time, and not only were they longer than the legal limit permitted by the subsequent Road Traffic Act, but when they were converted to pneumatics they were also significantly wider, at about 7ft 10in (2.4m) – there was a special dispensation for conversion to pneumatics but buses of this size were eventually legislated off the road.

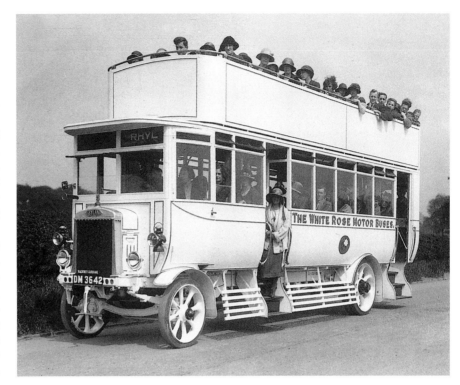

DM 3642 was one of two SG7s delivered with double-decker bodies and enclosed staircases (well, from the back at least!). They were built to seat sixty passengers (some reports say sixty-four!), and were absolute monsters! (BCVM Archive)

DM 2842, No. 31 with White Rose, is seen later on in its life looking rather dirty and fitted with pneumatic-tyred wheels on the front. Pneumatics made the steering very difficult indeed!

Takeover by Crosville

White Rose continued to buy Leylands, and by the time the company was bought by Crosville Motor Services in 1930, fleet numbers had reached No. 101 – this was the solitary Leyland Titan TD1. It is interesting to note that some of the later purchases for the fleet included some Shelvoke & Drewry 'toast-racks' that ran on incredibly small, solid-tyred wheels, for the seafront service, and also six Leyland

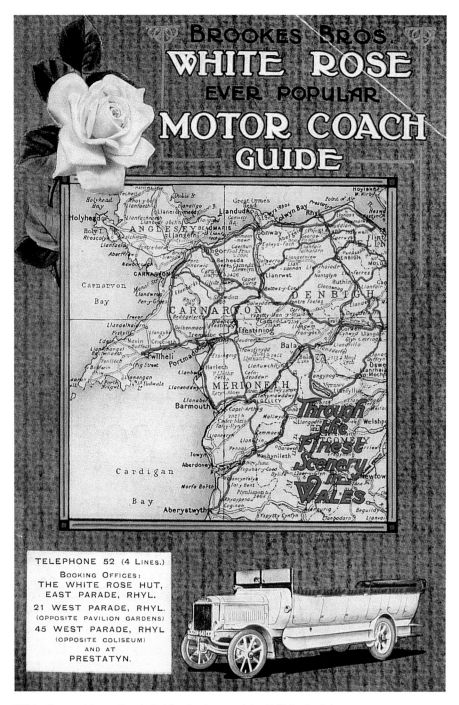

White Rose – Motor Coach Guide, *showing one of the 1919 Leyland charas.*

the chassis was in use as a farm trailer carrying a water tank, and guess what? It was devoid of engine, gearbox, controls … the usual story!

Brookes Bros carried on the removals side of the business, still carrying a white livery, right up to the 1960s.

Rescuing the SG7

On bringing the 'farm trailer' home, carefully leaving the water tank behind, out came the wire brush for some vigorous rubbing at the front nearside of the chassis frame. The chassis was clearly a Leyland SG7, but which one? 12535 was confirmed as the number, so there was yet another sprint up the drive to dive into the records and establish its identity. 'It's a Brookes Brothers!' What a fantastic find! All I needed now were an engine and a lot more bits to make it go again, and, of course, a body.

Finding the Running Gear

I recalled having seen a fairly complete Leyland SG9 chassis that had originally been a single-decker bus for Hebble Motor Services of Halifax, but which had been converted to a removals van; it had then been set on fire! Nevertheless, that model was virtually identical to the SG7, and could provide most of the missing parts if it could be found, and if someone else hadn't already restored it. On making several enquiries I located the Leyland at a little village in Dorset with the charming name of Sixpenny Handley – so it was off to Dorset. Having located the owner, he took me to the farm where it was kept. In the meantime the previous owner, who had not been able to get the Leyland in his garage due to its enormous length, had very kindly cut the back of the chassis off behind the rear wheels! On making enquiries, yes, the vehicle could be bought, and a couple of weeks later the SG9 arrived at Valley Forge. It was soon dismantled and the engine, radiator and other bits of running gear transferred to the White Rose chassis.

'Lioness Six' luxury coaches with Burlingham bodies. These were very powerful and handsome-looking machines – fortunately one is currently preserved, owned by Peter Stanier.

On takeover by Crosville, No. 27 became Crosville No. 440, by which time the solid-tyred wheels had been replaced by 38 × 7 pneumatic-tyred wheels. By the way, it is interesting to note that Crosville valued the bus at £300 for fire insurance purposes, the road fund licence was £67 4s 0d (£67.20) per annum, and the unladen weight was recorded by Crosville at 5 tons 14 cwt (5,791kg), presumably on pneumatics. The bus was disposed of fairly quickly by Crosville, and when its remains were found on a farm in North Wales, the body had gone and

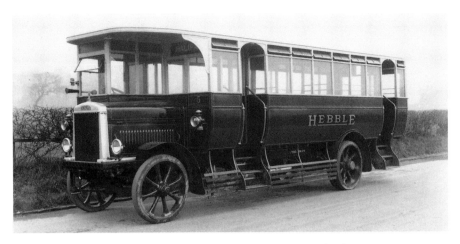

Photographed when new, the Hebble SG9, No. 5, CP 3804. (BCVM Archive).

The ex-Hebble Leyland SG9 in its second life as a removals van.

Finding the Wheels and Dash Panel

Next the chassis had to be put back onto solid-tyred wheels. Fortunately these were already in stock at Valley Forge, and naturally there is also a story attached to them. Many years earlier, when I was looking for bits for the Todmorden bus, a vintage vehicle enthusiast/dealer in Hertfordshire told me that he knew of the whereabouts of an 'RAF-type' Leyland that had been converted and rebodied as a removing van. Every year the body had been painted with a tar substance that had preserved it very well. It had been partly extended into a building, and was on a farm somewhere in Hertfordshire; but he would not tell me where. I made a point of seeing him every year, specifically to ask him about the Leyland: but all I could get out of him was that he was 'Keeping an eye on it'. This was exceedingly frustrating – it might have bits on it that I needed! Eventually he capitulated and told me the address of the farm and the name of the farmer. So off I shot to Graveley, near Stevenage, to see the farmer, only to be told 'No, there's no Leyland here, and there never has been!' Was he lying? Or even just mistaken? Or was my contact wrong? At the time there was absolutely nothing more I could do, other than look very hard at all the farm buildings as I retreated; but there were no visible clues.

A couple of years later a local friend told me that there was a new building development near Stevenage: 'They're clearing the site and an old lorry had been found!' On hearing this I went back to the farm – and yes, it *was* the same place and yes, it *was* a Leyland – the only problem being that the scrap man had already cut the chassis into four sections, had bulldozed the change-speed quadrant to smitherines

At Valley Forge, before the White Rose garage was built: the SG9 stands under a temporary scaffolding and plastic sheet cover, in the company of the Barnsley & District chassis. My timber store is to the left, full of ash, mahogany and Douglas fir gradually seasoning.

(gear lever quadrant), and it was already loaded onto his lorry to be taken off to be melted down. I had got there in the nick of time! After a quick deal the lorry carrying the remains was diverted to my home – and yes, another pile of junk had arrived.

Out came the wire brush once more, and this time the chassis turned out to be a Leyland G5 char-a-bancs new to Wood, Blackpool (later of Seagull fame). The guts had gone from the worm-drive back axle as usual, but it had a good set of wheels, a steering box and, best of all, it had the Leyland-shaped dash panel, associated with early 1920s buses and

building ('The Motorhouse'), known as 'The Grotto'. This is like an enormously long 'L'-shaped carport – or perhaps I should call it a 'Leyland spare-parts port': it is in fact merely a timber frame supporting a tin roof surrounded by fence panels, but it is about 70ft long by 12ft wide (21 by 3.6m). In it are racks full of front axles, back axles, wheel hubs, brake drums, bonnets, mudguards, engine undertrays, fire walls, complete Leyland chassis frames and a large quantity of solid-tyred wheels, and so on and so forth. In addition, the spare parts department extends to two enclosed lorry containers, one full of Leyland RAF-type

nuts and bolts red hot to clear the rust before they would undo!

Finding a Leyland SG7 Body
The next problem was to find a Leyland SG7 body, similar to the Leyland 'Edinburgh type'. I instantly recalled that when going to the Brewery at Charnock Richard to investigate the char-a-bancs bits, bonnets, wings, etc. we passed a farm on which stood the body of an identical 1920s Leyland single decker and two LT1 Lions, all being lived in as static caravans. So, Barry and I jumped in the car and off we went to Lancashire. We found the site, but there was only one of the Lions left, with empty spaces where the other two vehicles had been. Was it worth trying to find them, or were we too late? We noticed someone around the back of the farm and went to investigate. It was the farmer, and when I asked him about the 1920s Leyland body he replied 'Oh dear! I set fire to it yesterday!'. He pointed to a big pile of ashes, some twisted metal and remaining lumps of wood, all of which were still smouldering and emitting a small plume of smoke. We explained why we had come to see him and I'm sure the farmer was as upset as we were – just missed it, by one day!

I found a rake and began to scratch around in the dirt (again!), and all sorts of goodies came out of the ashes of the bonfire, much of it still warm. All of the floor-frame steel support brackets were there, as were all of the internal body irons, albeit some being badly twisted when the body collapsed in the flames. Various lumps of wood came out, and roof support brackets, window hinges, handrails, door fittings. Some of the aluminium fittings had melted in the heat, as had the yellow hammered glass from the ventilator windows – there were globules of melted glass and aluminium everywhere. After several hours searching and rummaging, we amassed a very large pile of treasures, and these were carefully loaded up and brought home, and proved to be absolutely invaluable in constructing the body for the White Rose, Leyland SG7. Clearly the woodwork would all have to be

Part of the remains of the Graveley G5 char-a-bancs chassis, which donated the rear wheels to the SG7.

chars-a-bancs. This scuttle, and indeed the front wheels, would come in very useful for the L&NWR char-a-bancs that I subsequently restored, though I didn't know it at the time. It has also helped the restoration of another Leyland on the Isle of Wight belonging to Geoff Golding, to whom I lent the scuttle for some time while he copied it. The back wheels, of course, are now on the White Rose, Leyland SG7, and the curves of the dash panel could be copied for the White Rose.

Those of you reading this who have not visited us here at Valley Forge, may like to know that there is an area to the side of, and behind, my biggest garage

engines and gearboxes, the other full of the small spares, arranged around the perimeter of the container in open tea chests, stacked one above the other. These spares are an invaluable source for finding the missing bits or even repairing broken parts when restoring one of my Leylands. I suppose it's really like a mini version of the Ham Works at Kingston, Surrey! I'm sure they had an easy life at Kingston rebuilding Subsidy 'RAF types', the oldest of which at the time must have been ten years, compared with the sort of things that I and my team of helpers have had to put up with. I don't suppose they had to get the gas out to get new, but these were all genuine Leyland fittings and structural ironwork and they helped enormously in ensuring that the dimensions and design of the body were exactly right. Unfortunately, because of the fire I do not have any photographs of the body as it was.

Restoration Begins

Before the restoration of the White Rose, Leyland SG7 could start I had to build a new garage for it, as it was just too long to go into my existing two garages. It is not easy to get planning consent for such big buildings in any

event, let alone when they are in the curtilage of a Grade II listed thatched cottage. But as it turned out, this was not a major stumbling block, and having obtained permission I erected a garage to a really high standard, particularly with regard to its thermal qualities, which are probably better than the average new house.

Restoring the Chassis

First to be restored was the chassis, and I wanted to get this completed before starting on the body so that there was a frame on which to construct it. At the time I was restoring the London

& North Western Railway 'Torpedo' char-a-bancs, so work on that was halted for six months while I restored the White Rose chassis. First we had all the major units sand blasted, then we tackled the wheels, removing the front stub axles – with great difficulty, I might add – and putting them back onto solid-tyred wheels. I already had one front 140 × 720mm new tyre in stock that came from a farm in Somerset, and – another stroke of luck! – Mick Giles telephoned me to say there was a farm auction coming up with some solid-tyred wheels. Among them was a brand new 140 × 720 tyre,

ABOVE: *The front wheels and solid tyres (size 140mm for 720mm rim).*

RIGHT: *Repairing the original radiator.*

BELOW: *Steve comes up for air while working on the cardan shaft brake (foot brake).*

BELOW RIGHT: *The Ricardo head E36HP/2 engine is fitted with new (old stock) cylinder-head gaskets.*

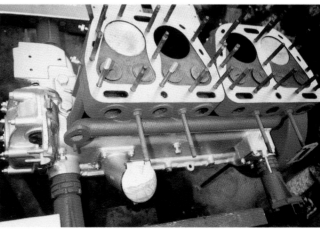

The completed SG7 chassis, ready for road testing.

What a long beast this is!

The elaborate paintwork on the wheels – a feature of many Leyland products of the time (note the ex-Midland Red wheel chock).

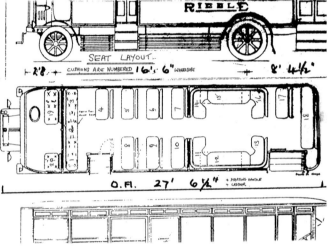

The seating layout, taken from an original drawing – note the unusual layout of the smoking compartment (we call it 'the snug').

and he kindly purchased it for me: so I now had a matching front pair of wheels and tyres! The tyres on the back wheels were already quite useable, though very old.

Restoring the Body

After completing the L&NWR chara in May 2000, work commenced in earnest on the enormous body of the White Rose SG7; I prepared very detailed drawings of the framework, pillars and so on. In anticipation of this, three years earlier I had bought a large quantity of kiln-dried American and English ash, which I then kept to season properly, and Nick Downes (in Shropshire) machined the structural woodwork. He also made the more

complicated parts such as the bulkheads and doors, that have ash framework with inlaid mahogany panels. The floor frame, pillars, cant rail, waist rail and light rails and roof hoops are all in ash, as usual, with the ceiling boards and decorative side panels in Douglas fir (Colombian pine) stained alternately light and dark, as it was when the vehicle was new. The floor is made of Douglas fir 1in tongued and grooved boards, and the steps are in solid ash. All the structural steel parts and fittings from the body in Lancashire have been used in the restoration, and have proved invaluable after straightening and repairing them.

The restoration of the body of the White Rose SG7 was completed in

the record time of two years, after a target of entering the 2002 London to Brighton Run had been set. This included having some White Rose 1920s moquette woven at Holdsworth of Halifax, and with the help of many interior photographs supplied by the British Commercial Vehicle Museum Archive at Leyland, I have been able to make the seats exactly to pattern. There was very little time to do any road testing prior to the Brighton Run, and we only managed to go up and down the road outside the house a few times. On the first occasion we noticed that there were three cracks in the cylinder blocks and a cylinder head, which fortunately were overcome with a good dose of Radweld.

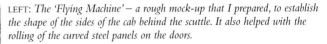

LEFT: *The 'Flying Machine' – a rough mock-up that I prepared, to establish the shape of the sides of the cab behind the scuttle. It also helped with the rolling of the curved steel panels on the doors.*

MIDDLE LEFT: *The ash frame of the body starts to take shape, mounted on the restored chassis, in the 'White Rose Garage'.*

BOTTOM LEFT: *Youngest son Ricky laying down the floorboards.*

BELOW: *Building the full-width cab, with all its curves and shape, was an exceedingly difficult task, particularly the doors.*

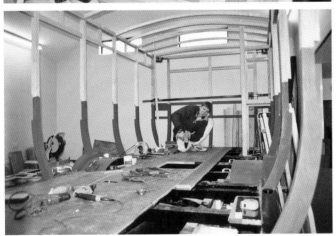

However, on the second time out we noticed that the rear cylinder block was heating up much more than the front cylinders. There had to be a blockage in the waterway somewhere – so off came the water manifolds, which we had not previously removed, and the cylinder water jacket sideplate, only to discover that the waterways were totally blocked up with hazelnuts and acorns. Clearly we had had a visitor while the chassis stood awaiting restoration! Who would have believed that you could have an engine full of nuts? Having removed them, the bus ran much better. With its Ricardo detachable heads, the engine is much more lively than its predecessor, and the bus is quite a fast vehicle on the flat (approaching 30mph/50km/h). However, its performance is not so good on the hills, particularly because of its heavy weight – on the weighbridge at the Totternhoe Lime Kilns it measured just over 6 tons (6,096kg) – a very heavy bus for its time!

I had thought that the L&NWR char-a-bancs was a very difficult restoration, but so was the White Rose SG7 – mainly due to its enormous size, but in particular because of its shaped front end where we had to make the two front doors and curved dash panel. All these had to blend in perfectly together when finished, and this was helped at the planning stage by constructing the 'flying machine', a mock-up of the shape of the front of the cab. Furthermore, as well as having to cope with the curves and the angles of the door framework and cab pillars, the windows of the doors had to slide up and down: this caused problems because the glass, which was straight, had to fit into the curved door – not easy, as glass does not bend, which caused some funny angles for the window channels. Also the doors taper towards the bottom, whereas the sides of the window channel have to be parallel – the depth of the rebates and

ABOVE AND RIGHT: *Nearing completion and only a few weeks to go before the Brighton Run and a lot yet to do! Note the striped interior lining panels, stained dark and light.*

BELOW: *Under its own power for the first time, the White Rose SG7 emerges from the garage, exactly twelve months after starting the body restoration, at the Valley Forge Crank-up and Barbecue, June 2001. (Bob Kell)*

window channel therefore varied: again, not easy!

Restoring the Fittings

Another complication with this bus is the large number of fittings. Fortunately many of these had been rescued from the bonfire, and they proved very useful as patterns for the casting of additional fittings. There is a huge quantity of bits of brass all over the bus, and one particularly difficult job was bending the 1⅛in (28.8mm) handrails into shape. I hired a hydraulic pipe bender for the weekend, and we set about trying to bend this enormously expensive brass tube. We annealed it, filled it with sand, annealed it, filled it with wood, annealed it again, put coiled springs in it – and every time the tube collapsed, even around some of the shallowest of bends. So out came the gas again, and we melted what seemed like a huge number of bars of solder into the tube until it was filled right up. It worked a treat, and with a lot of trial and error we managed to achieve the complicated bends and angles for all four handrails without a single kink in the brass. Once bent to the right shape, we lit up the gas again and warmed it up, and out came the molten solder into an old saucepan. (I would strongly recommend this practice for anyone trying to bend any difficult tube – it was really easy, and did not leave any stretch marks anywhere on the brass tube.)

I did not have any interior light fittings, but found one of the correct pattern at Beaulieu Auto Jumble; we therefore made patterns in Jellutong and had some more cast in brass. And the 'Sutcliffe luck' came into play yet again, in that the Nazeing Glass Works, who blew the globes for the London Central Leyland X2, found just the right quantity of an obsolete saucer-shaped globe and supplied them from stock – we were *very* careful not to break any of them!

The first outing of the White Rose SG7 under its own power was exactly twelve months after starting the bodywork, with three or four trips up and down the drive. It was on the occasion of our Sixth Valley Forge Crank-Up and Barbecue (Open Day) in June 2001. On swinging the handle, the engine burst into life perfectly, accompanied by a tremendous cheer from the one hundred or so spectators. At this time the panelling was nearly finished, and we had started to fix the special half-round aluminium beadings that were a discontinued size. I had managed to find a stockist with a die, and provided I had a minimum quantity (enough for ten to fifteen buses!) I could have some extruded. I took the risk of getting it made, and was surprised at just how quickly I managed to sell all the surplus to cover my costs!

On the roof there should be six 'torpedo' ventilators. I had not seen these close-up, but I had noticed some on the roof of the railway carriage when Pat and I went for a trip on the Orient Express. They were exactly what we wanted, and on making enquiries I managed to find another at the Quainton Railway Society from an L&NWR 1886 railway carriage. They very kindly loaned it to me to copy, and we made six scaled-down (bus-size) torpedo ventilators. For the inside part of the ventilator, mounted on the ceiling, I was given one original and made the other five in brass. The original has

The destinations carried by the White Rose buses of the period.

RHYL
PRESTATYN
RHUDDLAN
MOLD
DYSERTH WATERFALLS
DENBIGH
OCHRYFOEL
MELIDEN
HOLYWELL
LLANDUDNO
RHUALLT
CEFN
RHYL
TREMEIRCHION
ST ASAPH

PLAS HARRI
GYFFYLLIOG
RUTHIN
LLANFAIRTALHAIARN
ABERGELE
KINMEL BAY
FFYNNONGROEW
GRONANT
RHYL

'L&NWR' stamped into it, and as I have an L&NWR char-a-bancs, I decided to leave the initials on the ventilator (the one over the driver's seat, so that I can look up at it from time to time!).

Another complicated job was the destination boxes and blinds. Fortunately I had acquired an early 1920s destination box complete, and this enabled me to remove all the fittings and have additional ones cast for the second box. The winding gear did not fit, so we had to make everything from scratch, using some 45-degree bevel pinion wheels that I found on the Internet. Having made the whole thing from scratch, we found that the winding handle fouled on the opening windscreen, and so we are going to have to make it all again – back to the drawing board! The destination blinds were made especially for me by Norbury & Co. Birmingham on linen cloth, having been through a White Rose timetable of the period to obtain the destinations and to ensure their correct Welsh spelling!

The Paintwork

Seven coats of paint have been applied to the side panels: etch primer, Bondaprimer, two white undercoat, two white gloss, and finally old-fashioned yacht varnish. The first coats were sprayed and rubbed down, and I applied the final coats myself. Prior to the varnish, a good rub down with 1200 grit wet-and-dry, and then the signwriting – lots of it. Pip Darnell (a friend who is now a school caretaker) and I did this between us, with me planning it out and Pip doing most of the lettering and lining. The lining-out process involved over one mile of lines, painstakingly carried out at a snail's pace – what an enormous job this was! The most difficult part was the ⅝in (1.5cm) gold-leaf lining along the half-round beadings, which had to be edged with an ⅛in (3mm) red line at each side, and round all the corners and wheel arches – not an easy job. From my collection of 60,000 photographs I found interior views of Leyland SG7s and scanned

Pip puts on the gold leaf. Compare this with the picture of the White Rose Leyland G double decker in Chapter 8.

I put the finishing touches on the maker's 'transfer'.

them into my computer, enlarging the Leyland maker's transfer to its exact size.

Unfortunately the White Rose expert, John Nickels of Rhyl, did not live long enough to see the completed restoration, although I am very glad that I sent him pictures of the completed chassis, which he received just before he died. One of the things that he helped me with was the 'White Rose' oval emblem on the side of the bus. Many years ago John had made

friends with the man who was in charge of the paint shop at Brookes Bros – when the firm sold out to Crosville he took one of the White Rose transfers and put it onto a white bathmat - where else! He had shown the bathmat to John, but did not really want to part with it. However, John was obviously very persuasive and managed to get the man to swop it for forty Woodbines. Since John died I haven't been able to find out what happened to the bathmat, but he had kindly

A copy of the White Rose emblem, taken from the bathmat.

The emblem on the side of the SG7 painted by myself.

ABOVE: *The signwriting on the front doors.*

ABOVE RIGHT: *The rear of the bus with hackney licence plates issued by the various Police Watch committees.*

arranged to have it put on a laser copier, and I at least have a colour copy of it with dimensions. I have myself painted these emblems onto the side of the SG7, religiously copying the originals to the best of my ability, although not being an experienced signwriter.

Specification – Leyland SG7	
Operator	Brookes Brothers (White Rose) Rhyl, No. 27, registered DM 2583 in May 1923
Model	Leyland SG7
Chassis No.	12535
Engine	Four-cylinder, 36/42hp, Model E36HP/2C, built by Leyland No. 27025
Body	Leyland 40 seat bus, with full front and dual entrance, the body being split into two saloons
Length	28ft 8in (8.74m) (including starting handle and ladder)
Width	7ft 5in (2.21m)
Height	10ft 7in (3.23m)
Weight	6 tons, 0cwt 2qtr 4lb (6,123kg)

I found the Leyland 'Royal Coat of Arms' radiator filler cap in Florida (on the Internet!). A man whose father was a bus driver in North Wales (White Rose or Crosville?) had emigrated, and agreed that it would look right on the White Rose SG7 – more Sutcliffe luck!

After all the last-minute panics in the week before the Brighton Run, such as fixing and painting 120 roof slats for the luggage rack, we actually made it to Brighton, where the bus caused quite a sensation and won many prizes.

My sons Matt and Ricky hard at work fitting roof slats, three days before the Brighton Run: 'Don't worry, Dad, you'll do it, you always do!'

On the Brighton seafront, May 2002.

The off-side of the White Rose SG7 shows the different window spacings, and also two removable centre windows for warmer weather.

A study of the roof and bulkhead in the driving compartment (with L&NWR ventilator).

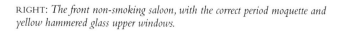

ABOVE: *The rear of the bus has an adjustable stepladder to reach the luggage on the full-length roofrack.*

RIGHT: *The front non-smoking saloon, with the correct period moquette and yellow hammered glass upper windows.*

CHAPTER ELEVEN

The Chocolate Express, Leyland LB5, of 1924

Arthur Partridge would have been proud to have seen the Chocolate Express Leyland LB5 XU 7498 running again – it was his favourite bus, and was probably the most famous bus of all of the London Pirates. Michael Plunkett and Alan Lambert discuss its merits in the driving compartment.

Leyland's London Bus

The first example of Leyland's next major attempt to build stage carriage buses for London was delivered from the coachbuilders, Christopher Dodson, to Arthur Partridge's Chocolate Express Omnibus Co. and ready for service in August 1922. Plans to build this bus had, however, been going on for quite some time as it was first mentioned in Leyland's drawing office records in January 1922. There are references to drawings (now long since gone, unfortunately) relating to the rear brakes and a special London Bus frame; there is also a reference to a 'G7, fifty-five-seater double-deck submission drawing to London'. Just who these drawings were submitted to is a mystery, but a number of specifications were demanded by the Metropolitan Police, and these had to be met.

One was the fitting of a 'silent' gearbox, and Leyland Motors already had one of these in production – the S8 helical gearbox, already mentioned. Another requirement was evidently the fitting of two brakes on each of the back wheels, a hand brake and a foot brake. Leyland's conventional braking system was to have the hand-operated lever connected to internally expanding shoes in the rear brake drums; generally what we would think of as the handbrake. However, with these early vehicles this is not just the hand brake, but also the driving brake. It is only in emergencies, or when carrying a heavy load and extra braking is needed, that one uses the foot brake. On a Leyland the foot brake is very effective, being externally contracting shoes on a wide but small drum behind the gearbox, acting on the cardan shaft. It therefore seems a possibility that, as this foot brake was standard with Leyland, there may actually have been two brake pedals, as well as the hand brake on these Leyland LB's, with two sets of brakes on the back wheels plus the cardan shaft brake. I have not seen any evidence of this,

although I have been told that there were three brakes.

The other major change was the adoption of roller bearings for all four wheels, which meant alterations to the front axle and wheels. At the same time, larger 850mm front wheels were fitted (using tyre size 120 × 850mm), and because of the additional height of the centre of the front wheels, the front axle had to be redesigned and lowered, with different-shaped jaws to hold the stub axle. It is interesting to note that this revised design was later adopted for all Leylands in the 4- to 6-ton range from about 1924, when all of these solid-tyred road wheels were standardized at the same diameter, 850mm. The development of the London Bus therefore pushed ahead the design of the larger Leyland models.

The Leyland LB (London Bus) soon became the LB2, later the LB4, and the majority of the examples built

were LB5. I do not know what each of these model designations meant in terms of changes to the chassis, but they must have only been minor alterations. Photographic evidence does, however, suggest that one or two Specials were built for London (and Ortona, Cambridge), which had the 43in (109cm) wide frame instead of the usual 38in (96.5cm) wide. It would be nice to know more about this subject, but who is there to ask!

Apart from the above alterations, the LB was basically a G7 chassis, with low radiator, 15ft 10in (4.8m) wheelbase, worm-driven back axle and S5.36/40hp engine. In terms of performance, with their 6.6 litre engines, the Leyland LBs could easily out-perform London's B types, K types, S types and NSs, despite the fact that the LGOC vehicles were generally lighter. The only serious competitor to the Leyland LB with the London Pirate

Leyland's second version of the London Bus, the LB2, is shown here in the shape of XP 435 carrying a Dodson forty-eight-seater body, new in August 1923 to Drake & McCowen. The livery was cream and black, the firm being taken over by Birch Brothers in February 1929. (Dodson)

operators, was the Dennis 4-ton. They sold in similar numbers, about 170 vehicles each, although Dennis had the slight edge, but operators generally favoured one make or the other. It is interesting to note that there are only two preserved Pirate buses, one being my Chocolate Express Leyland LB5, and the other the Dennis D142 that was restored by Prince Marshall and is now owned by the London Bus Preservation Trust at Cobham Bus Museum. The Dennis was new to Dominion in April 1925, one of two that had passed to Redburn's Motor Service and to London General in January 1928. The bodies of both vehicles are very similar, being built by Dodson, although the body on D142 has been extended forward over the cab since it was built. As with the Chocolate Express LB5, Prince Marshall found the body only, and had to find a suitable Dennis chassis. As there were no 4-tonners left, he used a late 1920s 3-ton chassis, with a later Ricardo detachable head engine, and this very much improves the performance of the engine. When in service in the 1920s the two makes would have been very comparable, and a real threat to the London General.

The Development of the Leyland Double Decker

Before turning to look at Arthur Partridge and the Chocolate Express fleet, it is worth looking at the development of the Leyland double decker up to the Leyland Titan TD1. Like the LB5, the G range was based on the 'RAF-type' model range, and the G7, later the GH7 with the higher radiator, became the most popular model. These continued in dwindling numbers up to 1927.

However, Leyland's attempts to make forward-control models could not leave out the double decker, and the first to appear was an enormous sixty-five-seater in December 1921, designated the OP2 'Manchester type'. A demonstrator was built clearly with Manchester in mind as a customer, and it had the 5-ton bevel back axle, hence the 'P' (5-ton range). It was not

The over-type demonstrator for Manchester, Model OP2 'Manchester type'. (BCVM Archive)

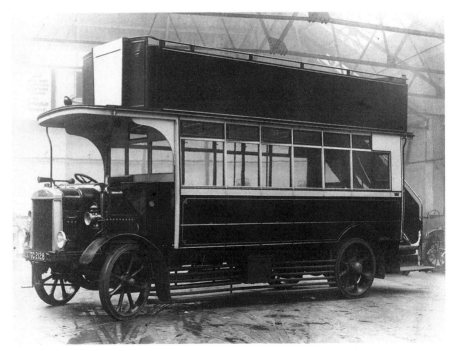
TC 2128 was a Dodson-bodied Leyland SG7 demonstrator to Birmingham. Note the similarity between this body and the Dodson body on the Leyland LBs. (BCVM Archive)

a success, and after being demonstrated to other operators, the bus disappeared into obscurity – possibly it was just too heavy (it was certainly very ugly!). A second attempt was made in March 1923 with another demonstrator, this time aimed at Birmingham. It was a half-cab side-type based on the SG7 chassis and carried a Dodson fifty-four-seater body. Again this was unsuccessful, and the bus was sold a couple of months later to the United Counties Omnibus & Road Transport Co. via – guess who? – William Benjamin Richardson: it's a small world, again!

With the introduction of the 'L' range in 1925, the double-decker variant was the Leviathan. The design incorporated a new chassis frame with 'joggle' at the front end and swept up over a new back axle; otherwise the components were basically existing designs. This gave a slightly lower overall height that enabled the top deck cover to be added although, compared with the Titan, the overall height was more like that of a tram. A total of ninety-seven Leviathans was built between 1925 and 1927, when it was well and truly ousted by the Leyland Titan TD1, developed by G. J. Rackham. Here, we will leave the development of the Leyland as it takes us into another era. Perhaps it would be true to say that I am really an enthusiast of the pre-Rackham-ite era!

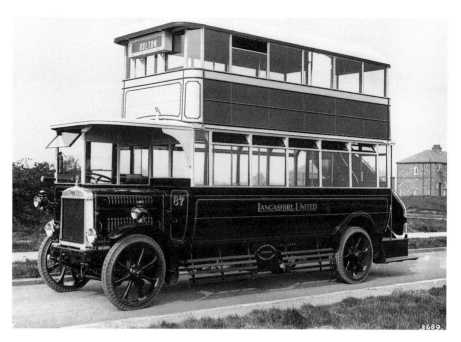

Lancashire United operated this Leviathan LG1, No. 87, TD 5990. The body from one of the LUT Leviathans still exists on an allotment near Harrogate. (BCVM Archive)

Arthur Partridge, Chocolate Express, and their B6

The Chocolate Express Omnibus Co. Ltd was not only the first of all the London independents of the 1920s and 1930s, it was also the best remembered. This pioneer independent bus operation embodied all that was best in private enterprise, and deservedly won a reputation second to none for service, cleanliness and reliability. At the end of every journey (not just every day) the buses were swept out with dustpan and brush provided for the crew. Even in the roughest weather its buses appeared spotless, and there was probably no other city operator in the country to match them. Arthur George Partridge, who started the company in August 1922, was a completely unknown quantity and a man whose business ability was so far untried. He soon turned out to be a man of great determination in the face of relentless opposition by the London General, who aimed to drive him out of business. His business skill later became apparent, and he became accepted as the unofficial leader of, and spokesman for, the many men who were to follow his example and become independent

What better photograph to end this brief history of the products of Leyland Motors than this wonderful picture of a Thames Valley Leyland Titan TD1, with open staircase bodywork by Leyland: TVT No. 165, RX 1754.

London bus proprietors. Even Frank Pick of the LGOC, who had little time for most of the 'Pirate' operators, held Arthur Partridge in high esteem. For several years he was the chairman of the Association of London Omnibus Proprietors, and at their annual meet-

ings he was an outstanding and eloquent after-dinner speaker.

Arthur Partridge had been a driver with the London Road Car Co. in the early 1900s, and later a taxi driver, and he could not help noticing that the London General bus services couldn't

The London 'Pirates'

Before the Great War, the London General Omnibus Company, under the control of the Underground Group, had gradually acquired nearly all of the other London motor-bus operators, and it had a monopoly in the capital. There were four other operators, all of which had pooling arrangements with the General, whereby each operated an agreed proportion of the total London bus mileage on specific routes. There was no competition between any of these companies and the General.

The LGOC fleet in the early 1920s consisted of the residue of a once large number of B-type buses, built mainly between 1910 and the outbreak of war. The B type had been designed and built by London General, leading to the formation of AEC, and many of these buses had been sent off to the war effort, several never to return. In 1919 the General started to replenish its fleet, first with the forward-control AEC K type, built with a capacity of forty-six seats within the stringent Metropolitan Police Regulations, soon to be followed by the larger S type when weight restrictions were relaxed, and the NS type with its dropped frame. These newer buses gradually replaced the B types, and although they contained some modern and novel design features, they were somewhat under-powered and slow.

There had been a large upsurge in bus passenger traffic after the war, although even by 1920 the number of buses operating in London was considerably less than before the war. This led to long queues at the bus-stops, and a large amount of public dissatisfaction at the bus services in London. A London taxi driver by the name of Arthur George Partridge became aware of this situation and decided that he would run his own omnibus.

In the summer of 1922, Partridge ordered a Leyland 36/40hp 4-ton chassis specially designed to pass the stringent London Police regulations, and the body was built by Christopher Dodson at their Willesden premises. The bus was painted in a dark brown and cream livery, with 'Express' written in gold leaf on its side panels, and it was declared to be the best bus ever to run on the streets of London. On Saturday 5 August 1922 the 'Express' bus entered service on General's route number 11: the first of the 'Pirates' had arrived. Right from the beginning the new bus was harassed by the General, although, as will be seen later, they withdrew their chaser buses to a certain distance and just kept a close eye on operations of the 'Express' bus. By this time the brown and cream bus had been affectionately called the 'Chocolate Express'.

This was just the beginning. The following month the coach firm Samuelson put into service three double deckers, and this was soon followed by Percy Frost-Smith with petrol-electric buses that he had designed himself. These were followed in turn by two more independents that carried the fleet names 'Primrose' and 'Admiral' and, by the end of 1922, there were five independent bus operators running thirteen vehicles in London. Over the next two years there was a vast increase in the number of independent London bus operators: by 1925 these had grown to nearly 200, with approximately 630 buses in the Metropolitan Police area. They were painted in a variety of different liveries, giving a new dimension of colour to the London streets. The fleet names carried on the sides of the buses were as varied as the liveries, and included names such as 'Chariot', 'Earl', 'The

Timpson's were early on the scene with a large fleet of the modern but unsuccessful Straker Squire Model A, with bodies built by Straker and painted silver and maroon.

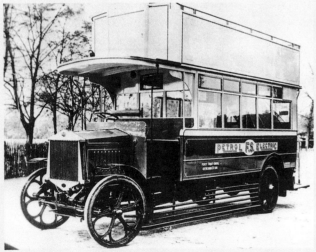

Percy Frost-Smith's blue and cream petrol-electric buses of his own design saw only three and a half years' service prior to withdrawal.

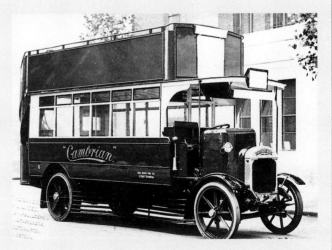

Cambrian operated a massive fleet of green and white buses, including this forward-control Thornycroft J with Dodson body.

continued overleaf

The London 'Pirates' *continued*

Hawk', 'Meteor', 'Nil Desperandum', 'Peraeque', 'Premier', 'Pro Bono Publico', 'The Royal Toots', 'St. George', 'Supreme', 'Uneedus', 'Venture', and even names such as 'The Pirate' and 'The Rogue' – what a sight it must have been!

At first the travelling public liked the independent buses because they broke up the General monopoly, and were fast and efficient. However, they soon attracted the nickname 'Pirates' because there was no restriction on licensing for the services they could operate, and some less scrupulous 'Pirate' bus operators went for the most lucrative routes. This meant that as many as fifty different firms could be chasing the passengers of one single route, causing heavy congestion. If passenger loadings became low, these less reputable operators might suddenly switch to another route, even though they still had on board the passengers from the previous route! It had become a mad scramble to carry the largest number of passengers possible and, as tempers heated, buses raced with one another along the streets! As this was going on the General were introducing large numbers of additional S types and NS types into service in an attempt to beat off the competition. Something had to be done about the situation, and on 1 October 1924, the London Traffic Act came into force. This required each bus operator to deposit schedules of routes and times, and once deposited, these schedules and times could not be changed without the approval of the police. Furthermore, the Act empowered the Minister of Transport to designate streets as restricted, thereby limiting the number of buses travelling along these streets. The new regulations helped to stabilize the situation, and brought a halt to massive increases in independent buses in London.

Turning to the buses operated by the independents, the first was the Leyland LB (London Bus). This was much more sturdily built than the London General buses, and had a bigger engine. The Leylands had a considerable turn of speed and could easily outmanouvre any of the General buses, and were therefore very popular with the 'Pirates'. Late in 1923, Dennis introduced a London version of their 4-ton chassis, and this also sold in large numbers during 1924 and 1925, reaching a peak of approximately 250 vehicles in 1926. Of these 'Pirate' buses, both the Dennis and the Leyland were far superior to any of the other makes, and many lasted up to the final demise of the independents in 1934.

Carlton (later Overground) had a number of brown and white Leyland LB2s with exceptionally wide chassis frames and bodies by Christopher Dodson.

'Pro Bono Publico' ('For the Benefit of the Public') was the fleet name of this Dennis 4-ton. Note the white-wall tyres of this chocolate and white painted bus, again with Dodson coachwork. (W. Noel Jackson)

Another popular bus at first was the Straker Squire 'A' type. This had a modern monobloc engine with coupled gearbox, but it also had a long and troublesome propshaft, and they were not reliable; moreover, many Straker Squires did not last long. Other less common makes included a forward-control version of the Thornycroft 'J' chassis (there were just over thirty of these), and the Daimler 'Y' type, of which there was a similar number – these were rebuilt Great War lorry chassis that had been reconstructed by the firm J. M. Roberts of Shepherd's Bush. There were also a handful of rebodied Tilling Stevens TS3A petrol-electric buses and the six petrol-electric double deckers designed and built by Percy Frost-Smith. None of these lasted very long, however. There were a few single-deck buses, comprising four small Crossleys built on the RAF-type light-tender chassis, three Fiats, about fifty Dennises on 2½-ton chassis and some Leyland Lions.

The vast majority of bodies on the 'Pirate' buses were built by Christopher Dodson Ltd of Cobbold Road, Willesden, North London. Towards the end of the last century Dodson had been a builder of horse buses, and the natural progression was to build motor-bus bodies. The sudden influx of 'Pirate' buses in the early 1920s must have resulted in a big increase in business for Dodson. The design that was introduced on the first of the 'Chocolate Express' buses was later copied by the Wilton Carriage Company Ltd, and similar bodies were also built by Strachan and Brown Ltd, and Birch Brothers. Christopher Dodson himself was very sympathetic to the 'Pirate' operators, and arranged hire-purchase terms at reasonable rates. He did not personally like the large monopoly of the General and would therefore not undertake any coach-building work for General in later years. This situation continued until near the end of the 'Pirate' era in 1933, but it became clear that Dodson would lose a large part of its market share overnight, and he ceased to build omnibus bodies, and moved to the Isle of Wight.

At the beginning of May 1926 came the General Strike, which brought the General almost to a halt; however, the independents were able to continue, as very few of their employees were union members. This caused great problems, and the angry strikers did everything in their power to bring the independent buses to a halt. Many vehicles were damaged, and it was not uncommon to see a policeman riding 'shotgun' by the side of the 'Pirate' drivers.

From 1926 the General decided that it would buy up as many of the 'Pirate' businesses as possible in order to reduce the ranks of the competition; fifty-four operators were taken over in the following two years. These were probably the weaker businesses that were unable to expand their operations due to the new regulations. In July 1927 a new company was formed, the London Public Omnibus Company Ltd, by the amalgamation of a number of the independent operators; by May 1928 'Public' had acquired seventy-seven operators with 219 weekday schedules. At first, many of these operators felt that by joining Public at a handsome purchase price for each scheduled bus, they were joining a stronger organization that could beat the General. However, after some time, people became suspicious that Public was just a front for London General to acquire as many independents as possible. Their suspicions were proved right in May 1928 when London Public sold out to the General.

By the end of 1927 there were only sixty-four independent bus operators left in the Metropolitan area, running just under 250 buses, a situation that was to remain virtually unchanged until 1933. The late 1920s saw a revolution in the design of buses due to the introduction

The General Strike, 1926. One of Gray's Leyland LB4's is seen with its windows boarded up and with wire mesh to protect the driver.

The blue and white livery of the London Public Omnibus Co. looks resplendent on this Dennis 2½ ton single decker. It was originally new to P.H.R.H. (Philip Henry Roper Harris) who sold out to Public without realizing that it was the 'General' in disguise! (W. Noel Jackson)

'Nil Desperandum' ('Don't Despair') must have been a welcome fleet name for the potential passengers waiting in the long queue. This Birch-bodied Leyland Lion PLSC3 was painted in a crimson and cream livery with white-wall tyres. (J. Higham)

A crimson livery was applied to Pioneer's buses, this one being a Dodson-bodied Leyland Titan TD1. Note the absence of any windscreen or headlamps, at the insistence of the backward-thinking Metropolitan Police Authority.

of forward-control vehicles, with the driver sitting beside the engine, and a low load-line chassis frame that enabled the body to be mounted significantly lower on the chassis. Up to that date most chassis frames had been completely straight, and could be fitted with either lorry or bus bodies. With these changes in design came a whole new generation of buses, although London followed a couple of years behind the rest of the country. After a small number of Guy six-wheelers and Dennis Hs came the first Leyland Titans that were delivered to 'Chocolate Express' and 'Triumph'. These buses were the last word in comfort, and had Leyland six-cylinder petrol engines, the 'Express' Titan being exhibited at the 1929 Commercial Motor Show at Olympia.

Over the next four years, many more of these Leyland Titans were purchased by the majority of independents to replace ageing Leyland LBs and Dennis 4-ton buses. In total, 132 entered service, including the three City six-wheel Leyland Titanics. They were far more successful than any of their rivals, which entered service in very small quantities, including the Dennis H, HS and HV, some of the first

continued overleaf

The London 'Pirates' *continued*

'Pirate' buses with covered tops. These Dennis models were in turn rather belatedly replaced by the Dennis Lance in 1930, and a few were bought by the 'Pirates' and by 'Overground', but the Lance was not a realistic competitor to the Leyland Titan and later the AEC Regent. After the introduction of the Leyland Titan, London General had to do something to update its fleet. Its most modern double deckers were the NS introduced in 1923, sluggish and cumbersome machines, and the LS six-wheeler, a lost cause in bus design. General experimented with a few of their own designed and built vehicles, but a breakthrough came when AEC poached G. J. Rackham from Leyland. He had designed the Titan, and now set about designing the AEC Regent double decker, the Regal single decker and the Renown six-wheeler along similar lines to the Titan.

City had an immaculate fleet of buses painted in their fawn, brown and white livery, with plenty of lining-out. CS1 was the first of the six-wheel rebuilds from former Leyland LBs. (D. W. K. Jones)

The epitome of the London Independents was surely Westminster's Sunbeam Sikh with Dodson body carrying sixty-four seats. It was built in 1933 (still without windscreen), and in its red, maroon, white and black livery, it was surely the most impressive vehicle of its time. (H. C. Casserley)

There was no doubt that the existence of the 'Pirates' had influenced the standard of the London bus. The new General AECs were to a much higher specification and were a match for the Titan (well, nearly! – who's biased?). Only a handful of 'Pirates' purchased AEC Regents, the largest quantity going to 'Pickup' who specified open-top Park Royal-built bodies. 'Gordon' purchased a solitary Maudslay Mentor ML7 with a new design of Dodson body: this vehicle was shown at the Olympia Show in 1931. Another one-off was a six-wheeled Sunbeam Sikh, bought by 'Westminster' in 1933, following an earlier demonstration of a Sunbeam Sikh with 'Ambassador' and later 'Westminster'. The demonstrator was not purchased, and ended up with Derby Corporation. Single deckers included about twenty or so Dennis Es and a similar number of Leyland Lions and Tigers. Bodies for these later buses were almost all built by Dodson, with a few by Birch Bros, but also some double deckers by Duple. There were some double-deck bodies built on single-deck Leyland Tiger chassis, and single deckers built on double-deck Leyland Titan chassis. Other oddities included six rebuilt earlier vehicles by 'City'. These were Leyland LBs, extended to six-wheelers and rebodied by Dodson (one) and Ransomes, Simms & Jeffries (five) – rather odd-looking vehicles with forward control.

Throughout this time the 'Pirates' were updating their earlier vehicles, converting solid-tyred wheels to pneumatics, and the backward-thinking Metropolitan Police had even been persuaded to accept four-wheel brakes. Their stringent regulations significantly held back the design of the London bus, and even as late as 1933, modern buses were entering service without windscreens or any real protection for the driver. They had no headlamps (or sometimes one) and many still had open staircases.

In the early 1930s the power struggle to control the buses in London re-emerged. A new Labour Government had been elected to power and in 1929, on the advice of the Minister of Transport, Herbert Morrison, the London Passenger Transport Bill was promoted to bring public ownership to the transport of London. Despite a change in government in August 1931, the bill slowly made its way through Parliament, becoming law in April 1933. This gave the new London Passenger Transport Board powers to compulsorily acquire all of the bus operators, tramway operators, the Metropolitan railway and underground. It was therefore only a matter of time and negotiation before the rest of the London independents vanished. Some saw this coming and expanded into coaching operations and long-distance stage work. These included 'Allitt' (with a six-wheel Karrier char-a-bancs), 'Westminster', 'Premier Line', 'Gordon' and 'Birch'. Some, following takeover by General/London Transport, used their sale proceeds to expand coaching/express operations, a good example being the City Coach Co. The remaining 'Pirates' were gobbled up by the giant London Passenger Transport Board one by one; the last operator, 'The Prince', was taken over on 5 December 1934. This was indeed the end of a very colourful sight on the streets of the capital; but the memory of these enterprising little companies has lived on, helped by the existence of my Chocolate Express Leyland LB5, and Cobham's Dennis 4-ton, saved by Prince Marshall.

cope with the volume of passengers, especially at rush hours. He felt there was room for private enterprise which, wisely operated, would help to fulfil an urgent public need and at the same time show a reasonable margin of profit. With two former wartime colleagues he ordered a bus, through Dodson, to be bought on hire purchase. Its construction was completed in July 1922, and on the 25th it was presented to the Metropolitan Police who did not pass it immediately, as they required certain minor modifications to be made. On 2 August it was

RIGHT: *The first 'Pirate' – Chocolate Express XL 7513 caused a sensation when it appeared in August 1922. (Commercial Motor)*

LEFT: *The Chocolate Express Omnibus Co. Ltd prospectus of October 1922 was not a financial success.*

BELOW: *At the last presentation dinner and dance of the Association of London Omnibus Proprietors Ltd held on 25 February 1936, Arthur Partridge was the guest of honour. Note the names of some of the pirate operators around the artist's impression of the Chocolate Express bus.*

This Prospectus has been filed with the Registrar of Joint Stock Companies.

NO PART OF THIS ISSUE HAS BEEN OR WILL BE UNDERWRITTEN.

The Subscription List will be open on Tuesday, the 17th October, 1922, and will be closed on or before Saturday, the 21st October, 1922, for Town and Country.

THE CHOCOLATE EXPRESS OMNIBUS
COMPANY, LIMITED

(INCORPORATED UNDER THE COMPANIES ACTS, 1908 to 1917.)

CAPITAL   -   ~   ~   £15,000

Divided into 15,000 Shares of £1 each.

Under an Agreement set forth herein, 3,750 Shares have been issued to the Vendors as fully paid,

leaving an

ISSUE OF 11,250 SHARES OF £1 EACH,
WHICH ARE OFFERED FOR SUBSCRIPTION AT PAR.

PAYABLE AS FOLLOWS :

5/- per Share on Application,
15/- per Share on Allotment.

Directors :
Mr. ARTHUR GEORGE PARTRIDGE, 36, Gayville Road, S.W., Omnibus Proprietor.
Mr. DAVID FRANCIS JERMYN, 5, Crab Tree Lane, Fulham, S.W., Omnibus Proprietor.
Mr. ALBERT SYDNEY GRIFFIN, 32, Crab Tree Lane, Fulham, S.W., Omnibus Proprietor.
Two members of the public subscribing, being men possessed of business experience, will be invited to come on the Board of the Company after allotment, so as to afford to the Company the benefit of their experience.

Solicitors :
LAWSON & LAWSON, 181, Queen Victoria Street, London, E.C.

Auditor :
THOMAS L. SUMMERS, F.A.A., F.I.S.A., 64, Victoria Street, S.W. 1.

Acting Secretary and Registered Offices :
W. A. JEWELL, 181, Queen Victoria Street, London, E.C.

PROSPECTUS.

This Company has been formed for the objects set out in the Memorandum of Association, and more particularly to acquire, and take over as a going concern, the well-known and celebrated Omnibus now upon the streets of London, popularly called the " Chocolate Bus."

VENDORS.

The idea of placing this Omnibus upon the streets of London was conceived by three ex-Service men, namely, Messrs. Arthur George Partridge, David Francis Jermyn and Albert Sydney Griffin. These enterprising men ordered and purchased the Omnibus themselves and then proceeded to run the same, as a private enterprise, in partnership with each other, under the name of the Express Omnibus Company."

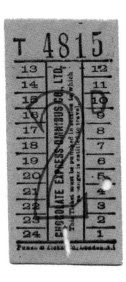

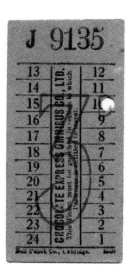

A selection of tickets from the Chocolate Express Omnibus Co. Ltd.

finally approved and licensed as XL 7513, and it entered service three days later. The 'Express' was soon to make the headlines in the national press, and was plagued with 'chaser' buses stationed fore and aft by the London General. As the days and weeks went by, the LGOC chasing persisted unabated and Arthur Partridge began to get despondent. One day in desperation he turned abruptly into the cobbled forecourt of the Houses of Parliament, only to be evicted – but not before complaining bitterly to interested Members of Parliament about the persecution to which he was being subjected. The incident came to the ears of the Home Secretary who called for a report. This was duly made, and eventually public opinion, aroused by the press, forced the General to abandon its tactics.

Headlines such as 'Fair Play for the Ex-Serviceman's Bus' could not be ignored even by an organization as vast and powerful as the LGOC.

Chocolate Express expanded to a fleet of five Leyland LBs, all with Dodson bodies. Between 1929 and 1931 they were replaced by five brand new, enclosed top, Dodson-bodied Leyland Titan TD1s; these became B1 to B5 in the fleet. Partridge's favourite bus was, however, Leyland LB5, registered XU 7498, new on 3rd September 1924. Despite the fact that it had effectively been replaced, he fitted it with pneumatic tyres in March 1930, numbered it B6, and ran it together with the Titans right up to the end in August 1934.

London Transport Takes Over
With the threat of compulary acquisition it was only a matter of time and negotiation before the rest of the London independents vanished, and Chocolate Express was one of the last to be taken over by London Transport. On the last day, Friday 10th August 1934, the first of the Titans, UV 9097, made the last run from Liverpool Street and headed to the garage at Ethelburga Street, Battersea, for a farewell party. There the staff removed all route boards, numbers, vehicle badges, fare boards and everything

White-wall painted tyres were a feature of many of the pirates, including Chocolate Express Leyland LB4, XT 4951.

that had anything to do with Chocolate Express, and I am fortunate enough to have some of these. The late S. L. Poole, an enthusiast who was there, recalled the moment:

> Farewells are always sad things. Each went his way leaving the buses alone in the garage, the silence broken only by the creaking and cracking sounds of contracting metals as the engines cooled off. Just before 8 o'clock the next morning the six buses lined up outside the garage for the last time. The empty white glass of the front stencil holder seeming to stare ahead like a sightless eye. Arthur Partridge passed down the line, shaking hands with all the thirty-four men who had made up the staff, including the

ABOVE: *XU 7498, Arthur Partridge's favourite bus, seen here on white-walled, solid tyres.*

RIGHT: *The bus again after conversion to pneumatics, and photographed by D. W. K. Jones, fifty-five years before he saw the bus again.*

BELOW: *The second of five Leyland Titan TD1s operated by Chocolate Express.*

garage staff and others in the open topper, which was to lead the way to Chiswick [B6 – *my bus!*]. As the clock struck eight, engines were started amidst a cheer from quite a crowd of people who had come to see this last act played through – they drove away one by one until only a faint haze of blue smoke remained, dwindling away as the memory of the Chocolate Express was to do.

Arthur Partridge could probably never have dreamt that the memory of the Chocolate Express would live on in rural Bedfordshire! (By the way, Pat and I got married on 3 September 1994 – the Choc Box's seventieth birthday!)

The Rescue of B6

After their purchase by London Transport, the Titans went on for further service, but the LB5 was not required for long and was therefore sold; it became a showman's vehicle for a while, and at some stage the body became detached from the chassis. I first heard of the Chocolate Express bus, or at least the body of B6, almost to the day that I finished my restoration of the 1921 Todmorden Leyland G. I received a 'phone call from a colleague who had found an ex-Great Yarmouth Corporation 1920s Guy single decker on a farm near Norwich. He wanted to know if I knew where there were any mechanical parts for the Guy, as he wanted to bring it home to restore. Just as the 'phone call was finishing, he added: 'By the way, there's another old bus body with the Guy, which the farmer has told me to remove at the same time. It's a bit of an embarrassment because nobody wants it.' He told me that it was extremely difficult to find out what it was, as it was covered in corrugated iron, but the interior looked very similar to Prince Marshall's London Pirate Dennis, D142.

A 'Pirate' bus? I would love to own a 'Pirate', and indeed had come very near to it once when I found a similar body near Salisbury, though that had gone long ago. So off I went to Norwich the following weekend, and confirmed that it was definitely the lower deck of a London 'Pirate' bus, and almost certainly built by Dodson. It was not at all easy to see because of the cladding, but there were a number of 'tell-tale' signs, particularly around the driver's cab area. At some time it had been on fire at the rear off-side corner, and this had done some minor damage.

On going inside the shed I was delighted to see all the original fittings – brass handrails, interior lights, opening windows and even the trap doors in the floor for access to the rear axle, gearbox and cardan shaft brake. It had

ABOVE AND BELOW: *On the farm in Norfolk, the corrugated iron cladding helped to preserve the Dodson body.*

RIGHT: *Inside the body many of the fittings were still intact.*

ABOVE: *The white stallion took us straight to the Leyland S5.36hp engine in Ben Jordan's yard at Coltishall.*

RIGHT: *With cladding removed the body was clearly recognizable, though the rear offside corner had been badly damaged by fire.*

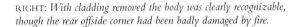

LEFT: *All we need are a few seats, and off we go!*

Rescuing the Engine

Sure enough, the following week a Leyland Freighter complete with a Hyab crane was there to pick up the body, and it was lifted on with no difficulty. Then, while the body was being tied down, quite amazingly an interested by-stander said: 'I know where there's an engine for that – just down the road in Ben Jordan's yard at Coltishall.' He described the engine to me, and we immediately sped off to the yard leaving the lorry to take the body back home. I had been to Ben Jordan's yard many years before with Michael Plunkett in search of a radiator for his Leyland Titan TD1. I well remember there being a 1930s single-decker body ex-Eastern Counties, absolutely stuffed full of TD1 radiators, Guys, Associated Daimlers, Tilling Stevens, in fact all sorts, and Michael was able to pick out the best one! Ben Jordan himself was quite a character – he didn't walk around his scrap yard, but had an enormous white stallion on which he rode through the yard, pointing to things with his cap. The stallion seemed to know its way around quite well, and was able to step around all the

been fitted out inside with benches and a whole series of timber pigeon-holes that had clearly been made from the timber decency boards from the upper deck. I immediately told my colleague that he need not be embarrassed any more, and that a lorry would be there the following week to pick it up.

different engines – Tilling Stevens, 1920s' Dennis and AECs – with no trouble. There were TD1s, TD2s and all sorts of interesting things in the yard. The stallion took us straight to the engine we were seeking, and sure enough, it was a Leyland S5.36/40hp engine; it looked rather sad, but it was absolutely complete. Unfortunately, however, it would not quite go in the boot of my car, so a pick-up truck was hired the following weekend and the engine safely rescued, together with some of the others aforementioned for

Barry Weatherhead. Even today there are some very early items remaining in Ben Jordan's yard.

Finding and Restoring a Chassis

The big problem now was, where could I find a chassis? (I seem to have been here before!) And as I discussed in Chapter 3, was it really worth restoring this body? There was still plenty of it there and very original, and certainly restorable, but whatever I did there was no way I was going to find its original chassis, or even another London Pirate

Leyland, as none existed. Should the body therefore be scrapped? I think not! If vehicles like these were not restored using authentic parts from other surviving and original chassis of virtually the same model, there would be hardly any pre-1925 buses in preservation. Some years ago I had obtained a few bits and pieces of an incomplete Leyland chassis that lay in a loft over a factory at Willment's Yard in Twickenham. Willment had operated a number of 'RAF types', and had even kept one back to restore, together with the

ABOVE: *The Willment chassis is lifted out of the loft.*

RIGHT: *It just came apart in my hands!*

The Barnet 'T'-type chassis buried up to the axles in concrete.

remains of another. These remains – the whole of the spare vehicle minus engine and radiator – were up in this attic and could be purchased – in fact, I finally swopped it for some photocopies of Leyland manuals! Fortunately there was a crane nearby, and having completed the transaction, the chassis was lifted down into the yard. Barry and I immediately set about dismantling it so that it would be easier to transport it home.

The chassis frame was a terrible mess – hardly worth having. It had started life as a petrol tanker for Red Line Motor Spirit, but had later been cut down and converted into a tipper for the contractor. It must have had a very hard life, as looking along the frame it

Welding the best parts of both chassis together, and filling up the ninety-six holes.

was shaped like a banana – the driver presumably had severe difficulty preventing the vehicle from just going round in circles – either that, or he had to be continually turning left! There were no fewer than ninety-six holes in the frame, which were completely superfluous, and all of these would have to be welded up.

We immediately set about getting the chassis frame into a usable condition – the holes were welded up and the frame straightened, and the back portion of the Barnet 'I type'

(remember, the one buried in concrete?) was welded onto the back to bring it back to its proper length with 15ft 10in (4.82m) wheelbase. The rest of the chassis was cleaned up, sand blasted and reassembled, together with the engine from Ben Jordan's yard, suitably renovated. This all sounds very simple in a few words, but there was a lot of work involved including lowering the top water manifold in order to make it suit the low-type radiator.

Finding and Restoring a Radiator

The only major mechanical part now missing was the radiator, and that would have to be made from scratch. Fortunately I was able to borrow some radiator parts to make into patterns allowing for the shrinkage of the molten LM6 aluminium, and the castings were then made and machined for the two tanks and side standards. This time there were 155 radiator tubes, each with 141 or so square gills – 21,850 in all. They each had to be threaded onto the tubes, one by one the right way round, and being square, *exactly* in line before being solder-dipped and then the tubes individually soldered into the tube plates. Fortunately Vic's wife, Doreen, liked knitting

while sitting in front of the television – well, threading gills on radiator tubes is pretty well much like knitting, isn't it? And there must be about as many stitches in a jumper as there are gills in a Chocolate Express radiator! A deal was done, and two weeks later the jumper, I mean radiator tubes, were delivered. Ironically, after the radiator was finished and the bus restored, an advertisement appeared in *Exchange & Mart*: 'Leyland Bus radiator, in Blackburn'. Having just done the Trans-Pennine Run, I drove the Chocolate Express from Harrogate to Leyland, via Blackburn, of course, and pulled up outside the three-bedroom semi. The owner was mowing his lawn and couldn't believe his eyes! He took me to the radiator in his garage and, lo and behold, it was identical to the one on the 'Choc Box' – just think of all that work that would have been saved, had I known about it sooner! Nevertheless, £50 changed hands, and the radiator did get used, though later, on the L&NWR char-a-bancs.

The Restoration of B6

Restoring the Body

At the same time as the chassis was being restored, work on the body – sitting on a spare 'RAF-type' chassis in my 'bus port' – was commenced. The first task was to remove the corrugated iron to see what lay beneath – and it was not a pretty sight: cobwebs, dry and wet rot, and the decayed skeleton of a dead rat. Some of the panels had been replaced by wooden boarding, and the full extent of the fire-damaged offside could be seen. All the windows were still intact, but the side framework was in a very bad state, and it was clear that most of the pillars would have to be replaced. The cant rails, although badly damaged with 4in (10cm) nails, were salvageable, and this was clearly good news. The roof sticks were good, and most of the ceiling boards only required minor repairs. The front bulkhead was sound, although all the horizontal rails had rotted at the ends where they met the pillars, and pieces would have to be let in.

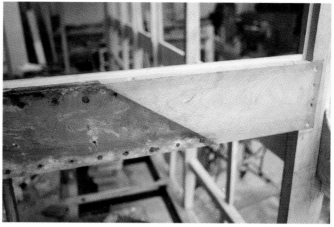

The bulkhead and roof were strung up to the roof of my 'bus-port' so the new side pillars could be fastened one by one. Matthew sits on the chassis.

New pieces are let in to repair damaged woodwork, with as much of the original as possible being retained.

ABOVE: *The framework now ready for panelling.*   *With the panels on, the body begins to take shape.*

The first task was to make the body sound, so ropes were tied around the bus roof and then taken up and attached to the roof of the bus-port. Each pillar was then sawn through, leaving the roof and front bulkhead dangling from the bus-port roof. It was then possible to build a new floor framework underneath the bus roof, and to fit in new pillars, one by one. The wheel arches, waist rail, light rail and panel rails were then fitted, and by May 1985, a year after starting, the basic framework was completed. The panels were then fitted, and once again the Chocolate Express started to look like a bus, although at that point the restoration work was less than 20 per cent complete. One of the worst jobs was tackled next: stripping off the old paint and repainting the ceiling boards.

Assembling the Chassis and Fittings

Returning to the chassis, the front springs of my Todmorden Leyland G had originally been set too high, so this was an excellent opportunity to have two new front springs made for the Todmorden G and transfer the re-set Todmorden springs to the Chocolate Express. With the springs, axles and wheels assembled to the chassis it was then a question of finding a decent set of tyres – what an awful problem that has been, far worse than with the solids, finding seven good

38 × 7 pneumatic tyres – these pneumatic balloons with bladders are nothing but bother! Eventually I found a set of six Goodrich tyres with diamond pattern tread, absolutely brand new and looking really good. The only problem was that on the London to Brighton Run, two of them actually burst and we had to limp home with just one wheel on

one side at the back. They had clearly been stored in poor conditions, and the canvas in the tyre walls had rotted.

As for the bonnet, well, do you remember those bonnets that were found in the brewery in Lancashire? Well, one of them fitted perfectly, the only problem being that one side of it had been lying on the ground and was badly rusted. I had it sand blasted,

very, very carefully, but when holding it up to the light, it looked like a star-filled sky! But it was a shame not to use it, so out came the filler and polyester spray, and now it looks as good as new.

The Metropolitan Police always insisted on engine and gearbox undertrays to protect the streets of London from splashes of oil and grease. The undertrays that came from the brewery in Leyland were not good enough to use, but they were useful for patterns, and yielded a number of important fittings that could be affixed to the new sheet metalwork; so Vic Elliott, a brilliant motor engineer who helped me with many of my restorations, fabricated a replacement undertray out of the cover of an old washing machine that he had just thrown out. I'm sure it said 'Zanussi' on it somewhere, though that will now have been painted over! The haul from the brewery also helped to provide mudguard stays, lamp brackets, many fittings for the petrol tank including taps and the right type of Leyland filter, chassis plates, hinges – in fact all sorts of things. However, some of the body fittings, such as the 'spider'-shaped signal bell and mechanisms, the

TOP: *Assembling the chassis in my garage in exceedingly cramped conditions.*

ABOVE: *Now, which bonnet or undertray shall I pick? Some of the huge pile of rusty tin that came from the brewery in Lancashire.*

RIGHT: *This original bonnet fitted perfectly.*

rear lamp on the body and the destination stencil indicators, had to be made; though at that time I was attending metalwork classes on Tuesday evenings, which came in very handy for making many of these myself. The fares board, on which there are some 5,400 letters and numbers, each individually put on with

TOP: *Nearing completion in winter 1986 underneath the open bus-port, with young Ricky learning how the engine works!*

ABOVE: *Trying out the driving seat for size.*

RIGHT: *The first trip out onto the road, on a really dreadful day.*

Letraset, has been started but the job has not yet been finished. One other important bit of equipment was the 'pruning' saw, affixed to the ceiling over the driver's head, and one of the correct type was very difficult to find. After asking around for some time I found one in a very old-fashioned ironmonger's shop in Bletchley. The saw was a Metropolitan Police requirement, its intended use being to saw through the lifeguards between the wheels to get at anybody you might have run over! Presumably there had been a serious accident in London that had sparked off this bright idea!

The Paintwork

Next came a major disaster: the chocolate-coloured paintwork that had been so painstakingly applied (six coats, all carefully rubbed down between coats), broke out in microblisters: they were popping up everywhere, so badly that the surface began to feel like sandpaper. The paint representative who came to have a look confirmed the worst: the whole lot had to come off, right back to bare metal, as damp had got in at some stage of the painting. This is just the sort of problem that the amateur has to suffer when restoring vehicles in poor working conditions, almost out in the open. The only way to paint a vehicle properly is either in the heat of the summer or in a properly heated workshop and not to leave very long between coats. The offending paint had to be removed with paint stripper before it could be rubbed down and the work started afresh. What a terrible waste of time and effort!

Having made the seats, a suitable moquette was found and applied not only to the seat cushions but also to the lower deck interior lining panels – some of these 'Pirate' buses were very well appointed in order to attract passengers from the London General. The original signwriting and gold leaf on the front bulkhead proclaiming the ownership by The Chocolate Express Omnibus Co. Ltd, and also the two makers' signwritten boards on each side on the bulkhead, are

magnificent to behold. They have been copied exactly, and if you ever get to see the bus, do please have a look – they are really excellent! And I trust that everyone who sees the bus will get as much pleasure from looking at it as I have had in restoring it. I sincerely hope it is a fitting tribute to Arthur Partridge and all that he achieved – possibly the memory will

not dwindle away as Mr Poole once feared that it would.

An Outright Winner

Finished just in time for the 1987 London to Brighton Run, again with wet paint drying on the Saturday whilst driving it to the start, the Chocolate Express Leyland LB5 had a successful run, albeit with some major magneto

At the start of the 1987 Brighton Run, complete with white-walled tyres.

ABOVE: *Photographed by D.W.K. Jones on the 1988 Brighton Run. He had previously photographed the same bus in 1933, fifty-five years earlier!*

BELOW: *The Chocolate Express Leyland LB5 won many major prizes.*

problems at the half-way stage; however, we made it. That year it took every prize that it could – six firsts, including the outright winner in the Concours – and the following year it was runner-up. With two major restorations of Leylands then under my belt, I was successful in getting into the finals of the Scania/Transport Trust Award Scheme, a most prestigious event. Out of the twelve finalists it then came second overall, chosen from some pretty impressive restoration projects, not only of road vehicles, but aircraft, railways and boats/ships. This happy result was rewarded with a most enjoyable dinner attended by Prince Michael of Kent, followed by a trip to Sweden and a monetary prize. Several other prizes

ABOVE: *Runner-up in the Scania/Transport Trust Award scheme, with Prince Michael of Kent.*

LEFT: *The Team, from left to right: Vic Elliott, Mike Street, Mike Sutcliffe, Steve Wootton and Rob Andrews, at Brighton in 1987.*

Specification – the Leyland LB5	
Operator	The Chocolate Express Omnibus Co., No. B6, registered XU 7498, new August 1924
Model	Leyland LB5
Chassis No.	12920
Engine	Four-cylinder, 36hp, Model S5, built by Leyland, No. E16457 (14/5/24)
Body	Dodson, 48 seats (26 outside, 22 inside)
Length	25ft 11in (7.9m)
Width	7ft 2in (2.19m)
Height	12ft 10in (3.92m)
Weight	5 tons 5cwt 3qtr (5,372kg)

have been won with the 'Chocolate Express', too. Furthermore it was featured on the television *Top Gear* programme in 1987; and its most recent film appearance was briefly in *All The King's Men*, the story of the soldiers from the Sandringham estate during World War One, starring David Jason. What a magnificent vehicle this bus is!

RIGHT: *The pruning saw.*

FAR RIGHT: *The signal bell, made from scratch.*

BELOW: *Christopher Dodson maker's 'transfer'.*

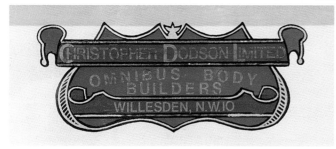

RIGHT: *The driving compartment.*

ABOVE: *Interior with 'Beware of Pickpockets – Male & Female'.*

RIGHT: *The ornate Dodson paintwork in gold leaf.*

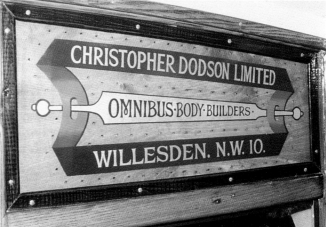

ABOVE: *Upper-deck rain covers.*   RIGHT: *The 'Zanussi' engine undertray.*

CHAPTER TWELVE

The Todmorden Tiger TS6

Once we have completed the Barnsley & District 'Combination Car' (in 2005/06?), the next planned restoration is of a different type of Leyland, rather more modern – in fact, ten years newer than the Chocolate Express. There had been a revolutionary change in design, in lower chassis frames and in the oil engine (diesel, in modern parlance) – so why is this of interest to Mike Sutcliffe? Well, as already mentioned, I am interested in all buses and coaches up to about 1968: after this, with the demise of the half-cab, the coming of the National Bus Company and the mass destruction of the original municipal operators, the face of the bus world changed. Up to 1968 my interest diminishes as time progresses – although I have fond memories of my younger days in Todmorden, and well remember the Leyland Tiger TS6 operating in service as a towbus – need I say more!

We have already looked at the early history of Todmorden Corporation, and as mentioned earlier, the undertaking became jointly owned with the LMS Railway on 1 January 1931. One of the most elaborate of coats of arms ever applied to buses adorned each side of every Todmorden bus, and this is reproduced here, clearly showing the LMS crest. The whole fleet, which at its maximum was forty vehicles, was equally divided, with each bus being owned by either the Corporation or the LMS; No. 15, YG 7831 – my Tiger TS6 – was owned by the Corporation throughout its life.

Todmorden Corporation, followed by Todmorden Joint Omnibus Committee, were always loyal to Leyland Motors right from the start in 1907, and for the whole time that Leyland were building their own bodies, from about 1910 to 1954, they religiously

One of the first photographs that I took was of the Todmorden Tiger TS6 as converted to a towbus.

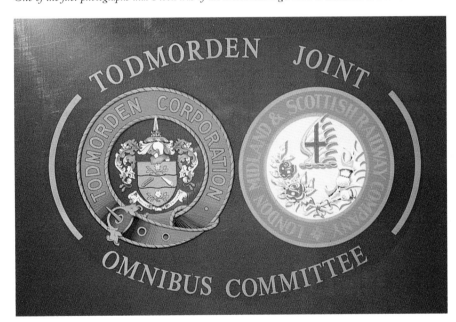

Todmorden Joint Omnibus Committee coats of arms, surely one of the most attractive in the country.

bought Leyland bodies – most of the time. One exception was in 1934 when the Leyland body-building shop was experiencing a major trauma. Having recently introduced metal-framed bodies, all previous framework having been of ash, it all went wrong because there were faults in the metal-framed designs; this

entailed the recall and rebuilding of many of the metal-framed bodies (the tale of this is described very well in the booklet *The Great Disaster* written by Ron Phillips and published by the PSV Circle). In 1934 Todmorden JOC needed four new buses and purchased two Titan TD3s and two Tiger TS6s, but had to go to Northern

The only picture I have seen of a Todmorden Tiger TS6 in service is this rather poor copy taken during the war.

Counties at Wigan for the bodies to be built. These were to the standard timber-framed (composite) Northern Counties design at the time, and were delivered in June 1934.

Service History of the Todmorden Tiger

No. 15 did not have a very long life in service as a saloon bus, due to the fact that Todmorden JOC were gradually replacing their single-decker fleet with double deckers. It was withdrawn in 1941, and was left unused in the garage for some time, its diesel engine removed to keep another vehicle on the road, as spare parts were difficult to come by in the war. Around 1945 it was decided to convert the bus to a break-down vehicle, or 'towbus' as it was called in Todmorden. Its chassis was cut and shortened, thereby removing one of the two propshafts, and also the back portion of the frame was removed. The front portion of the bus body was retained, to provide seating accommodation and a small workshop for the fitters, and the entrance position was transferred to the front. A Harvey Frost crane was mounted on the back. A petrol engine was fitted, possibly from bus No. 17, and from then

onwards the vehicle ran on trade plates. In October 1951, as other vehicles were withdrawn, an oil engine became available – the 8.6 litre engine which had been removed from Titan TD5 No. 24.

As a towbus the Tiger had an extremely long life, an incredible forty-two years' service. It remained with Todmorden until after the Calderdale Joint Omnibus Committee was formed in August 1971, after which the crane was removed and it was sold to

Jack Mulley of Ixworth, West Suffolk for continued use as a towbus. I tried to buy the Tiger from Jack Mulley on two occasions, but felt that he wanted far too much for it. Time went by, and by 1987 it was sold to a Mr B. Reynolds of Bardwell Hall, a couple of miles from Ixworth. Mr Reynolds was a dealer, although he had some interest in older vehicles, but after a year under cover the space was needed, and the Tiger was put outside to graze (or should I say to rot away).

Rescuing the Tiger

I was unaware of its whereabouts for some time, but a few years later, by coincidence, a letter was published in Gavin Booth's excellent *Classic Bus* magazine asking about the whereabouts of any surviving Todmorden buses. I replied with the details of those vehicles I knew about, and questioned what had happened to the Tiger TS6 with Mulley. Someone kindly replied, saying that it was at Bardwell Hall, and I thought to myself 'It's now or never...'. Pat and I jumped in the car and went to West Suffolk, where we found Bardwell Hall, and the Tiger sitting in the back of the yard looking very forlorn. A price was agreed, and we were there the following week with a low loader to bring it home.

The towbus at the end of its life in Todmorden after it had lost its Harvey-Frost crane.

The plan now is to restore it to a full-sized bus, as it will then stand a much better chance of continued preservation than it would if it were converted back to a towbus. I was fortunate enough to find an ex-East Midland Motor Services Tiger TS7 chassis that will help me to repair the frame and return it to its proper length, and also provide the missing propshaft. I expect to start this work as

RIGHT: *Layers of paintwork removed to reveal its original identity.*

BELOW: *My two Todmorden buses meet. They never met in service, as the Leyland G was withdrawn six years before the Tiger was built!*

soon as the Barnsley & District 'Combination Car' is finished – so again, watch this space!

Life is full of coincidences – some would say luck – nevertheless I believe that in life you make your own luck! It seems poetic that the very first bus that I restored (the little Chevrolet LQ) came from Jack Mulley at Ixworth, and probably the last that I will be able to restore (the Tiger TS6) also came from him. Another coincidence is that the first of my major Leyland restorations originally came from Todmorden, as will the last, the Todmorden Tiger!

Specification – Leyland Tiger TS6	
Operator	Todmorden Joint Omnibus Committee, No. 15, registered YG 7831, new June 1934 (owned by Todmorden Corporation)
Model	Leyland Tiger TS6
Chassis No.	4829
Engine	Six-cylinder oil engine, Model E136, 8.6ltr, built by Leyland, No. 13465 (originally fitted to Titan TD5 No. 24, new January 1940)
Body	Northern Counties M.E., thirty-six-seater, rear entrance, single decker
Length	27ft 6in (8.38m)
Width	7ft 6in (2.3m)
Height	9ft 5in (2.87m)
Weight	Approx. 6½ tons (6,604kg)

CHAPTER THIRTEEN

The Ones that Got Away!

I have so far recovered the remains of fifty-two Leylands, plus some other makes, and it would be too laborious to detail them all here. I will, however, comment on a few of the more interesting aspects and anecdotes relating to some of them.

In addition to all those Leylands, I purchased a little 1929 Chevrolet LQ lorry around 1972, only to sell it nine years later. Having decided to dispose of it, it was advertised in *Exchange & Mart* and a buyer was quickly found. The only trouble was that the advert right next to it in *Exchange & Mart* was for the sale of a 1919 Karrier WDS (War Department Subvention) chassis registered in Bradford, AK 6063. This Karrier was on solids, and had been the subject of a major restoration that had not been quite finished. I couldn't resist buying it, as it was the only surviving Karrier from World War One, and I planned to build a full sized char-a-bancs body

on it. That, however, was not to be, and as I have now been able to restore a full-sized Leyland char-a-bancs that is much more authentic and original, I plan to dispose of the Karrier.

In 1986, a very attractive 1918 Crossley 20/25hp chassis became available locally, and this ended up in The Sutcliffe Collection. It had been a light tender, used by the RAF during 'the Troubles' in Ireland – again, it was partly restored and it was the intention to build a new four-seater open tourer 'RAF Staff Car' body on it to replace my Swift tourer. However, one can only do so much, and the restoration of the buses continued to take priority, particularly as they were much bigger – I like to have something to get my teeth into! Although it would have been a lot of work, the Crossley was also not to be, and so I sold it recently to a man whom I am sure will do a good job on it. A derelict 1927 Clyno 12/28 saloon car came

my way and was ultimately passed on, as was the second 'RAF type' from Willment of Twickenham. The Imperial War Museum at Duxford was looking for an 'RAF-type' chassis to put under a very original First War workshop body that had been found in Lincolnshire – very nice it is too, and still with all the original tools and equipment. The ex-Willment chassis therefore went to Duxford and, as it had been converted to pneumatics, I was able to also pass on the solid-tyred disc wheels and axles from the Barnet Leyland 'I type' – remember, the one buried in concrete!

Side-Types and Harems

Having always had a soft spot for the Leyland side-types of the 1920s, I rescued the remains of four Leyland SQ2 6- to 7-tonners, from Dartford, Carterton, Gloucester and Barnsley – all of which could have been put together to

The first of the Leyland SQ2s, Dartford.

The Barnsley Leyland SQ2 – what a state!

make two good vehicles. Also, a Dyson trailer came along, together with two very attractive 'lift' containers with their 'herringbone' boarding, and complete with 'greedy boards' (hinged boards on top of the roof that enable more luggage to be accommodated on top of the 'lift'). As the restoration proceeded on my Leyland buses, I had to make decisions on priorities, as I was quickly running out of space and money; and so all these SQ2s were sold in the first major rationalization of the Sutcliffe Fleet. I also sold the 'RAF-type' chassis from Shenley, which had yielded solid-tyred wheels for the 'Charabus', to Stephen Hubbuck, who is doing an absolutely splendid job restoring a rebuilt Subsidy 'RAF type' that had once belonged to the Stoneham Motor Co. near Southampton. The Eastbourne Aviation-built body of his saloon bus was recovered from a timber yard at Ringwood, near Bounemouth. I well remember going to see it with Barry Weatherhead, long before it had been recovered by Stephen, where it sat on a World War One Ryker 'Locomobile' chassis. It is reputed, no doubt with great accuracy, that the owner of the yard once had a harem, and at one time all of his ladies lived in the Stoneham bus body – just how true this is, or whether there is an element of exaggeration, I suppose we will never know! (You may think this is far-fetched, but I well remember seeing a photograph of three Star Flyer Harem Wagons, supplied to a wealthy Arab sheik.)

There is, of course, the ex-Ribble Motor Services, Leyland Lion LT2 of 1931, that we found in a wood near Windsor, and rescued about twenty-five years ago. We will probably never have the time to restore it, but at least it is saved, and hopefully someone will come forward to take it off our hands and do a proper job on it.

The Bus in a House

This was followed in the summer of 1980 by one of the stranger, and seemingly more bizarre exploits of the 'intrepid duo'. Michael Plunkett had taken me to the site at Purley Park, near Reading, in the 1960s to see some of the old buses being used as caravans. It was an amazing sight, with row upon row of elderly buses, mainly dating back to the 1920s. There were no fewer than three Maidstone & District Tilling Stevens B9As all together; across the road was a Western National Leyland Tiger of 1929, still with its original body and enormous fleet name along its side; a Guy six-wheeler with three floor levels and a veranda; Lions and Lionesses; and a Bristol B 'Superbus'. Around

The Ribble Leyland Lion LT2, woken up from its sleep in the woods.

the corner was a very interesting old bus with an aged lady occupant, and this turned out to be a Dennis 2½ ton of about 1923. It was one of a small batch bought by Greyhound of Bristol, to open up the very first long-distance coach service in the country, between Bristol and London. These Dennises had Strachan & Brown bodies and ran on large, spoked, cushion-tyred wheels. If ever an important coach was to be found and restored, it was that one; but a few weeks later it was gone, burnt by the gypsies.

In that summer of 1980, Michael, Barry and I were in the Purley Park having a good 'sniff around'. Having been to see three ex-London General B-type double-decker bus bodies in some woods near Reading, we drove around the area and stopped outside a bungalow called 'Takiteezee': it was a tidy house, with a large, well kept garden, and another chalet bungalow standing in the middle of the orchard. We looked at each other: 'There's a bus inside that bungalow,' I said; 'I'm going to knock and ask.' The others waited patiently in the car while I knocked on the door and cheekily asked, 'Excuse me, but is there a bus inside your house?' (What an obvious question for anyone to ask!) The owner, surprised at the question, answered: 'Yes, come and have a look.' I beckoned to the other two, and we were escorted round to the back of the bungalow. A panel had been removed, and there for all to see, was a solid-tyred front wheel. After some scratching about in the dirt – we were all used to that! – the initials 'LML' appeared: yes, it was another Leyland! Could it be an 'RAF type' like mine? I needed some more wheels – or even a pre-World War One model? How could we find out?

It transpired that the owner, an elderly man in his seventies, used to live

ABOVE: *'Takiteezee' – obvious, isn't it? The trained eye will instantly recognize this as a 1920s single-decker bus – with bay windows, pitched roof, veranda and half-timbered cladding added for disguise. Note the five ventilator windows below the eaves – they are the giveaway!*

LEFT: *The rear of the 'chalet-bus', with Leyland solid-tyred front wheel. The offside front window and bulkhead behind the driver can clearly be seen behind the ladder. Barry Weatherhead, disturbed from his demolition work, looks out from the lounge (after knocking the wall out!), and Marc thoroughly enjoys the demolition work.*

in the bus. He had subsequently bought the bungalow next door and moved into that, and let the 'chalet-bus' to holidaymakers. But recently the County Council had ordered its demolition, which presented the old man with a problem: how to get rid of it? Well, he should look no further! We managed to persuade him to put his sledgehammer down before he wrecked any more of it, and to leave it to the three of us – now demolition experts. (We have incidentally demolished four houses in order to extract vehicles!) We arrived the following week with the necessary tools, and bit by bit the house was dismantled: first the pitched roof, immaculately built over the vehicle with proper tiles; next the wooden veranda; and then the chimney stack – yes, the lounge had a brick-built fireplace right in the centre of the vehicle. This was followed by the two bedrooms at the back of the bus, together with an extension to the rear of the chassis frame.

Gradually the bus emerged – but what was it? The roof cross-member over the kitchen portion was covered in a black, greasy film, but one could still read 'Spitting is Forbidden' – some people really do have some nasty habits – in the kitchen of all places! The next roof sticker said 'To stop Car push Bell once only' – what a find!

As we got nearer to the ground the back wheels emerged, and the chassis frame. The frame was very long and flitched, and it soon became obvious that it was a Daimler Y type, built in February 1916. Further research showed that it had once belonged to the East Kent Road Car Co., being re-registered FN 6050 after reconditioning. However, at some stage it had obviously acquired some Leyland front wheels, and these were to come in very useful later. The body turned out to be off an Associated Daimler 415 chassis that had operated for the United Automobile Services. To cut a long story short, we managed to winch the vehicle out, across planks carefully placed so as not to damage the lawn, and we brought it home. We still own these remains, and are currently looking for someone who may want them to restore.

At a later stage Barry and I went to rescue the mechanical parts from a very early AEC/ADC(?) from a yard near Shaftesbury. The bus had once carried a Dodson body, and had operated for the firm of White's in South Wales. White had a large number of AECs in the 1920s and early 1930s.

The Bus Too Far

In 1990, when enquiring about some 1920s' Leyland mudguards that a man in Yorkshire had for sale, I asked him

Looking out of the hole in the wall. On the left is the body framework (offside) with the lounge extension and brick-built fireplace. Being used as a home frequently means that alterations have been made, but this is sometimes a small price to pay for the vehicle's ultimate survival!

After all the building materials have been removed, the remains of the vehicle. Compare this with the photograph of the building before demolition work commenced.

how he knew they were definitely Leyland. He replied that he used to have the lorry that they came off, and in fact he still had its original bus body that had been removed to convert the vehicle into a lorry in 1930! Pat and I went up to Knottingley to have a look, to discover that it was a saloon bus body of 1925, built by Barnaby of Hull, and still carrying the original livery of East Yorkshire Motor Services. The body rested on three RSJs let into the wall of the garage, about 12ft (3.6m) in the air, so that lorries could be driven underneath it. A long stepladder went up to the body that had been in use for many years as an office – dry stored for sixty years! So the body was available, but how could we get it down? We do get ourselves into some real pickles!

We returned home, and after a number of telephone calls were offered the use of two forklift trucks, free of charge and with drivers, provided we could transport them the 9 miles to Knottingley. No problem! Another series of telephone calls found a friendly company with a low-loader, and everything was set for a week on Friday. Pat and I booked ourselves into the local hotel on the Thursday afternoon, and I made a telephone call to the low-loader firm to confirm that everything was still OK. But it was *far* from OK, as the firm had been declared bankrupt that very day and the liquidator had seized all the assets, including the low-loader. This was very depressing news indeed – what could we possibly do to find another low-loader in such a short time, bearing in mind that the job was to be done on Friday at the latest?

We jumped in the car and drove all around the area looking for haulage companies, with absolutely no success – there just didn't seem to be any about. However, at one point we passed the gates of a firm called Plasmor, who make concrete building blocks: they have an enormous fleet of very smart eight-wheeler Fodens, and I did happen to notice in the corner of their yard, a Foden tractor unit with a low-loader trailer. We made a quick 'U' turn, but the premises were closed. The next morning, at first light, we were back at the yard, and drove up to the office block. I asked to speak to the transport manager and told him of our plight. I think he uttered the word 'No' about three times, but I wasn't listening! I persisted with my story, and suddenly realized that his stance was weakening: well, they weren't very busy that day, and if I could hang on till lunchtime, the lorry could be made available (and for a sensible price, too) – excellent!

The appointed time came, and from then on everything went like clockwork. The forklift trucks arrived and got into position alongside the body, one at each end, and with fork extensions fitted. Together they lifted the body off the RSJs, which were then cut by gas and lowered to the floor. The body was lowered gently down and taken outside ready to load up onto a wagon to bring it home the next day.

The Barnaby body, still in East Yorkshire colours, dry-stored for sixty years.

Pat's garden shed – a 1910 tram from York, built by Brush. You can almost hear the whine of the electric motors!

I knew of an appropriate Leyland C-type chassis that could be used for the restoration (it had originally been a tower wagon for Leicester City Tramways – No.2), and so this was duly purchased and the body put on the chassis. Restoration was started: but then it all had to be put on ice while we moved house and started on the Leyland X2 restoration. And finally, in 2001, we came to the decision that there is really only so much you can do in this life, and that one must be realistic about what is achievable in order not to 'short-change' the other important projects; in short, Pat and I decided that this was likely to be the 'bus too far'. Some of the chassis components of the Leyland C type would supply the missing bits for the restoration of the Barnsley & District 'Combination Car', and the garage space was very much needed. So very reluctantly we decided to sell the East Yorkshire body, and it has now gone to a new home, back in Yorkshire, where hopefully the new owner will restore it as a bus.

The Garden Shed

When we moved to Valley Forge we built two large garden sheds in addition to the garages. One was designated as the workshop, and the other as the garden shed, particularly as Pat is a very keen gardener, and somewhere was needed for all the garden tools and suchlike. However, this did not last long, as it is also important to store paint tins and so on away from garages housing old buses because of the potential fire risk; so guess where they ended up! Realizing that these paint tins were multiplying as the weeks went by, Pat said that the next time we acquire an old bus body, she would like to have it in the garden as a store shed.

Amazingly, the very next evening I received a telephone call from a man in York who wanted to part with a tramcar body. It had been operated by York City Tramways from about 1910, and was still in its York blue-and-white livery, albeit the lower saloon only. It was absolutely ideal, and in extremely good condition considering that it had been out of use for about sixty-five years. The car was built by Brush of Loughborough under sub-contract from British Thompson Houston at Rugby, and was built to a very high specification with double sliding doors at each end. A deal was struck and the man towed it all the way from York to Valley Forge at Tottenhoe on a trailer behind an ex-London taxi – he hardly got out of second gear all the way! The tram is now situated next to our driveway at Valley Forge, and is a pleasure to look at every time we pass it. This tram is not really one that got away, as the title of the chapter would suggest, but we don't propose to install an operating tramway along the drive, and so are not planning to restore it. It has, however, been saved for posterity, and when we both leave Valley Forge in our wooden boxes, hopefully someone will save it and make it run again.

CHAPTER FOURTEEN

The Future – Where Next?

So, where do we go from here? With the Barnsley & District 'Combination Car' currently undergoing restoration, and the Todmorden Tiger TS6 yet to do, with my previous track record I would estimate that the Tiger will be finished around the year 2008/09 – assuming that my excellent team of helpers will be able to continue with me, and of course, that I can carry on working and providing the income to enable the projects to be financed. After that, who knows? There will still be a lot of work re-restoring bits that I'm now not satisfied with – for example, the Charabus window frames – and finishing off certain parts, such as the Chocolate Express and Wellingborough vehicles' fares boards. There will, of course, also be on-going maintenance – when the restoration of a bus is completed it becomes an enormous liability – to keep it clean and polished, and in a roadworthy condition. The more I restore, the more work I make for myself! It is my intention however, that *all* the Leylands are capable of being started and driven out at any time. They are always kept taxed and insured for road use, as this is what they were always intended for. Static exhibits in museums are very nice, but it is so much better to see them running, to hear the sounds they make, the various smells they make, and, of course, to feel them come to life again. There are those who would say that a 'national treasure' like the 1908

OPPOSITE PAGE:
TOP: *Regular maintenance of the restored vehicles is absolutely essential to keep them in proper running order. So the more I restore, the more work I create for myself: is this really sensible?!*

BOTTOM: *Cleaning the buses ready for the next summer season – always a big job, especially with so much brass to polish.*

Leyland X2 is a very valuable and delicate piece of our national heritage, which should not be worn out or damaged by using it on the road. This may be correct, particularly if it were owned and operated by a national museum, where possibly the interest and dedication of the individuals let loose on the vehicle was not as great as my own personal dedication. I have seen early vehicles damaged in museums by people who do not fully understand the vehicles. My dedication will only last as long as I do, or am capable of operating the buses and keeping them up to scratch. And after that …?

The Valley Forge 'Crank-Up'

To this end, Pat and I hold an annual open day known as the Valley Forge 'crank-up and barbecue', and by the time this book comes to publication we will be in our ninth year of open days. Unfortunately this has to be by invitation only, as we can only accommodate about a hundred people at our premises. It is basically a relaxed social event to which we invite enthusiasts and visiting vehicles – for example, Barry Weatherhead's K type or Tilling Stevens petrol electric, the Tate & Lyle McCurd, Fraser Clayton's Cheetah, David Powell's Todmorden PD2 and Miles Glen's Bournemouth PS2 – and we generally have a good get-together with early vehicles. The highlights of the day include trips round the local villages with vehicles going in opposite directions, where you can see the other buses coming towards you for quite a long distance – this always causes a great deal of excitement, with honking of bulb-horns/blowing of exhaust whistles, and a merry time is had by all. These events will continue as long as we are able to hold them, and as long as we get pleasure in oper-

ating the buses, as well as attending rallies all over the country.

We also cater for personal or society visits to come and see the vehicles – we are always pleased to see people and show them around and these visits occur several times each year. However, this has to be by prior arrangement, as we run a very busy business from home, and for obvious reasons that has to be. Recently we had a visit from the Nottingham branch of the Omnibus Society, who arrived in a large coach. One of the members wrote to thank us for the visit and commented that 'the visit was the best day of his life'. It is so nice to know that the restoration of these vehicles gives so much pleasure to others. This is also evident when driving to rallies, when so many people, particularly older people (even though they would not remember my vehicles in service), stop and look at the buses with a smile from ear to ear.

I have often heard it said that the Leyland buses in my possession are 'safe' and 'in good hands' – and yes, they are, but this only applies as long as *I* last, or am able to look after them properly! What will happen after that? Just because they are historically unique and a 'national treasure' does not necessarily secure their future. A number of early vehicles have come to grief once they have left the hands of their original owner – the person who lovingly restored and cherished them. Examples of these are now becoming numerous: for instance, Jack Mulley's Gilford AS6, Bob York's little Albion bus, formerly belonging to a convent, Mr Goodey's Ryker/Locomobile with early London Bus body (though this is not a genuine bus), and the Glasgow Omnibus Co. Metcalfe-bodied AEC Renown. At least three of these buses have decayed so badly that they

THE VALLEY FORGE CRANK-UP AND BBQ

Some pictures which capture the atmosphere and operating of the vehicles together.

The 'meeting of the buses', viewed from inside Fraser Clayton's immaculate Leyland Cheetah. (Alan Townsin)

Barry Weatherhead cranks his London General K type.

ABOVE: *Three bonneted buses meet. You can almost hear them say, 'Have you heard about the latest vehicle rescued …?'*

RIGHT: *Luxury coaches old and 'new'.*

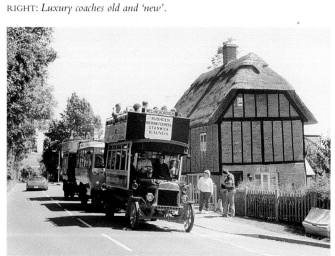

The 'Wellingborough' sets off from Valley Forge.

A study of front ends, parked up at one of our outings to a local narrow-gauge railway.

may never be restored again (what an utter waste!). One of them was actually purchased at auction by its new owner for over £40,000, and this just goes to show that even when serious money is spent on them, it doesn't guarantee their future! With all of these vehicles, they simply cannot be replaced – it is not as though, like a Bristol RE or London Transport RM, there is another just around the corner – there are simply no other survivors!

It is my view, depressing as it may seem, that as my generation of vehicle restorers gradually disappears, so will many of their vehicles. There are simply not enough youngsters coming along with an interest in the *older* vehicles. There are plenty of 1960s and later buses being preserved, and in greater and greater numbers, but these are the vehicles that their owners remember in service, or are slightly older, and these are the vehicles they prefer. There are too few dedicated enthusiasts who will go back further in time, to restore or even re-restore the earlier buses.

This is also a tendency at some major bus museums for some of the older restored vehicles, and indeed unrestored buses, to take second place to Daimler Fleetlines, Bristol REs, Metropolitans, and so on. Some even get put outside to deteriorate further to make way for these 'modern' buses. Good undercover accommodation for such big vehicles is always at a premium, and several major museums allow duplicate and triplicate examples of the more modern buses to overwhelm the available accommodation. The people in charge of these museums – meaning the trustees – have a duty to ensure that a proper balance is achieved, so that future generations can enjoy seeing a representative 'national collection' of buses and coaches, going back to the early days. As said in Chapter 3, everyone is entitled to preserve and run their pride and joy – nobody should try and take anything away from that – but we have the situation where sometimes virtually whole batches of vehicles have been 'preserved'. There will be, and has to be, a great shake-out of these over time – let it not be the earlier vehicles that suffer, as there are too few of them.

The 'Headache'

So, what is going to happen to the Leyland buses in 'The Mike Sutcliffe Collection'? This is quite a headache, and a problem that is discussed by Pat and myself virtually every week of every year. It has been recommended to me by senior staff of the Science Museum that I should dispose of the Leylands during my lifetime, so that I can have some measure of control as to where they go; and also to benefit me financially, to recompense me for all the effort and money that I have put into them. But could I bring myself to do that? I found it exceedingly difficult to part with the little Chev coach, and other 'surplus' vehicles, on the two occasions I thinned out my collection. If I don't manage to achieve this, all of the buses will have to be disposed of when I die, and they could end up anywhere, purely for financial gain.

If I do dispose of them, where would this be to, and how? I suppose the two extremes are these: one – I sell each of them at auction, and for the highest price; as opposed to two: I give them all away to a museum or

ABOVE: *The original Totternhoe AA sign, now fixed to 'Valley Forge'.*

RIGHT: *The 'Hippo in the hall' – one of the forty radiators.*

Some of the large collection of Leyland badges.

The oldest restored British-built motor bus. (Bob Kell)

organization that can't afford to buy them, but would give them a good home. However, even with this second scenario, what I deem to be the best possible home may not have the room, and may not want them or the responsibility that they will attract in terms of maintenance and upkeep – this is a very, very difficult problem! I do believe that my collection is of 'national importance' to this country's heritage, and I would like to think that the vehicles could all be kept together – possibly Heritage Lottery Funding may be the answer, to extend an existing museum and buy the eight vehicles. One thing is for certain, it would be an enormous wrench to part with the vehicles, and something that I may never be able to do – who knows? For the time being, this will have to remain an enormous unanswered question.

The same applies to a lesser extent to my collection of photographs, books, documents, badges, radiators and other commercial vehicle ephemera, which must amount to one of the largest personal collections. These will also have to be found a home one day, and I don't envy the job of the person who is going to have to deal with it! I do, however, keep most of it very well filed and documented.

Over the next two or three decades I would personally like to learn more and more about the history of bus operations and vehicles operated in the first half of the twentieth century (not

just Leylands!), and to help and support the preservation movement, either on a personal basis or through organizations of which I am a member.

It is encouraging to see that, over the fifty years of the bus preservation movement, the hobby has continued to grow, and provided that people have money in their pocket and time for leisure pursuits, the interest will grow further. There are more and more rallies, and museums go from strength to strength with both their establishments and exhibits (I think that Crich Tramway Museum is the shining example to all; also Amberley Working Museum has worked wonders on a negligible budget). It has been suggested that there should be a National Bus Museum, though I am not personally convinced that this is the correct way to go. By far the most important asset of any vehicle museum is its regular supporters, who give their time and enthusiasm free of charge. Without this, a museum is doomed – look at the experience of the Transperience debacle in Bradford, where millions of pounds were pumped into a 'clinical' and uninteresting project, badly conceived and poorly administered. Lottery and other funding is best spent developing and encouraging existing museum projects, which can then go from strength to strength, as we have seen at Crich.

It is also heartening that organizations such as The Transport Trust and

the National Association of Road Transport Museums (NARTM) are developing and becoming stronger, thereby helping the sector to grow in an organized way. One other organization that was started only recently is The Leyland Society, with about 600 members, formed to promote the study and preservation of Leyland vehicles. As with my own collection of Leyland buses, it is guaranteed to pass on the knowledge and experience of Leylands for future generations to enjoy. Leyland Motors were the undisputed leaders for excellence in their day, and I am proud to own and operate this collection of magnificent buses: 'The Mike Sutcliffe Collection'.

> " ——— opportunity comes once in every man's life; whatever your walk in life, however humble, however monotonous and routine, be sure of this; train yourself and prepare to seize it when it comes; if you are not ready when opportunity knocks this once it will pass you and leave you in your rut, at your office desk, for ever."
>
> *A. G. Partridge.*

Sid Poole, who was there and wrote about the last day of The Chocolate Express Omnibus Company in 1934, planned to write a book on Chocolate Express and the 'Pirate' operators in London. His manuscript, which still exists, was unfortunately never put into print. He had the foresight to ask Arthur Partridge to put into words his philosophy on life and this is reproduced here. It totally mirrors my own outlook on life.

Some Important Organizations

The National Association of Road Transport Museums (NARTM)

NARTM was formed by a group of UK museums and larger private collections to promote a unified approach to issues facing these groups, and to act as a lobbying body to various authorities with whom its members inevitably come into contact. It meets two or three times a year at members' locations on a cyclical basis, with one or two representatives from each member.

The association is involved with the on-going development of a database of preserved buses, and during the last four years this has grown to a comprehensive listing of over 2,500 buses and coaches: that is, about 50 per cent of the vehicles in preservation. The details cover most of the existing museums and the larger private collections, and the database is growing all the time – it is envisaged that smaller collections and even individual buses will be added as time goes by. NARTM is a substantial partner with Ian Allan Publishing in the production of *Buses Restored*, an annual book that lists preserved buses in museums and collections throughout the UK and Ireland, many of which are not themselves NARTM members, and each year the book has proved to be a best seller in its field.

A sub-group of NARTM has brought the bus and coach preservation movement to the forefront of transport preservation bodies in that it has developed a scoring system to identify the more important buses and coaches that have been saved for posterity. The application of this system will enable candidate vehicles to be selected to form a 'National Collection' of the most important vehicles, and this can be used to advise funding bodies such as the Heritage Lottery Fund when making grants to house or restore particular vehicles. This sub-group of NARTM has been working closely with The Transport Trust throughout this prioritization process.

Contact: NARTM, PO Box 5141, Burton-upon-Trent, Staffordshire DE15 0ZF
Website: www.nartm.org.uk
e-mail: nartm@btinternet.com

The Transport Trust

The aims of The Transport Trust, founded in 1965, are to promote and encourage the permanent preservation, for the benefit of the nation, of transport items of historical or technical interest, books, drawings, films, photographs and recordings of all forms of transport by road, rail, air and water. In furtherance of these aims, the trust sets out to co-ordinate the whole transport preservation movement, and generally seeks to advise and assist in all respects of preservation, including the raising of funds. Additionally it arranges displays and rallies of historical transport.

Britain's place in the history and development of transport is second to none, and the trust's aim is to ensure that future generations have the opportunity to study and enjoy our achievements in all forms of transport, by preventing the loss of irreplaceable relics and material, and to assist with providing accommodation and maintenance facilities for those that are saved. The trust makes available legal, insurance and planning advice, so that the overheads of affiliated societies are kept to a minimum, and their own locally raised funds can be deployed directly into restoration, preservation and maintenance. The trust's brief is wide-ranging, from advice to local authorities and other bodies setting up transport museums, to obtaining the proper insurance cover for small society rallies. It maintains a library and archive at Ironbridge, which is available for research and for the receipt of documents related to transport history.

The Transport Trust is therefore a facilitating body with a potentially significant influence in that it gives advice to funding bodies such as the Heritage Lottery Fund – its motto is 'Preserving the Past for the Future' (the trust is currently producing a book on the history of transport preservation).

Contact: Tony Walker, Director General, The Transport Trust, 202 Lambeth Road, London SE1 7JW.
Tel: 0207 928 6464.

The Leyland Society

The Leyland Society was formed five years ago, to promote the study and preservation of Leyland vehicles. It has about 600 members worldwide, and has built up a very lively communication system between members through its quarterly magazine *Leyland Torque*. The magazine is of an exceedingly high quality, containing articles on the history of Leyland and its products, two major regular features to promote research into Leylands, and a lively 'Letters' section.

In addition to *Leyland Torque*, the society produces an annual journal, again of the highest standard achievable. With these quality magazines, the Leyland Society stands out amongst most 'one marque' societies, and is proud to be associated with what was once undoubtedly the greatest commercial vehicle manufacturer of all time – Leyland Motors Limited.

Contact: Mike Sutcliffe, Hon. Secretary and Magazine Editor, The Leyland Society, Valley Forge, 213 Castle Hill Road, Totternhoe, Dunstable, Bedfordshire LU6 2DA.
Tel: 01525 221676; e-mail: sutcliffes@valleyforge.fslife.co.uk

Index